D1036819

Rebirth
of the
Corporation

D. Quinn Mills

John Wiley & Sons, Inc.
New York   Chichester   Brisbane   Toronto   Singapore

Copyright © 1991 by D. Quinn Mills.
Published by John Wiley & Sons, Inc.
All rights reserved.

Published simultaneously in Canada.

Library of Congress Cataloging in Publication Data

Mills, Daniel Quinn.
    Rebirth of the corporation / by D. Quinn Mills.
      p.   cm.
    Includes index.
    ISBN 0-471-52220-1
    1. Organizational change—Management.   2. Corporate reorganizations—Management.   I. Title.
HD58.8.M55 1991
658.1'6—dc20   90-39272

Printed in the United States of America

91 92 10 9 8 7 6 5 4 3 2 1

To Shirley and Lisa
and
Michelle and Scotty

ACKNOWLEDGMENTS

I owe a significant debt to G. Bruce Friesen who drafted substantial elements of this book and who did much of the field research which contributes so greatly to it. Lydia desGroseilliers, Mark Cannon and Linda Medin made important suggestions.

I am grateful to Paul Lawrence for encouragement. The Division of Research of the Harvard Business School provided support for much of the analysis.

Brian Forst gave the manuscript a critical reading and made valuable suggestions.

All errors and omissions are my responsibility alone.

D. Quinn Mills

CONTENTS

Contents

Rebirth
of the
Corporation

INTRODUCTION

The Road Map
to the Future

Whether you are a manager, employee, or investor you have heard about flattened organizations, delayering, getting closer to customers, and cost cutting. But these visions of a rebirth of the corporation have not been accompanied by road maps about how to get there. Now, the dreams of the past are becoming a reality. After years of efforts, some companies have marked out the route to the organization of the future. This book tells you what they are doing and how.

If you are a manager, you have read about theory X and theory Y. You have been told that your organization should be less bureaucratic, that your people should be more innovative and risk taking, and that you should pay people by results.

You know that the work force is changing. In the 1990s almost 85 percent of the new people available for jobs will be women and minorities. What will make these people feel positive about their work and cause them to bring real commitment to their jobs?

You know that productivity has not been growing rapidly enough. Substantial investment in computers and communication equipment does not seem to be paying off, perhaps because the technology has been modernized but the organization has not.

To keep up with more rapid change, your firm is attempting to become more adaptable and flexible. You are trying to be more responsive to customers and to be more in touch with the marketplace. You are also delegating more responsibilities to those closest to your customers; and it feels as though the organization may be turning upside down.

You see that a number of managers in your organization have been dismissed. You know that there is now more to do with less resources and the demands seem to be increasing. Your company has been reorganized again and again. You hear people below you in the organization demanding more say in what they do; but you are responsible, and you do not know if you trust them enough to let go.

You know that blue-ribbon groups like the Commission on the Skills of the American Work Force are urging companies to reorganize—to emphasize teamwork, rigorous training, and high skills in order to be more competitive.

You want your organization to work better. You know that some people are not doing much, but there seems to be no way to motivate them. Despite the downsizing there is still inefficiency. Morale is low, and some managers around you say it cannot be avoided. You are working hard and the company is making a profit, but you know that the organization has much unrealized potential.

You want to adapt new ideas to your company. Your objectives include minimizing managerial layers, using modern communications technology, providing direct accessibility for clients or customers, having accountability for results fully defined, and providing much more flexibility in work and program structures.

You are frustrated by books and articles that tell you what kind of a company you should have but fail to provide a clue to how to bring it about.

You have begun to hear about organizations that are quite different from yours. People have told you about visiting companies where there are flat organizations and managers have an unusual role. You've heard about a "network" organization and a large international construction company that has told its employees that the new organization chart was the company's phone book. You wonder if this can be true, and if so, what it means for you. Does a very different organizational structure work better? If it does, how do you start to make the change? Can it be done from the bottom up, almost like spontaneous combustion in the company, or does it have to come from the top down?

Suppose you were to try something really different. How would you go about it? What hassles would you meet along the way? How much leeway could you find for changing things in a bureaucratic company? Or what if you were given carte blanche: What would you want to do? If you took some venturesome steps, where would they lead you?

This book gives you the answers to such questions through a new and radical idea I call the *cluster organization*. The main obstacle to the rebirth of the corporation is the hierarchy. A cluster organization breaks down the artificial walls that stifle creativity, innovation, communication, and productivity. Isn't doing away with hierarchy impractical? Hardly, as you will see when you meet Andrew Harriss of Du Pont (in Chapter Thirteen) and see how much leeway and room for productivity growth there can be in a huge, well-established company. Or when you listen to Julian Darley of British Petroleum (in Chapter Five) and see what can be done if your company would give you a free hand.

A cluster organization changes and simplifies the role of corporate headquarters, sends down financial authority and responsibility in a flattened structure, and eliminates committees and layers of control and planning. The end result is to force individuals to take accountability and initiative. How much can be accomplished when this happens? Watch a new approach brought to the activities of Royal Trust of Canada in Chapter Eleven.

A cluster does not mean chaos, anarchy, or lack of central direction. It does not mean the end of management. What it does mean is a new role for managers through the exercise of what I have come to call counter-conventional leadership and establishment of an effective and meaningful vision of strategic goals.

Could you find a competitive edge if you reshape your organization in the new way? Do you think reform isn't for everyone? See what the military is doing. The hierarchy originally found its way into business centuries ago from the military, but in today's high-tech, high-cost world, the Army has been moving its battlefield commands a long way from tradition while hundreds of firms, facing a market battlefield no less high-tech and high-cost, are mired in the old traditional ways.

Historically, firms have depended on large numbers of production or clerical workers doing narrow, repetitive tasks. In consequence they have used management systems based on a hierarchy that provides strict direction and control.

In the future most firms will not have armies of production or clerical workers because they will produce goods and services by automated processes. Some employees will develop, maintain, and service equipment rather than perform physical work. Others will handle sales, design, applications, and various staff functions such as finance, planning, marketing, and human resource management.

Employees in such activities require support and development rather than direction and control. Hence the need for a different approach.

Nonetheless, many firms remain mired in the old organizational structure. A shift may already have occurred in the company's work force so that a new system is needed. Yet the old system remains firmly in place.

The challenge for any individual is to determine whether he or she fits the new world. Do you understand it? Can you work within it? If you are an executive, how can you tell when the transition should occur in your firm?

The best clue is whether things are already moving in that direction. Following is a list of characteristics of firms that are responding to revolutionary changes. If these fit, your firm is already partway down the road to becoming a cluster organization. In this book you will learn how to take advantage of this opportunity.

By recognizing where your firm is headed, you may be able to lessen the confusion and cost that might otherwise occur in a misunderstood evolution. And by moving quickly and effectively, you might seize an advantage over your competitors. You might also be the first in your business to merge happily the new work force and dramatic technological breakthroughs through a new management system.

Firms that show few of the characteristics listed are firmly mired in the old ways. Yet if you are in such a firm, should you not ask yourself whether your competitors will be using these new ideas? Can your company afford

4

to let its competitors be the first to employ these modern organizational techniques? Consider:

1. Employees ask for more involvement in decisions about their work.
2. Narrow job descriptions seem a thing of the past as people work to accommodate customers.
3. One or more layers of management have been eliminated to cut costs.
4. The average span of control of managers is increasing as efficiency moves delayer the organization.
5. Decisions are being moved closer to the point of action to be more responsive to customers' needs.
6. Organizational units are being asked to do more with fewer resources as costs are cut because of competition.
7. The firm is experimenting with profit sharing or other variable compensation at nonexecutive levels in an effort to motivate workers.
8. Employees are communicating through electronic mail or networks of personal computers.
9. The firm is using satellite teleconferencing to cut travel costs and to increase the frequency of interaction among its workers.
10. The company uses quality circles, self-managed teams, project teams, or "matrix" management as it tries to be more productive.
11. The company is beginning to measure customer satisfaction directly in order to be more responsive.
12. Information about the business is being decentralized in the belief that better-informed employees will be more effective.
13. Ideas have been advanced about upending the hierarchy to improve customer relations.
14. Managerial decisions increasingly involve more people through collaboration, consensus, or multiple input.
15. More information reaches workers through informal channels, indicating that the old stove-pipe hierarchical structure is breaking down.

16. Multidisciplinary task forces are being used on key issues to assemble the breadth necessary to tackle today's problems.
17. Performance reviews now require input from more than an immediate supervisor (for example, customers and peers) to get a fairer and fuller picture of each person's contribution.
18. The organization is trying to give greater encouragement and reward to individual initiative in order to be less bureaucratic.

Some executives believe that they are already changing fundamentals. But many are fooling themselves. The pressures of the changing business world make it apparent that traditional practices have to change, so executives modify their behavior a bit and announce that all has been transformed. It has not.

For example, often in recent years I have been told by managers that they put a high priority on empowering people to take more risk and responsibility in their jobs. Sometimes top executives have told me that empowerment is a central theme of their activities. Yet people in the same firm report that the culture remains unforgiving of mistakes, so no one takes seriously the exhortations of top management to take greater risks. Instead, people still want prior approval from supervisors before taking any but the most routine steps, and the company is as slow and bureaucratic as ever.

In general making employees subject to a large corporate hierarchy enfeebles them and thereby hurts the company's responsiveness to customers. Empowerment is the liberation of those who do the work from rigid oversight and direction.

When the fundamentals of management have really been addressed and transformations made, life is very different in a corporation. Empowerment is real. Everyone is aware that things are different. But the problem is how to communicate the change to outsiders, especially to outsiders who use the same vocabulary of change but don't really transform themselves.

"Oh, yes," said one executive, "we do that delegation stuff, too." But his firm makes only a motion in that direction, although he may think his efforts are significant.

"We do top-down goal setting and bottom-up implementation," another told me. But the top-down was real and the bottom-up was only an illusion. Supervisors set the goals, closely directed the work, and monitored performance carefully. There was no real delegation.

Finally, some companies do get into counterconventional leadership: They provide employee involvement programs, set up semiautonomous units, and delegate extensively. But these transformations are done only as an island of change in the midst of a sea of tradition. In these companies true empowerment is a yard wide and an inch deep.

So common has become the practice of acknowledging the need for greater delegation without really changing the old ways that many firms have moved away from empowerment themes to question their own degree of commitment. "We talk the talk," they say, "but do we walk the walk? We discuss change, but do we really do it?"

To recognize the degree of change necessary, we must see current business practices as they are, not in an idealized fashion. Executives who talk of delegation, accountability, and risk taking by subordinates generally know that they are not very successful at accomplishing these objectives, no matter how hard they try. Much of what is proposed is not accomplished. Executives who say that the firm empowers workers and has transcended bureaucracy are merely dreaming.

The nontraditional business approach, which is the subject of this book, is a dramatic change from traditional management. Consequently, it may appear to many to be fraught with unknowns and risks.

Surely, there must be an hierarchical alternative. And if so, is it not to be preferred because it is more familiar?

The answer is no. Evidence to date suggests that a hierarchical organization cannot achieve what a cluster organization can. It cannot be as responsive to customers. Clusters are better because they put true decision making much closer to the customer. A hierarchy cannot be as cost effective because of its high administrative expenses.

A hierarchy cannot utilize the talents of its workers as well as a cluster because it is continually telling them what to do rather than gaining from their imagination and initiative.

Finally, a hierarchy is handicapped in exploiting the new communications and computer technology because its vertical reporting and functional divisions inhibit networking. Clusters are the only form of organization that allow a company to realize fully the potential of the new information and communications technology.

Certainly, there are excellent businesses that are hierarchies. A company does not have to be organized as a cluster to be successful. But any business can probably be run more efficiently and with a greater potential for the future in the cluster format.

"Hierarchy is dying," a top staff officer of one of America's largest companies told me. "Everyone is sick of the rituals, delays, and inefficiencies. It's almost a corpse and soon will have to be buried."

"My father was in the military," the president of a medium-sized manufacturing company told me. "I was brought up with a chain of command and I've been part of that environment all my life: initially while I was in military service myself, and then in the corporate world. I understand it and I'm comfortable with it. I've done well in it. But now I think the hierarchy just doesn't work anymore. Our young people hate it. They're insisting I change it."

The conclusion is inescapable that continuing to cling to the traditional hierarchical system without taking a careful look at alternatives is nothing more than resistance to the future.

So this question is left: What exactly is the alternative? What is the nature of the posthierarchical firm? Some writers have pointed to directions in which beginnings are being made, but this book is the first to stress how fundamental is the divide between the old ways and the new, and to show what the new organizational structure is like in practice. Here you will find the first road map on how to get to the organization of the future.

PART I

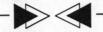

Counterconventional
Leadership

CHAPTER ONE

Shortchanged by Traditional Ways

Today the living standards of each of us are being shortchanged because the traditional managerial hierarchy is failing our economy. The only solution is a radically different approach.

A bitterly competitive environment puts a premium on quick reaction to a changing world. The conventional hierarchy is too costly and too slow to give an effective response.

New technology promises an answer. Personal computing is advancing to interpersonal computing. Linked computers make communications more direct and give people more information so that they can act more quickly and provide better service to customers.

But will employees be able to use the new technology to work smarter? Not in conventional settings, it appears. Already the most talented employees are calling for new managerial approaches.

The hierarchy is under siege because it's increasingly inefficient and many of the most effective workers in our companies are sick of it. They're tired of the rituals, the lack of real communication, the delays in making decisions and taking actions. With new technology diffusing information widely, many feel that the issue isn't who you are in the structure but what you get accomplished.

With an economic push, a technological pull, and the changing aspirations of knowledge, workers are each calling for a new type of organization. This book is about how some executives are responding with dramatically nontraditional approaches.

Down the Hierarchy

Something important is happening, something that requires us to rethink the fundamentals of management and that offers great, new opportunities when recognized and mastered. Companies and markets are in rapid flux. "Where," you wonder "is change taking us? Where are we headed?" The questions are especially critical since a business revolution is in the air.

Inexorable, long-term forces are compelling companies to adapt. At the forefront of these forces are intense competition and rapid economic change. These developments impose on companies the need for speed in action, for staying close to customers and markets to anticipate their needs, and for high quality in the products and services they offer. Agility, quickness, and innovation are needed as never before.

But corporate bureaucracies stand in the way. Bloated hierarchies slow responsiveness, suppress innovation, crush aspirations, and retard productivity.

Often it's difficult for people who are forward looking and innovative to accept how stodgy and resistant to change are many other people, and their companies. This was brought home by an executive who had once attended a top management-development program. "I screwed up the use of that good education I got," he said. Asked what he meant, he replied,

It's my fault. It wasn't what I learned. The teachers did a great job. But I was naive. I should have known better. It's my fault.

I'm the youngest on our top management team. The company is over 100 years old and we've had essentially the same products for all that time. We sell the same things to the same small group of customers, and we do it well. It's a cyclical business, but over the long haul we make money, so you can't say it's bad. But there's so much more we could do.

We're very bureaucratic. Our chairman believes in committees to plan everything. Unless he has complete consensus in the management group, he

12

won't do anything different. Everyone has to sign off on the other's plans. The president even says he's a bureaucrat. He believes in it. He tells me I'm the only nonbureaucrat he has.

When I was at school I talked to the other participants and I learned that most other companies don't operate that way. There was only one other firm like ours in this regard. Everywhere else they'd assign a project to someone and let him go do something with it if he could. In our place everything he does has to be approved by the committees.

Last year our company lost $80 million. It's by far the biggest loss we've ever had. I thought that gave me my opening, so I made a bunch of proposals for doing things differently. I couldn't believe they'd be rejected; they all seemed so sensible to me. The company has such unrealized potential. With the big loss, I figured people would be looking for a new way to do things.

I was wrong. Instead of saying, "What can we do different and better?" they said, "Let's go back to how we did it before—that seemed to work." So they're less ready to change than ever.

In a way I can understand it. This way of operating is all they know. The company has been successful for many years. They just want things to go on as they have in the past: making some money; being left alone; doing what they know how to do.

I'd like to leave, but I've had two big heart attacks in the past, and the medical insurance ties me down. It's all right; I can stay where I am. They're nice people, and I don't think I have to worry about losing my job. But I used to love to go in to work. Now I don't.

The traditional hierarchical structure of our companies is more than just a system that has outlived its usefulness—it is a clear and present danger to the economic welfare of all of us. How do we know this is true? Companies with access to great natural resources, with the incentive of an enormous domestic market, and with the most advanced technology nevertheless give up markets to competitors whose only real advantage is greater imagination and effort in meeting the desires of customers.

Companies that only a few years ago dominated their industries have now sunk into insignificance. Working people struggle to make ends meet by having every adult in the family work, some at more than a single job, and yet living standards have begun a slow and inexorable decline.

Perhaps in the past companies needed to be organized as if they were old-time military units. People were poorly educated and required precise direction. They were reluctant to work and poorly self-disciplined, so they needed close supervision. Because communications were slow and information difficult to obtain, many people were needed to collect information and prepare reports for top executives. The result was a pyramid of supervisory managers who kept the business humming and rewarded themselves with good salaries and high status.

But all this has changed. Much of our work force is fairly well educated and can direct its own activity. Many are highly motivated—before the corporate hierarchy discourages them—and want considerable autonomy in their work. Communications are rapid and information pours in floodlike volume from computers. All this is now too much for the corporate pyramid. It no longer makes the business hum. Instead, bureaucracy slows it to a crawl.

The world will not wait for bureaucracies to hurry up; rather, the pace of change accelerates. In every major aspect of business there are dramatic transformations. The future shows us a world with

- Intense and increasingly international competition
- A work force splitting into educated professionals, on the one hand, and persons who have only rudimentary math and reading skills, on the other
- Human attitudes that stress autonomy and individual recognition, but also want involvement and inclusion in a group
- Further and extreme specialization of knowledge and experience

Some have recognized that the only option is to try to keep up with the changes by modifying our corporations. So in some places hierarchies are being modified dramatically to bring down administrative costs, to speed marketplace adaptations, and to reenergize those who can make our companies successful. The people who are making these experiments are today's pioneers. Their efforts to increase productivity and performance in their companies will help improve the lives of each of us.

Advances in our living standards are tied to productivity improvement. Technology that is now emerging from corporate laboratories is a key source of potential for productivity advances. And the opportunity is enormous. What the personal computer was to the 1980s—the linkage of computers in communications networks—the *interpersonal* computer will be to the 1990s—a key driving force toward a new way of working.

Today, technology is following its own dynamic direction toward distributed computing of greater and greater power and diffused, not centralized, information. Communication and information technology are the great sources of productivity advances in the future. Their potential is not in the factory but in the office.

Much of the potential advances in human productivity have already been accomplished in our factories. Automation has proceeded very far and there are few people left in the plants. But there are enormous gains to be made in the offices of our companies. Specifically, the productivity of "knowledge" workers has lagged while technology has advanced greatly. The great opportunity of the next few years is in improving the bottom line through enhancing the productivity of knowledge workers.

The real question is this: How is it to be achieved?

Technology alone is not the answer. Advanced communication and information networks contribute to enhanced productivity only if people are able to utilize them fully. This is a management—not technical—issue.

People often think of an information network as if it were a form of organization. It is not. An advanced communication and information network is an infrastructure or base around which people can rearrange themselves to improve productivity. Executives who spend large sums on a new network but do not know how to permit people to use it fully are shortchanging not only their companies but the rest of us as well.

The Economic Push

Facing a substantial drop in business activity during the recession of the early 1980s, most firms found they had to cut costs to survive. The standard approach had been to cut from the bottom up—beginning with production workers, sales staff, and other wage labor. Many firms followed this practice and discovered a terrible truth: What had worked in the past somehow was backfiring in the 1980s—reducing competitiveness instead of enhancing it.

As employees were fired, morale and loyalty in offices and manufacturing facilities alike slumped. Key employees, even those not threatened by layoffs, jumped for better opportunities. Key orders from managers were only half obeyed, as people kept one eye on job opportunities and one eye on current responsibilities. Turmoil and confusion at the staff level became the order of the day. Customers began to respond negatively to poor service and shoddy product quality, which were the result of understaffing at the employee level.

Some innovative firms, looking at the chaos around them, challenged the conventional logic of employee layoffs. Their leaders looked more closely at operating economics and concluded that (1) there were too many middle managers and professionals and (2) applied technologies such as personal computers, sophisticated software, and other tools could enable ordinary employees to do many of the reporting and analyzing tasks formerly assigned to expensive managers and professional staffs. These firms also discovered that service—all-important to competitiveness—suffered when customer requests were relayed through multiple levels in the organization for resolution.

With this logic in mind, senior executives cut middle management ranks to speed up their organizations and cut costs without impairing direct service. The results of this shift were striking. Costs were reduced and competitiveness at least partially restored. The numbers of people for whom a manager was directly responsible (technically referred to as the *span of control*) grew substantially. Managers were forced to respond to a novel situation.

Initially, many did so by running faster and working harder to maintain their traditional role, but they could not do the same things with subordinates as they could under a narrower span of control. They could not maintain close communications, make most decisions, and provide direction all at the same time. So they began to let things slide, and sometimes broke down themselves. Organizations, it seems, were cut to the bone.

Others asked themselves how to keep from being buried by the additional work. The answer was to adopt a different approach to management by centering on a new sort of team.

Teamwork permits managers to have broad spans of control. Work units no longer need expensive middle-level managers and staff to coordinate and collate information. Instead, employees are trained to take the initiative themselves and to work with minimal supervision. Close communication among specialists from different functions through teamwork eliminates the need for middle managers to provide communication links. Information technology makes business data readily accessible up and down the organization and thereby reduces the need for middle managers to review and repackage information for top executives. Finally, customers are put in direct contact with those in the company who do the work, eliminating the need for a buffer zone of managers. Since some companies have discovered this method of permanently lowering costs, competitive pressures in the economy are pressing others to follow suit to avoid being priced out of business.

The Technological Pull

The rapid advance of computer and communications technology is pulling business toward dramatic changes in management itself. As the chief executive of a major retail chain commented,

> We're run without any substantial bureaucracy. Our stores are largely autonomous. Each store manager orders separately and is responsible for his or her profitability. What has been our problem is how to communicate between our stores directly, since there are too few of us at corporate headquarters to see that messages are transmitted up and down the hierarchy.
>
> Our managers often run into similar situations and want to get advice from each other. The fax machine and new computer linkups have been lifesaving for us. Now our units communicate laterally and we are able to grow the business again by adding more units.

Traditional hierarchies are often hampered by inflexible lateral communications. Memos sent across functional lines are ignored; top managers from different functions meet but fail to get around to topics that are of great significance to their subordinates; people don't know whom to call at their same level in a different department to get things done. When coordination across functions is necessary, many companies rely on a few long-service individuals who know persons in other departments. But as people leave or retire, these channels may atrophy.

Where good service to a customer demands cooperation across departmental lines it may suffer. Getting "close to customers" demands more rapid analysis and decision making than a large, functionally organized hierarchy can deliver: Its employees and executives are separated by too many layers of "repeating transmitter."

Nor is the problem of the traditional hierarchy one of just speed in taking action. The layers of management that repeat and transmit messages often garble them. Each layer that is further from direct communication with those closest to the matter at hand often unknowingly alters the message in the process of transmitting it.

There is a parlor game that depends on exactly this phenomenon of human communication. The players sit in a circle and some person begins the game by whispering a short message in the ear of the person closest to him or her. That person turns to the next person in the circle and whispers the message. By rephrasing and misunderstanding, the message that reaches the last person in the circle is often distorted beyond recognition.

You can play a simpler version of this game yourself in your own work situation. Give a message of a few sentences to a subordinate or a colleague, asking him or her to repeat it exactly to some other person. Then listen when the message is conveyed. Usually all subtlety is lost, and sometimes the message is totally altered. For example, you might say, "Please tell Joe that I very much appreciate his message and I'll get to it as soon as I can." Probably you'll hear your message repeated somewhat akin to the following: "Joe, Susan said to tell you she has your message and will get to it when she can." Joe, on receiving this reply, may well be angered that his message did not get a more favorable response from Susan.

As this example shows, even one-to-one communications are fraught with error. How much more so are those that pass up and down the chains of command of large organizations? People who are essentially transmitters, as are many people in a large hierarchy, often introduce distortions and errors into the communications.

New technology can eliminate the difficulties of speeding and improving the accuracy of information flow by more often connecting the sender of a message directly to the ultimate receiver. Electronic networks connecting groups—regardless of level, position, or function—can be created as easily as direct-dialing telephone conference calls. A multinational company can put people in different countries on the same project and have them work simultaneously via computer screens and satellite transmission. What used to be occasional and intermittent communications are now intimate and continual and without the need for intermediaries.

When local area networks are put together in businesses, they change the way people do their jobs. Suddenly, a group of people are connected by their personal computers. From a new network of PCs emerges increased collaboration among those included. As people work more closely together across departmental lines, the need for management to get daily reports and to provide direction and oversight declines dramatically. Productivity and performance both rise. Thus the new technology pulls a new form of organization into being.

For management, the challenge is to back off and let people do their work in the new way. Technology can speed up data flows and decision making inside traditional hierarchies, but only at a price: violation of the principle of unity of command. Employees no longer need to talk to each other through their bosses, keeping these people informed as they go; instead they can interact directly. In this sense the organization becomes flattened, cutting through layers of bureaucracy. As pioneers in organizations have formed informal ''rings'' to share data, firms have discovered how quickly things move when network wires replace human channels. The logic of competitive economics also suggests that before long the most rapid action-taking methods will prevail.

A manager at a major Canadian company pointed out that ''without E-mail'' (electronic mail) his firm would grind to a halt. Hewlett-Packard's engineering group at Lake Stevens, Washington, uses a worldwide computer grid to link its engineers. If someone wants the best solution to a design problem, he or she accesses the network to form a giant mechanical equivalent of a human brain. The system also stores a catalogue of parts that the company knows from experience already work, are cheap and reliable, and can be integrated into new designs.

19

In many businesses today information technology is not seen as a gateway into the organization of the future. The strategic significance of computers, faxes, and networks is being missed. Instead, advanced information technology is seen merely as a way to unify procedures centrally and improve cost accounting. What a missed opportunity!

The real opportunity in advanced information technology lies in mobilizing information about customers for marketing support, in identifying costs (not just counting them) for production rationalization, and in connecting people all over the organization who can work better together than separately. Computers should serve those working, not those working the computers. Networks should serve the business, not the business serve the networks.

It is crucial to recognize that computer networks are not an organizational form, a confusion that has crept into thinking about the effect of computers on organizations. Rather, they are the technological base that makes the new organizational forms possible.

Modern technology makes counterconventional management possible by providing intimacy and speed in communications and data transmission. But the causality also works the other way. *Without counterconventional management, the full advantages of modern technology cannot be seized by a company.* Without a new form of organization a company's large investment in desktop computers and electronic mail will not be fully utilized. The barriers between people erected by unit boundaries and a lengthy chain of command in a hierarchy prevent the optimal use of the new technology. For example, one manager in a company that had just introduced electronic mail instructed his employees that all such messages had to be cleared with him before they were sent. His motivation was understandable. He was trying to avoid being blindsided by people from outside his organization who might know more about his unit from E-mail than he knew himself. In a hierarchy this is often proper managerial procedure. He was trying to keep control. But such a directive restricting the use of E-mail deprives the system of much of its usefulness by introducing delay. Why invest in speeding communications only to have the messages stop at a middleman's in-basket?

A positive example to illustrate how technology and counterconventional management can interact to the benefit of an organization comes from General Electric's rescue of its old circuit breaker business. "We had to speed up or die," said GE's William Sheehan.

The business unit set itself the goal of reducing the elapsed time between a customer's order and delivery from three weeks to three days. A total business overhaul was required. Six production facilities were consolidated to one, reducing inventory storage, handling, and shipping time. An automated design system with about 1,200 interchangeable parts was created to replace a custom-design process supported by human engineers utilizing 28,000 parts.

This technology shift saved one full week, while maintaining 40,000 different product line configurations to meet customer needs. In the new system, a salesperson enters specifications into a computer at GE's main office, the order flows to the plant, and it is automatically programmed into the factory machines.

Even after the technology shift, the plant still had almost ten days to go to reach its target of three days. Where did it find the remaining time savings?

Because decision making and problem solving on the factory floor were slowing things down, the change team removed all line supervisors and quality inspectors, cutting the organizational layers between worker and management from three to one. All the functions of the middle managers—vacation scheduling, quality, work rules—became the responsibility of the 129 workers on the floor, who were divided into teams of 15 to 20. "And do you know? The more responsibility GE gave the workers, the faster problems got solved and decisions made," said a GE manager.

The result of combining new technology and organizational features was that a two-month backlog of orders dropped to two days. Productivity went up 20 percent in the past year. Manufacturing costs went down 30 percent, or $5.5 million, per year. The speed of delivery went from three weeks to three days. Said Sheehan, "We'd be out of business if we hadn't done it."

Positive impacts of this type are pulling computer technology toward a new role in management. No longer is it to be confined to the shop, the accounting department, production, or data processing.

Technological developments are enabling executives to make strategic choices about the role managers will play in firms. The work force is becoming increasingly professionalized and adept at utilizing the information stored in the communications and computer systems. As this occurs, more and more people are independently able to analyze data and make decisions without the need to defer upward. Not only is this speeding the responsiveness of organizations, but it is also making better use of employee talents in the automated age. As a result, opportunities are being taken to compress layers by moving managerial functions into computerized systems.

The consequence of these developments is that many managerial functions can be shifted to work groups without the loss of control over results by top management. As this occurs, traditional hierarchy begins transforming itself into something new.

The Changing Aspirations

Counterconventional managerial approaches have a nonconformist flavor. They provide greater freedom to individuals and are more intuitive and permissive of self-expression. In consequence their success depends critically on the competency of those involved. A company that has hired people of very limited educational and social skills will not be able to convert them to highly productive employees just by offering them greater involvement in their work. This has been a source of failure in some industries for self-managing teams and similar approaches. Novel organizational forms cannot work performance miracles with poorly trained workers.

Many companies have satisfied themselves with lesser quality in employees, believing that this system was cheaper and sufficiently efficient. "Don't give us your best and brightest," the head of a manufacturing company said. "Give us the people who are average or mediocre and don't know what they want to do with their lives."

The results for the company (which should not be unexpected) are rapid turnover, low productivity, high supervisory costs, and a certain inertia and lack of quick responsiveness. With poorly educated and poorly motivated workers, there is no alternative except a rigid hierarchy—despite its high administrative costs and low flexibility. The glaring weakness of this approach in a modern economy is causing business to look with more concern than ever before at the products of our educational system.

Many companies are trying to avoid the trap of low education, low motivation, low productivity, and high costs by searching for more competent and imaginative employees. There are still many competent people in our work force, and there are others in whom an investment in training will pay off handsomely. The problem for a company is to obtain them. Fortunately, counterconventional management is itself an attraction to such workers.

Today's work force differs from the previous generation in many ways. Far more independent, many workers have been insisting on a greater role in their work.

Nontraditional management is a means of reducing the binding and chafing of layers of supervision on the freedom of action that many people find confining. Firms can appeal to the most creative talent in the new generation by creating clusters—and to capture it, they may have to.

Caterpillar, Inc., now encourages its blue-collar employees to comment on things like product engineering, workplace layout, and quality improvement. "Five years ago the foreman wouldn't even listen to you, never mind the general foreman or the plant supervisor," says Gary Hatmaker, a 37-year-old assembly-line worker in a factory that makes the D10 and other giant tractors. "Now everyone will listen." When Hatmaker installs hydraulic hoses, he, not a spot-checking quality inspector, makes sure they are put on right. "I know how these things are supposed to fit," he says with pride.

From a broad perspective, then, businesses are being impelled toward nontraditional management by three forces. The first is today's business environment, with its demand for quick responsiveness to customers and cost control (the economic push). The second is the sudden availability of technology to support delayered, flexible organizations (the technological pull). The third is the desire of employees for greater involvement in their work (the changing aspirations).

CHAPTER TWO

Changing the Fundamentals:
A One-Way Ticket
to the Future

Reducing work forces, cutting out layers of management, and trying to be more responsive to the marketplace are providing businesses with a surprising opportunity: a new form of organization that is a true alternative to the traditional hierarchy.

Clusters emerge from two quite different business motivations: to permit employees to work more closely with customers and to cut administrative costs. Clusters are concerned with cost control and getting closer to the customer. In a business expansion, clusters promise greater productivity; in a recession, clusters offer lower costs. In either economic situation, clusters make higher quality of production and service a reality.

In a cluster organization, the behavior of people is changed so that the firm can better meet the demands of the business environment. Unfortunately, most people, even those directly affected by the changes described in Chapter One, do not understand them. There is general confusion about what is necessary to make the new form work and a failure to perceive the opportunities that it offers.

It is not surprising, therefore, that out of the confusion is emerging a way of working very similar to the new systems I will describe in this chapter.

What are the changes in fundamentals that must be made to address the new business environment?

Measurement of performance will shift from what people do in their specific area to what they help accomplish for customers or clients. That is, measurements will shift for today's focus on inputs (e.g., a person's effort) to his or her output (e.g., the value given to a customer and the customer's evaluation of what was received).

Financial controls will be enforced less through procedures and rules and more through training, dialogue, and different compensation criteria. When people understand that their pay checks are affected by their prudent use of resources, behavior will shift.

Individual responsibility imposed by supervisors will be replaced by the type of personal accountability that professionals accept for themselves.

Considerably more information will be made available to employees, and their role in the firm will be enhanced. Thus decision-support systems will increasingly support not managers but employees as they accept more delegation, computer-based expert systems will perform more work, and managers will monitor results by executive information systems. As this shift to employees in the locus of analysis, decision, and direction of work progresses, many managers will be free to place expanded emphasis on planning, coaching, and developing others.

What will ensure conforming to standard procedures; measuring inputs; setting detailed targets; making decisions about production; assuring quality; closely directing work; and limiting excessive use of labor, materials, and equipment if managers devote less attention to these areas? All of these duties are delegated to individuals and work groups.

Seen against the efforts of recent years to create more competitive corporations, what is most striking is the extreme nature of the changes now seen as necessary:

- Loosening of rules and procedures
- Delegation to individuals and groups
- Orientation to results

- Openness in communication
- Involvement of people at all levels
- Reorganization into a new type of structure

Thin Chain of Command

"I have 30 people reporting to me," said one manager. "Most are in the Midwest, but my office is in New Jersey. I get to the Midwest only two or three times a year. Yet we try to work as a team. I'm not readily available to the people who work for me, so they try to get feedback from their customers. They set higher standards of performance for themselves than I would set myself. Our company has been so downsized in recent years, especially in the managerial ranks, that when a person wants to send something up the chain of command for a decision, I say, 'You can't do that. There's no one there.'"

This manager's company has been evolving toward a new style but does not realize it. From the perspective of the top executives of the company, all that has happened is that they have cut costs by eliminating some workers. Yet in downsizing, they have forced managers and employees to develop a different method of working together. In place of the close supervision of the boss, there has emerged a team in which each person has considerable autonomy and looks to the others for support rather than direction.

Probably most of those involved think of the current situation as merely transitory, a brief period of adversity to be followed by a return to the old situation. New managers will someday replace those who were let go, they think, so that once again there will be someone there in the chain of command. Then the employees' autonomy will be gone, all will again work under close supervision, and things will be back to normal.

But those who hold this view are very likely to be wrong. New workers will not be added, the chain of command will continue to be very thin, managers will have more people than they can closely supervise, and employees will have to take more and more initiative. Rather than just a temporary phenomenon, the downsized company is a new type of organization, which is both inevitable in the current setting and likely to be permanent. It is the direction of the future.

Like the New Jersey manager and the people who report to him, thousands of people are struggling to understand how they should behave in the new environment. What will it take to be successful? Because there are so few opportunities for promotion, how can a person measure success?

When satisfactory answers are not available to such questions, there is no commitment to the changes that have been made. In the place of commitment is a determination to return to the past: to stop the cutting and to rebuild the old organization with all its imperfections, inefficiencies, and lack of competitiveness.

Organizations with only minimal hierarchies, self-supervising workers, and computer programs displacing middle managers may seem to be figments of imagination. Yet the cluster form toward which downsized firms are tending is the result of powerful trends in technology, society, and economics that have been developing for decades and will not stop in the near future. In combination they create revolutionary change in how an organization is managed and run.

Structure as a Litmus Test

Many companies have been trying to change. Efforts have been made to improve procedures, increase delegation, refine measurements, bolster communications, increase involvement, and restructure by downsizing and delayering. But for most companies these efforts have not gone far enough. In working with each area separately, executives have failed to understand that great gains can be made only by rethinking how each area relates to the others and by seeing that the consequences of change require a full transformation of managerial fundamentals.

We need a litmus test, that is, a way of divining whether a company has begun the process of overall change. The test is at hand. To make the new systems work, there has to be a dramatic change in the structure of the organization.

It is in a firm's structure that traditional managerial practices are most fully reflected. Everyone has a boss from whom he or she receives direction and evaluation. A chart defines the relationship of persons in the firm and the degree of power each exercises. Authority, decision making, individual responsibility, personal status—all turn on the organization chart.

The basic fact is that the hierarchy is not only an expression of traditional managerial practices but also their essence. Where a hierarchical structure suffuses an organization, there cannot be any rethinking of the fundamentals of management. There cannot be much delegation, or position in the hierarchy would cease to have meaning. There cannot be complete openness, or the authority of supervisors would be undermined. There cannot be loosening, or managers would feel a lack of control. There cannot be a thoroughgoing orientation to results, or managers would cease to be able to direct work closely. And there cannot be full employee involvement, or differences in status and reward based on formal position would be undermined.

When executives exhort employees to take greater risks, to pass information freely, to take initiative without waiting for their bosses' approval, and to think for themselves rather than await direction, but simultaneously maintain the full hierarchical structure, employees know that the exhortations are insincere at worst or misguided at best.

Executives commonly sacrifice potential performance in their companies in order to feel in control. People strafe under tight restrictions and productivity is diminished, but the hierarchical structure gives managers control. Hence it is the preferred organizational structure of today, even though market and technological forces are pressing for greater delegation and less direct supervision. Continued reliance on the traditional hierarchy is ironic because a careful examination of experience with nontraditional structures suggests that control need not be significantly sacrificed. Leadership, vision, education, and properly designed compensation systems can align autonomous units with the overall company so that the results hoped for from rigid controls in a hierarchy are achieved in an alternative form.

Thus, for there to be a true change in the fundamentals of management, the traditional hierarchy has to be largely abandoned in favor of a different form of organization: the cluster.

The Cluster Organization

The key new development in management is the cluster organization. It is a novel and long-term solution to many of the most difficult business problems of the future. Its exploitation for competitive advantage is the most significant managerial challenge of the 1990s.

Why the term *cluster*? There has been no common label for nontraditional approaches to structure so companies have come up with a variety of terms: *virtual teams*, *enterprise teams*, *networks*, and *autonomous business units* are among them. Yet each of these appellations has significant limitations as a generic label. *Team* is too broad a term because teams are also widely used in conventional hierarchies. *Network* is misleading because the word has too many meanings: A network is either a communications infrastructure or a group of people far more diffuse than a cluster. *Autonomous business units* imply profit centers and divisions of large companies, whereas clusters have more general applicability.

Cluster has the advantage of being new to managerial usage and has a meaning that closely fits counterconventional approaches. A cluster, says a major work guide, is "a group of people so arranged as if growing on a common vine, like grapes." In a business the common vine is the vision that corporate leaders provide of the company's future; the employees are in groups arranged by the vision; and the vine and clusters together produce the wine of business success.

For many companies, adapting to the modern world means that the now-dominant hierarchy will assume a residual role, confined primarily to the topmost reaches of an organization. Elsewhere it will be largely replaced by clusters: a new way of organization that changes the behavior of those in it to meet the demands of the business environment. Clusters succeed because they make it possible for a firm to hire the best people, develop an ongoing commitment to quality, be quickly responsive to shifts in the marketplace, and provide a process for rapid revitalization when performance declines.

A cluster is a group of people drawn from different disciplines who work together on a semipermanent basis. The cluster itself handles many administrative functions, thereby divorcing itself from an extensive managerial hierarchy. A cluster develops its own expertise, expresses a strong customer or client orientation, pushes decision making toward the point of action, shares information broadly, and accepts accountability for its business results.

As an example, let's say that the vision of a publishing company is to become the leading publisher in the field of accounting. Specific financial goals are set by senior management: sales of, say, $20 million per year; pretax profits of 20 percent; and costs at no more than 10 percent of sales.

Once the goals are set, the people from different specialties—the editor, sales manager, marketing manager, publicity director, production and manufacturing manager—would form a cluster to meet these goals. While each person would continue to perform his or her specialty—for example, the editor would continue to prospect for authors and work with them to write new books for the accounting series—roles would change. The editor would not just be responsible for authors and manuscripts. He or she would have an enlarged role in marketing, publicity, sales, and the financial performance of the cluster.

The editor may have wonderful authors, but if the books don't meet the financial goals of the cluster those involved will not be considered successful. A cluster moves people beyond responsibility for just their area and toward the performance of the cluster as a whole. The cluster, therefore, generates energy, benefitting not only the organization as a whole but also the careers of the individuals involved. The editor by necessity will need to become familiar with the nuances and skills involved in marketing and selling books, the details of their production and manufacturing, and the financial nuances involved in making a book a profitable venture. The editor's skills and career potential will be considerably enhanced through successful participation in a cluster organization.

Individual clusters inside an organization may vary in size, but a range of 30 to 50 members is common. Such a size is often necessary to provide the several functions and disciplines necessary to allow the cluster to run its business. Within a cluster, smaller work teams of 5 to 7 provide the intimate communication and easy accessibility that facilitates getting work done.

A cluster organization is made up of many such clusters and a small residual hierarchy, which administers the business as a whole. Is any hierarchy necessary? Maybe not, say the strongest supporters of clusters, but I know of no organization that has experimented with having no hierarchy at all. The complete absence of a hierarchy is, in all likelihood, an impossible dream. A typical cluster organization diagram is shown in Figure 1.

Several different types of clusters are represented. These are not the only types, because companies are often very imaginative about how they create and name cross-functional teams, but they cover most of the major uses to which clusters are put.

Six different types of clusters are shown in Figure 1:

A core team
Business units
Staff units
Project teams
Alliance teams
Change teams

A core team is comprised of the top management of the firm (or division or department of the firm). It has the central leadership role and is akin to the management committee of a European firm.

Business units are clusters that have customers external to the firm (or division or department). They conduct their own business, dealing directly with customers, in a semiautonomous manner. Ideally, they are profit centers, being measurable on both revenues and costs. Business units are

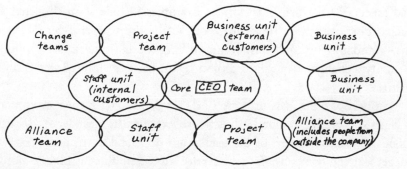

Figure 1   A Cluster Organization

the central elements of a cluster organization. Their flexibility, customer responsiveness, and autonomy in action allow a complex company to exhibit the quickness of far smaller firms.

Staff units are clusters that have customers internal to the firm (or division or department). In some firms staff units price their services to their internal customers. Examples include marketing, accounting, personnel, legal, and other staff functions which are organized as one or more clusters. The experience of General Electric Canada in converting a central financial services unit to teams very akin to clusters is described in a later chapter.

Both business units and staff units may be said to run their own small businesses. In fact, a staff unit may be converted to a business unit by permitting the staff unit to sell its services to customers outside the firm. A business orientation isn't characteristic in the same way of other types of clusters, which are therefore labeled "teams." The core team, for example, has leadership and administrative functions within the firm: it's more committee-like than commercial-like.

Project teams are assembled for a specific project. They lack the ongoing business orientation characteristic of business units, though some projects may be so large and enduring that they last a long time, and the teams may appear to be semipermanent.

Alliance teams are today's version of the joint venture. They involve participants from different corporations and are becoming common in marketing and sales in some industries (especially high-tech) and in product development in others.

Change teams are created for the purpose of reviewing and modifying broad aspects of the firm's activities. Examples include teams directed at reducing bureaucracy, cutting paperwork ("the great paper caper" in one firm), standardizing and simplifying billing of customers, and so on. Ordinarily a change team, like a project team, has a life limited to a certain objective.

Members of a business unit are in direct contact with their customers or clients. A cluster responds directly to what customers want. It also responds to what members of the team want done and to the desires of the managers of the company. In a hierarchy, however, the customers' needs are filtered through a managerial structure, often being distorted or lost in the process. Employees respond first and foremost to what the managers want, second to what managers say the customers want, and only to a small degree to what the customers say they want.

The emergence of the cluster organization is a phenomenon of the Western world. It is appearing in Europe and the United States. Clusters are not a Japanese system, although they have a limited and superficial similarity to quality circles. A cluster organization goes much further into the actual operations of a company and into its structure and the role of management than does any quality circle. In manufacturing companies the cluster is in fact an American and European response to Japanese competition.

What is particularly Western about the cluster organization is its imaginative combination of individual initiative and teamwork. It draws on both these strains of Western culture to respond to the Japanese emphasis on the group.

Teamwork in clusters enhances the individual. Playing for the Boston Celtics does not destroy Larry Bird's individuality; instead it gives him the support of others to maximize his own potential. The isolated individual can do only so much; as part of a team of talented people, he or she can do much more.

Teamwork is often enjoyable. In a survey done for a major business firm, several hundred professionals pointed to the cross-functional teamwork on particular projects as representing the firm at its best. What did they like about the teamwork? That it provided an opportunity to learn and grow, to meet new people and develop new contacts, and to engage in a competition with other firms in which there was a clear win or lose outcome. The cluster organization was an important addition to what was otherwise the unrelenting, isolated work of individual contributors.

Clusters involve the individual in both teamwork and separate effort. Clusters do not mean that everything is done on a common basis. The individual is able to meet his or her personal needs both for influence in the group and for autonomy, and to do so to a degree in each which suits his or her own personality and preferences.

Clusters are the key to survival in tomorrow's business world. They are a new way of tapping the full potential of an organization by breaking down the hierarchy, engaging the skills and aspirations of the workers, and improving productivity and quality. These are the things that will ensure the survival and success of a business.

Where are clusters to be found? British Petroleum has established them in its central engineering unit. General Electric Canada has used a variation for its centralized financial services. Many consulting, accounting, and law firms have clusters as a normal method of conducting their activities. Du Pont's Fibers Department, a multibillion dollar business, has them in its information services unit. And Xerox has used clusters to build product quality and regain market share from Japanese companies.

Empowering People

In the attempt to achieve greater initiative and risk taking in business organizations, managers and consultants now talk of empowering people. "Empowered" people, free from bureaucratic restraints, will act quickly at the customer's behest. But achieving such liberation of people from the system has proven very difficult in traditional organizations.

In contrast, clusters make possible the full empowerment of people. They provide an atmosphere in which the individual feels the freedom to act and the competence to do so. Clusters, far better than traditional hierarchies, provide the conditions necessary to make individual initiative possible.

What are the key elements that make empowerment possible? An example will help identify them.

A company had dispatched a team to open an office in a new section of the country. They'd been given very specific information about how to go about it, but on location thought that they should do things differently. They asked headquarters for permission to follow their own plan, and stressed that to have a chance of success, they must act very quickly. Headquarters had no time to investigate the local conditions and revise its plan. It could only approve the application or insist on its orders being followed. The quandary forced headquarters to think through the issue of extreme delegation—the question of true empowerment.

The danger of empowerment was that each person would do his or her own thing, and all would be chaos. What would happen to direction if each person felt free to substitute his or her judgment for corporate directives?

Yet people in the field were closer to the scene of action and often had knowledge of specific situations which was better than that at headquarters. Also, waiting for directions and clarifications from corporate was often a slow process that caused opportunities to slip away.

When, then, could top executives feel that they could safely empower employees to act on their own? In the past firms had answered this question by establishing careful procedures. Decisions could be made at the local level when they were made in accordance with procedures.

Unfortunately, procedures had grown so elaborate that they were both unduly time-consuming and so complex that they were unclear. A person in the field, anxious to avoid a mistake that could cripple his or her career, asked for guidance from headquarters about the procedures. The result was paralysis.

True empowerment meant lower-level decision making without specific guidance by higher levels. In what circumstances could top executives feel comfortable about such extreme delegation.

There were four main factors:

1. Each person must know and understand the mission of the team with which he or she works. Where the small unit is part of a much bigger whole, each person must understand the overall mission and where his or her group fits in. This is not a once and for all matter—a mission statement developed at one time and left unchanged while top executives return to ordinary administrative preoccupations. Instead, the overall mission is a living reality that has to be continually supplemented at the team level. Only if people know the overall mission and what it means to them in the near future can they act in accordance with it. Hence corporate leaders have to engage in a continual dialogue about the firm's mission and its meaning to each subgroup.

2. To act on their own initiative people must have the necessary competence. This requires not only technical specialization, but a grasp of the broader picture as well. It requires continual investments in the education and development of people. This can be done in a traditional organization, but the tendency is to see training as a cost item, rather than as an investment, and minimize it. Clusters are more clearly dependent on

35

the competencies of their members—rather than on the expertise and experience of a boss—and with the need for training more evident are more likely to make the necessary investments in people. This is a matter of attitude, and clusters have, in general, an attitude more favorable to human development than do hierarchies.

3. To make the correct choices in local circumstances people need information: not just local area information of the type they are closest to and to which they have the best access, but information as well about the overall setting in which they're acting. In today's world this means that they require a sophisticated information system that provides access to data bases and to networks through which they can communicate with those who have the information or knowledge they need. Traditional hierarchical methods deny them needed information (so that people must operate in the dark about the context of their activities) or require them to go up and down a chain of command to get information. This process is usually too slow and too fraught with potential for misunderstandings to be effective. Networks allow lateral communication which is both rapid and without risk of error due to intermediaries.

4. Finally, people need to know that they are trusted; that they will not be unfairly penalized for errors or failures that will sometimes accompany the exercise of their initiative. Higher-level managers must not sit in judgment over subordinates' decisions like Monday-morning quarterbacks after the game is over and the outcome clear. Identifying errors in that situation is really scapegoating, and subordinates will understandably avoid making decisions and taking actions that may turn them into scapegoats. Trust means knowing that when you act in good faith and things don't turn out right, you'll not be unfairly punished—you'll not lose your career or your job.

When are mistakes okay? When are errors to be tolerated? Unless a company has the correct answers to these questions it cannot empower its people. They will always remain frightened of being made scapegoats for error and will not act on their own.

Mistakes are okay when:

a. *They are made in pursuit of the mission.* Unfortunately, people often take actions not in furtherance of the firm's goals but of their own

36

or of those of their narrow department or function. When things go wrong for the firm because people were acting on their own narrow agenda, the error should not be excusable.

b. *Something useful is learned from the error*. When a mistake has occurred, it is important to investigate it to determine what went wrong. The purpose of the investigation is to learn so that further mistakes can be avoided, not to identify blame and find a scapegoat.

c. *The error is not part of a pattern*. If a person repeats the same error, or makes frequent, though different errors, he or she is either insufficiently trained or is in the wrong job. Empowering people does not mean tolerating errors unconditionally. When someone makes too many errors, then something has to be done.

d. *The error was made within the scope of the person's discretion, or one might say, authority*. Managers often fear that if people are empowered, they will make errors that grievously damage the firm. An error isn't okay, they say, if it costs too much. Unfortunately, many managers want to determine what is too much only after the event has occurred.

Instead, people ought to have a clear scope of discretion, and within that scope an error is tolerable. The scope of discretion is not, however, the same thing as the limits of authority that are granted in a hierarchy. First, for empowerment to occur, the scope of discretion must be much wider for many people than it is in a conventional hierarchy. Otherwise there is no additional freedom of action and there is no empowerment.

Second, in a cluster organization there can be some overlap of scope of discretion, a principle at variance with the hierarchical system. People in a cluster have accountability for both their own individual actions and those of the group; they have both a limited individual discretion for their own resources and a broader discretion for the resources of the cluster.

It is the combination of a broader individual scope of discretion with some discretion for the group as a whole that creates empowerment. Here the individual and the team come together. The individual can commit himself or herself, and in doing so commits to a degree the team as well, just as in any team sport.

We have just recounted briefly the whole theory of empowerment: that is, the conditions necessary for it to succeed. Unless all of these conditions are met, empowerment can be only partially and imperfectly achieved.

These conditions are difficult to create in a conventional hierarchical framework. Managers are too busy directing and supervising work to develop vision and communicate missions; they are too concerned with short-term costs to invest in developing competence; they guard information closely as a key to power in the organization; and they aren't prepared to trust people with discretion and authority. Some hierarchies overcome these limitations to a degree; most do not.

In contrast, empowerment is real in the cluster organization. It is made possible by communication of missions; by training to establish firm competence; by full availability of needed information; and by the trust of those in charge of the firm as a whole. Trust is made possible by making mistakes okay, when they meet certain criteria. The criteria are that the mistake is made in pursuit of the mission; the mistake provides a basis of learning for the future; is not part of a pattern of mistakes; and is within the broad limits of discretion of the person making the error.

Leadership means providing the vision; helping to develop missions; and providing inspiration, example, and challenge to people.

Thus the cluster organization makes both empowerment and management by leadership realities. This book describes in the chapters that follow how the conditions for empowerment and leadership are created through clusters.

Examples of Clusters

This book contains many examples of clusters and clusterlike organizations. I will summarize here one especially important story, which I will cover in greater detail in Chapter Five.

At British Petroleum

In 1987 Julian Darley took over as head of British Petroleum's Engineering Technical Centre (ETC) of more than 1,000 engineers and support workers. The center had to find a method of being far more productive in its delivery of services to its clients.

Clients told Darley they thought ETC expensive, distant, and unresponsive. The engineering specialists and the project team members from the client organization were not communicating well. In the words of one person, "You get the idea that the Centre's people are sitting back and watching you cock it up." On the other hand, the engineers' view of the attitudes of client personnel was "they don't want us to call them, they will call us."

Pondering the problem, ETC's executives decided more effective use of engineers for clients could be made by reducing specialization and enhancing flexible working relationships, embracing career development, and not trying to do everything.

In September 1988, a new organizational structure was put in place and a new system of management was begun. Enhancing customer support meant fewer working groups and a limited hierarchy. Increased flexibility implied an expanded role for engineers and a reduced role for specialist managers and supervisors, with the engineers managing their own work and communications across ETC; the specialist managers were assigned to different roles.

The proposed organizational elements were gathered into a model that was neither a hierarchy nor a matrix. Each major function—Engineering Resources, Technology Development, and Business Services—reported directly to Darley, through a general manager (GM). Each GM had a small team of subordinates and staff. In form the function offices looked like project teams.

Inside the "ring" described by the three functions were 16 independent clusters of 30 to 60 engineers. These were to be self-standing units with no reporting link to any functional leader. Engineers in a cluster were expected to be more or less self-managing on the basis of their experience and qualifications.

Each cluster prepared its own statement of capabilities, which was circulated to potential clients. When a customer called, he or she dealt directly with the engineers working on that project. The imperfections in communication from customer to engineer, which in the past arose from having managers in the chain, were eliminated. Clusters had no internal managerial structure, and the engineers in the cluster had no boss to whom to report.

Each cluster had one senior consultant responsible for coordinating the interaction between the functions and cluster members—but not for work supervision. For example, this individual would help the resource manager assigned to the cluster evaluate trainees' progress toward journeyman status. The senior consultant would help the business manager find available engineers to pick up specific jobs or recommend the "right" engineer for a specific task.

Each functional group had individuals assigned to service the various clusters. For example, Engineering Resources contained resource managers, whose job it was to review assignments and career progress for the 45 or so engineers in a cluster. Business Services designated a person to handle contacts and solicit business on behalf of a particular client. Technology Development designated a person to handle technology issues for a particular client.

The results? Costs are down, and client service is much improved. Said a customer in the fall of 1989, "We've used BPE for years, but we weren't their largest customer. We found it very difficult to get their attention. But a year ago everything changed. We find them much more responsive today."

Did he know about the organizational change that BPE had instituted? "No," he answered, "my organization knew nothing of that. All we knew was that they were much better with which to work."

Clusters versus Self-Managing Teams

Because a cluster is a very different type of organization, it is initially easier to understand by contrasting it with more familiar forms. A cluster is somewhat akin to a self-managing work team of the type now found in some offices and factories. But the cluster concept is broader. A cluster is more diverse in composition, being ordinarily made up of persons of different specialties and disciplines. Most important, clusters emerge from a different spirit and philosophy.

Self-managing teams continue to a large degree to involve the hierarchical managerial processes, although persons in the teams do the managerial tasks themselves. Clusters depend less on direction, whether from management (as in a traditional hierarchy) or from team members (as in a self-managed team). From a cluster point of view, self-managing teams are best described as nontraditional hierarchies.

There is greater flexibility in a cluster, which may be established for a particular period and later disbanded or may be increased or decreased in membership as needs require. Clusters have more in common with task forces than with self-managing teams of factory workers.

Also, the business motivation for clusters is different from that of self-managing work teams in factories. Factory teams are an effort to deal with a motivational crisis created by monotonous work. The team is an attempt to increase employee involvement and to derive better product quality as a result.

Are self-managing teams a step in the direction of a cluster? The answer is both yes and no. The teams represent a form of radical delegation that has much in common with a cluster. By helping managers learn to let go, self-managing teams take a long step toward clusters.

But self-managing work teams utilize hierarchical ways of thinking. For example, both hierarchies and self-managing teams speak of reporting relationships and where responsibility is placed. Clusters involve a more fundamental rethinking of managerial fundamentals.

Change Requires Leadership

Many executives have worked hard at improving their leadership capability in recent years, and this is all to the good. But management by leadership—by vision, example, and inspiration—cannot be done well in a traditional organization. The leader's message is delayed and distorted as it makes its slow and tortuous passage down the hierarchy. People continue to expect and wait for detailed direction. At the end of the supervisory pipeline, there is far too little scope for people to exercise initiative, take risks, and go beyond their own assigned tasks. In a hierarchy, empowerment is a hoax.

Clusters provide a solution. They make management by leadership a real possibility by allowing workers the freedom to respond with imagination and initiative. The leader gains and so do others. Nonconventional leadership is true leadership.

Clusters give a leader something similar to the freedom of random

41

access in computer memory. The leader can touch any part of the organization without being afraid of violating a chain of command or angering a key subordinate by going over his or her head. And as in random access, the part of the disk touched is free to respond.

Often executives set financial goals for their subordinates in the belief that in doing so they are acting as leaders. They are not. They are acting as administrators. For most people, financial goals provide no inspiration. All they see in a new financial target is more work, more time away from their families, more drudgery. There is no inspiration or vision for them to seize. This is not leadership.

Think about how people are persuaded to act when there is a lot at stake. Suppose that the firm wants many employees and their families to relocate across the country. What do top executives say to motivate them? For some, there are promotions and pay raises. These help but may not be enough. For others, there is neither more pay nor promotion, although the firm needs them.

The move is being made to cut costs and improve performance, and it will result in greater sales and a higher return on investment. The targets are an 80 percent increase in sales and an increase in return on investment (ROI) of 20 percent.

If executives share this information with their employees, will the latter care? Will it help persuade them to move?

Probably not. "What's in it for me?" they want to know.

What the leaders can share is a vision of what life will be like in the new setting; variety, personal relationships, challenge, opportunity, individual growth, and fun are powerful persuaders.

To influence others, executives must provide vision to guide action, examples of how to act to achieve outstanding performance, and inspiration so that people encounter challenges with enthusiasm. Last, leaders can see in others the potential for contributions that others may not even see themselves, and leaders can provide a setting in which others can excel.

Individual Accountability

Clusters involve a philosophy of work and human behavior that requires a new way of thinking. Thus, we must speak of individual accountability rather than personal responsibility, requiring *accountability* and *responsibility* to mean different things. Responsibility is about doing something right; accountability is about doing the right thing. In a cluster the individual has to understand the overall goal and key aspects of the overall situation to be able to know what needs to be done. Knowledge makes accountability real.

When people are told exactly what to do, they do exactly what they are told and little or no more. Clusters are the mechanism that gives each person enough opportunity and information to go beyond the routine. There cannot be true empowerment in a hierarchy, and this is the source of the disappointing results many companies have had in trying empowerment.

It is the essence of a cluster that those individuals who have the knowledge to do something also have the obligation to do it. Speed of action comes from acting on their own. And they are accountable for the results of their actions.

The issue of accountability versus responsibility is central to the differences among clusters, self-managing teams, and traditional hierarchies, but it requires an effort to comprehend. The difference in attitude is a fundamental matter and must be understood by those who wish to understand clusters and the opportunities they offer.

Consider the example of a high school football team that had just lost an important game. The team had been headed for the league championship and had expected to triumph. Instead, it lost. In the bus, returning from the opponent's field, the quarterback harangued the team for its poor performance.

Finally, one lineman got angry. "Lay off me," he said, "I did my job. I blocked the people I was supposed to. I opened holes in the line for our backs. I did what I was told to do. It's not my fault. You do your job and I'll do mine."

The lineman's outburst startled the quarterback and he had nothing further to say. But the coach, angered by the lineman's outburst answered the boy. "You're wrong," he said. "It's not enough for you to do your own job if the team is losing. You have a broader accountability for the success of the team as a whole. You have to do whatever you can to make the team successful, not just stick to your own little area. Even though you did what had been planned for you to do, when we got in trouble you had to do more and different things to help us win. We won't win by each one doing his own thing as if the rest don't exist.''

In a hierarchy, managers let employees take the position that as long as they have done as instructed, they have met their obligation. The managers alone are responsible for the overall success of the business. But in a cluster every person accepts individual accountability for the success or failure of the group effort. The employee makes a total commitment to the group and its objectives and accepts accountability for overall results. In this sense he or she becomes a professional, whatever the nature of the work being performed.

An Energy Generator

The cluster generates energy—or to use a term now popular, generates *empowerment*. By removing the hand of direction and control inherent in a hierarchy, a cluster generates a much higher intensity of human energy than does a hierarchy.

Having a single cluster or a small group of clusters in a firm does not make a cluster organization. Instead, a cluster organization is one designed to take advantage of clusters as the basic building blocks of business. To do so requires changes in many of the personnel, budgeting, and other policies and practices that characterize hierarchical organizations. In the chapters that follow I will provide detailed examples that show the several steps involved, and I will describe the modifications in managerial processes, personnel systems, and technological infrastructure that are necessary.

Does the cluster organization provide higher productivity, better quality, and performance? Will it stand the strains of business ups and downs? Those involved in clusters insist that the answer to these questions is yes, and they offer the experience of their units as evidence. Yet there are not many clusters in existence in comparison with the vast number of hierarchies, and those that do exist have not been around very long. No one can say today that the advantages of the cluster over the hierarchy is proven in the way social scientists would like to have it proven.

But business people cannot afford to wait for careful research to demonstrate which is better. The marketplace requires action now. Executives have to place their bets against an uncertain future. Although the cluster is new, as a true alternative to the hierarchy, it already has some limited degree of success behind it. For the executive searching for a way out of costly bureaucracy, the cluster offers an alluring promise. It also carries risks.

Accountability, empowerment, and energy are the elements that make the new organizational form desirable but also irreversible. People who have experienced the freedom and creativity of clusters will not go back to the old repressive style of the hierarchy. If compelled to do so, they will leave instead. This is why the trip to the future is on a one-way ticket.

CHAPTER THREE

Letting Go:
Learning the
Gorbachev Lesson

Clusters are a frightening concept to many people. For the most part, this is because clusters are poorly understood.

Executives find it difficult to "buy in" to clusters because of fears derived from older structures. Also, they are loath to surrender the authority and power with which they believe their positions to be imbued. Finally, there is a reluctance to accept the new form because it displaces their investment in knowledge about the traditional hierarchy.

Patterns of thinking appropriate to a traditional system are misleading when applied to clusters. Experience in hierarchies even suggests to some that a profitable business cannot be run in the new manner. As a result, people who find themselves drawn into behaving in the new ways appropriate to network organizations sometimes feel guilty about it. They are ashamed to act in unfamiliar ways, even though that is exactly what the circumstances demand.

To be embarrassed about changing how one acts in a firm is normal. To feel insecure in the new setting is also common. If you feel that way, you have a great deal of company. But do not worry about it. There is an easily comprehended reason for it.

People have spent years gaining experience about how others behave, about what motivates them, about how to accomplish things, about the trustworthiness of individuals, and about how flexible or inflexible people are. This experience is often referred to as "street smarts."

Street smarts are, of course, highly situational. And if the context changes, they are suddenly obsolete. Lessons learned about human behavior in a corporate bureaucracy are wrong when applied to a cluster. Executives who persist in applying an outmoded pattern of street smarts risk destroying their careers and their companies.

There is a story called the carpenter's lament, which goes as follows: "Oh, darn, I cut it off again and it's still too short!" Apparently the carpenter had only one response to any problem: He cut. If the board was already too short, all he could do was cut it again. Obviously, the problem was not being solved.

Executives too much committed to tight top-down control in a company are like the carpenter. If their company performs poorly, they tighten up. If things get worse, they tighten up more. They never seem to notice that the problem may be that they were too tight in the first place.

Too-tight executives need to learn the Gorbachev lesson: When things go badly, loosen up! Just as the Kremlin learned it cannot run a modern economy with serfs, top executives must realize that they cannot run a modern corporation with old-style employees. So the right response is to let go. Give people in the organization a chance to use their initiative.

For managers who have made the shift to cluster organizations, the fears of those who have not seem misplaced. A cluster organization can be competitive and profitable. In many circumstances clusters make as much or more sense than a traditional hierarchy, but this can be seen only when the cluster is understood in its own terms. Loss of control, possible anarchy, and other fears derived from experience with hierarchies that failed are generally not applicable to clusters. Finally, loss of power is compensated for by greater influence and potentially greater rewards. Power in a hierarchy tends to be limited and is divided and contested between managers and employees. Power in a cluster organization can be shared without leaving anyone powerless. What is impossible in a hierarchy becomes achievable with a cluster organization.

The loss of an investment in existing knowledge is real, but all technological, economic, and social progress involves replacing the old with the new. New street smarts must be learned: how empowered people take initiative, how the desire to learn and grow can be a great motivator, how variety stimulates enthusiasm in work, and how control can be exercised through education and training.

Limitations on Comprehension

People are often skeptical about the believability or practicality of what they are reading. This is especially likely to happen in reading about clusters.

We approach clusters with deeply entrenched preconceptions rooted in our experience with traditional hierarchies. Often, we assume that certain characteristics of hierarchies and those who work in them are elements of human nature, and not simply behavior adapted to this traditional setting. As a result, the very different human dynamics that exist in clusters seem utopian—as they would be in a traditional setting. Experience makes people suspicious and cynicism causes them to reject evidence. They cannot accept the reality of clusters because their experience in hierarchies teaches them something quite different.

A thoroughgoing cluster organization is as different from a hierarchy as a hierarchy is from a mob. One cannot understand much about a hierarchy by relying on one's experience with a mob. Nor can one understand much about a cluster by relying on one's experience with a hierarchy.

Clusters are a new paradigm for organizations and so require a substantial suspension of disbelief in order to comprehend them. Just as nonlinear geometry requires a student to abandon deeply held convictions about spatial relationships derived from Euclidian models, cluster organizations require the reader to suspend deeply held convictions derived from hierarchical systems.

In this part I will answer the principal questions asked about the cluster model. By confronting difficulties so early in the book, the reader may be able to overcome them enough to study the chapters that follow with a more open mind. What opinion the reader ultimately forms about clusters is up to him or her, of course.

Later, after reading the entire book, the reader may wish to return to this chapter. Then he or she will understand its message far better.

Hugo Uyterhoeven of the Harvard Business School once commented that he sometimes gave the same presentation twice to students: once at the outset of a course and again at the end. Invariably, he said, at the end of the course students would demand, "Why didn't you tell us that at the start of the course?" "I did," he would reply; "but what I said then, just repeated, sounds totally different now that you've had the experience of the entire program."

So it is with clusters. What the reader comprehends when his or her mind is still fixed in the mode of hierarchical thought is dramatically different from what he or she will understand when traditional hierarchies are forgotten.

An executive once told me about his difficulty in coming to grips with cluster concepts: "It was as if I were in a role-playing exercise trying to be someone I wasn't. I had to learn new expressions and new behavior. Every time I opened my mouth I'd say the wrong thing and have to put my hand quickly over it. Then I'd say, 'Excuse me; that was old style language again.' This went on until finally I had learned the new language; then I could speak freely."

Four Principal Questions

When making presentations about clusters I am often asked about them in terms appropriate to a hierarchy: Who's in charge? How are different units kept in alignment? How do managers motivate their workers? What if a cluster gets out of control?

"In charge," "alignment," "motivation," and "control" are concepts more appropriate to a hierarchy than to a cluster. Questions that include these concepts are off the mark from the outset.

Nevertheless, they must be answered. In the pages that follow I will discuss clusters in terms appropriate to hierarchies. This is not at all unprecedented. The Apostle Paul found it necessary to talk to the Athenians about Jesus in the language of the pagan religions. The worldly scholars of the Middle Ages found it necessary to talk about science in the language of religion. Examples abound, but in each instance those who were explaining the new recognized that it could be comprehended only imperfectly in the categories of the old.

Honest answers to some of the following questions would be "You don't need to ask that" and "Don't worry; it won't happen, but if it does, it won't matter." Answers like these, no matter how merited, are always unsatisfactory to those who asked. So I will answer the questions in depth, regardless of their merit.

Question 1
In a cluster, who's in charge?

No one is "in charge" in the traditional sense. There is no one person who is designated a supervisor by higher-level management and to whom individuals in the cluster have a reporting responsibility. There is no individual in whom responsibility for the performance of the cluster is placed. No single person has the authority to direct, discipline, or dismiss others.

But this does not mean that there is no supervision, responsibility, direction, and discipline. In fact these elements of managerial control—much more necessary in a hierarchy than in a cluster—are exercised in several ways in a cluster.

First, the cluster itself performs each of these responsibilities. Its members or subunits meet to review the quality of their work, to examine how well they work together, to make decisions, to decide direction, and to take disciplinary action against individuals and subgroups as necessary. Can a group discipline its members? Yes, it can. Can a group make decisions? Often it can, as we all know. But when it cannot, a leader must be identified who can act on behalf of the group as a whole. Clusters ordinarily do this.

Second, leaders—on both specific projects and in the cluster generally—who provide supervision, direction, and discipline are granted authority to do so by the others in the group. For example, many large corporations have a top management team that meets as a committee to conduct the business. Each member recognizes that the group brings more knowledge and experience to a problem than does an individual acting alone. With a common understanding of the business and years together, the management team rarely encounters deep differences of opinion.

But each executive also knows the dangers of relying on a committee when speed and decisiveness are needed. Hence, by common consent, one member of the team is empowered to make decisions on behalf of all when there is a dispute among them or when time is of the essence. That person is a kind of accepted tie-breaker. When the person who is accepted in this position of leadership is also the chairperson of the firm, the hierarchical structure is validated in practice. In many cases, however, it is not the chairperson who acts as the tie-breaker.

To act effectively, the cluster must have a method of resolving internal disputes and of making quick choices when necessary. Leadership in these areas goes to those who are accepted as the most competent—either best at the techniques involved or in handling people. Often different projects or different issues will have different members of the cluster in the leadership role. What is missing is the designation by higher-level managers of a particular individual to perform the tie-breaker function in all cases.

Finally, there is a residual hierarchy in the firm that interacts with the clusters and may, if necessary, exercise hierarchical authority in supervising and directing a cluster. A dysfunctional cluster can be eliminated. In fact, because clusters are fairly flexible units, to eliminate a demoralized cluster and start over is usually much easier than to eliminate a department in a hierarchy.

Question 2
How do you prevent clusters from degenerating into anarchy?

"What is anarchy?" my ten-year-old daughter asked me after seeing the symbol of anarchy scribbled on a downtown wall.

"It's chaos, confusion, and no rules," I responded.

Her face lit up. "Sounds like fun," she said.

Managers suspect that employees, like children, will find anarchy

51

irresistible. Just as adults do not trust children to do schoolwork when there are temptations to play, managers do not trust employees to work when there is no direct supervision.

The lack of trust takes two general forms. In many firms supervisors limit the discretion and freedom of employees about almost everything by giving them precise directions about the work to be done and by closely overseeing its performance. In professional service firms, research labs, and certain skilled trades, the firm trusts the employee with considerable discretion in the performance of the work itself but not in the business and administrative elements. In contrast, trusting the employee to do what is appropriate in both the performance of the work and in business and administrative elements is at the heart of the productivity gain and administrative cost reduction that clusters commonly achieve.

Trusting employees is based on more than faith. It is made possible in clusters by education about taking charge of one's work and training in needed skills. It is bolstered by developing human relationships between the managers and employees on an adult basis through training and informal interactions. Trust is built day by day and is a quality of the organization that is continually being worked on.

Proof of the value of trusting employees is given by the successes reported by many companies in clusterlike settings. In effect managers in clusters may in the vast majority of instances trust employees not to allow the clusters to degenerate into anarchy.

Question 3
How can you keep the activities of the clusters aligned with the company's mission?

People in clusters will align with the overall organization for several reasons. First, it helps them accomplish their business goals. Second, it facilitates interaction between a cluster and the rest of the organization. Third, the residual hierarchy in the cluster organization has as its principal task creating alignment between the clusters and the mission of the organization as a whole.

Alignment is created by having the clusters understand the mission of the firm and by sharing information about how other parts of the organization are pursuing the mission. Cluster organizations are designed to facilitate information sharing.

Question 4
*How does a company get its people to want to take broad accountability,
to learn, and to make decisions as required by a cluster setting?*

In brief the answer is by telling them, by letting them, and by supporting them. Education and training acquaint the individual with what is expected and help provide the necessary skills (for specific skill requirements, see Chapter Eight). Experience is provided by the flexibility of assignment that a cluster permits. Support is given by managers and, most important, by peers.

One firm experimenting with clusters has characterized ideal cluster members as "T people." The idea is that a person has depth in a specialty (probably his or her old job assignment in an hierarchy), which can be represented at the stem of the T. The cluster adds a band of general knowledge, which makes the person able to contribute generally in the team and which can be represented at the bar that crosses the stem to form the entire letter T.

"For years," said a team member to a new entrant to the cluster, "you've been preparing price quotations on the equipment we sell. That's your stem. Now you're going to learn about how we market to petroleum and chemical companies. That'll be the top of your T. Then you'll be a T person for our cluster."

Objections to Clusters

To help readers further comprehend clusters on their own terms, in this part I will list or comment on the 11 objections most often raised about the cluster concept.

Objection 1
Clusters ignore the innate human need for hierarchies.

Much of what we perceive as human nature in the workplace is nothing more than a thorough adaptation of individuals to a hierarchical context. People expect to be given direction, so they seek it out. To be without a supervisor means that one is on one's own in a way that is often profoundly disturbing.

The apparent search of the individual for a hierarchy to direct his or her activities is not truly an innate human drive, but instead is a sophisticated behavioral device for avoiding personal responsibility. Hierarchies permit people to demand specific direction from their supervisors and thereby limit their accountability to carrying out the boss's orders even if the business fails in the process. Responsibility is limited to carrying out orders, not to pursuing successfully the mission of the firm.

A U.S. firm was acquired by a Japanese concern. The American general manager went to Tokyo to see his new boss, the chairperson of the Japanese company. After pleasantries the general manager asked for his orders.

"Do what is right," replied the Japanese executive.

The American demanded greater specificity.

"Do what is right," was the reply.

Was this an inappropriate instruction? It was nonspecific, but the manager presumably knew his company's situation in America far better than his Japanese owner. Was the American not in a better position to set goals for himself?

How was the American to decide what was "right"? He could discuss it with his counterparts in the Japanese company, or he could consult his own judgment. But the responsibility was his alone because he had been unable to shift it to his boss.

No innate human need for a hierarchy tells a person what to do. To ask for detailed orders is simply a way of trying to avoid true accountability. But there is more to Objection 1.

There is a hierarchy of abilities among human beings. Human groups, like chickens in a barnyard, may have a pecking order, but one based on thinking capability rather than size or strength. Do clusters violate this innate characteristic of creatures—human beings included? No. Distinctions among individuals based on ability exist in clusters. Natural leaders emerge and play a disproportionate role in the activities of the group.

A formally designated hierarchy is not required for leadership to emerge. Quite the contrary. Executives frequently place in supervisory positions persons who turn out to lack leadership skills. The rigidity of a hierarchy then prevents natural leadership ability in subordinates from showing itself. In a cluster natural ability has more room to reveal itself than in a hierarchy.

Objection 2
It is impossible to motivate people without the prospect of promotion.

Cluster organizations lack the many-runged ladders of promotion that characterize traditional hierarchies. This is, as the objection suggests, a significant limitation on the cluster organization's ability to use promotion to motivate employees.

But it is a mistake to give too much weight to this factor. First, in many hierarchies today management ranks are full and the company has ceased to grow. The result is that there are few promotion opportunities actually available, despite the large number of management positions. Because promotion is not readily available in the traditional structure, the supposed advantage of a hierarchy in this regard is very much limited.

Second, most people can find considerable motivation in their jobs even if promotions are not readily available. I draw support for this assertion from a study of motivation I conducted at IBM. I asked a representative sample of 200 employees to express in their own words what motivated them at work. Later when I analyzed their comments for recurring themes, three factors emerged.

Pay and Promotion

One theme was the desire for higher pay and an opportunity to climb a career ladder. To be sure that those interviewed had not understated the importance of this theme, I coded and identified all substantive positive references to this factor as the key one. Even after this adjustment, only 22 percent of respondents cited this theme as an important motivator; this finding is a clear indication of the limited role that pay has in motivating the majority of IBM employees.

Pay is not, of course, missing as a motivator in a cluster organization. People in clusters can be compensated for performance on an individual basis, just as in a hierarchy (see Chapter Nine). Only the promotion ladder is much reduced in importance.

Recognition of Job Accomplishments

About 33 percent of respondents described themselves as motivated by recognition of their contributions and accomplishments.

Many pointed to specific recognition from the team of people with whom they work most closely as key. "What motivates me," said one, "is to propose new ideas and have them accepted."

Self-Motivation

The largest group, 44 percent, described themselves as motivated by their own feelings about the work they did and how they did it. These people stressed the importance of self-respect, which came from their own recognition of a challenge met and overcome.

"I always do a top job," one person said. Another reported, "Doing good work is part of my self-image." Yet another said, "I love the work that I do."

With promotion lessened as a source of motivation in clusters, recognition by peers and the interest inherent in work become key sources of motivation. However, as the IBM survey indicates, recognition and self-motivation already outdistance pay and promotion in some important situations.

Finally, it may well turn out in the 1990s that compensation practices become altered to reward business performance more substantially. Then how much money a person makes will no longer be a question of how many people report to him or her, so an ambitious person need not aspire to manage a big organization.

Objection 3
Individual performance in a cluster will "level down"
to the lowest common denominator.

In a hierarchy managers often must struggle against the tendency of employees to do as little as they can get away with. The employee who is able to do the least often seems to set the standard for the rest. In a cluster, where there are no supervisors to push people to higher standards, will not all performance sink to the lowest level?

Individual leveling down of performance in a hierarchy is to a large degree the result of a game in which the supervisor tries to force the employee to perform chores and obey rules, including production standards set by the company. Why does an employee try to get away with as little work as possible? Because the game of trying to outsmart the supervisor is more interesting than the work itself.

It is the hierarchy rather than the cluster that levels performance to the least common denominator. Not trusting anyone, hierarchical control subjects all to restraints intended to prevent malingering by the few. The restraints limit the initiative and performance of the best employees.

In a cluster there is no supervisor to outsmart. Employees working with the few managers who remain develop work assignments that are interesting and challenging. Peers, who depend on each other to carry part of the load, are very intolerant of shirkers. In effect the group creates an environment that encourages effort, something only the best supervisors can accomplish.

This response is not simply theory. The evidence is strong, though still largely anecdotal, that performance standards are higher on average in clusters than in hierarchical units.

But if a cluster does become demoralized and performance declines to unacceptable levels, the managers who remain in the organization can step in to reform or eliminate the cluster. What will signal that a cluster is demoralized? Its performance record and the exit of the better performers from it.

Objection 4
People will lose their individualism and privacy in
the close relationships that exist in working teams.

As contrasted with individuals doing their work separately and interacting only with a supervisor, people are thrown into closer contact in a cluster. Many people find working in teams a delightful antidote to the isolation of the traditional arrangement. Others already work in teams to a greater or lesser degree in hierarchical organizations. So to a large extent the change that occurs by going to a cluster is either welcomed or is not so great a change after all.

Nonetheless, clusters do substantially involve people in the group. To ensure that the individual is not thereby lost sight of, cluster organizations take many precautions.

First, individual performance appraisal is maintained. Each employee is evaluated and compensated on the basis of his or her own contribution. (I will describe how this is done in detail in later chapters.)

Second, work space is provided for the individual as well as the group. In Du Pont Fibers I/S, for example, everyone was assigned private office space when new quarters were obtained. This was a departure from the company's normal mode. In the hierarchy, clerical staff had never been considered important enough to have private space. A person's office (or *cave*, to use a term we'll meet later in the book) is as much his or her own as it would be in a hierarchy. It can be personalized and provides a refuge from the group when one is needed.

Third, the resource manager in a cluster organization prepares customized development plans for each individual. These career plans provide for learning and growth in both classroom and workplace.

Again, the individual is not lost in the group. Remember that a cluster is not a group of undifferentiated elements. Instead, a cluster is a multi-disciplinary and multifunctional unit in which each individual makes a unique contribution, and so is valued for herself or himself.

In hierarchies today some people—among them the most ambitious—have a career strategy of developing a close relationship with the boss while pushing aside all others. The boss, after all, is the key to promotion opportunities. These people do not want to be hindered in their climb to the top by having to work with others. Teamwork dilutes both their visibility and their contact with the boss.

In cluster organizations, people have to work together and support others. They must accept an accountability that goes to the performance of the group as a whole, not just their own work. Their ability to work with others in a peer relationship becomes an important part of their success or failure. They must acknowledge the contribution of others, rather than hog all credit for themselves. And they take the risk that the poor performance of others, or their own inability to work with others, will hinder their careers.

Objection 5
If I do not have an important-sounding job title, I will
not be able to get a good position in another company.

Because a cluster organization has fewer rungs on the job ladder, titles are likely to be different from more traditionally organized firms. In a cluster, for example, a person may have titles such as production associate, sales partner, or technical contributor. Probably these titles have few outside counterparts. So when a person seeks a job outside the company, will he or she be undervalued?

Not necessarily. Job titles already differ substantially among firms. In consequence better résumés carry not only a job title but also an explanation of the work involved. Many résumés also give examples of important assignments.

When assignments are given on a résumé or in a job interview, people who have worked in clusters are likely to have an advantage over those from hierarchies because experience is more easily gained in the fluid setting of the cluster. A cluster member may well have managed a project for the team. Although mainly a worker, he or she has had managerial experience to put on the résumé. That would not have happened in a hierarchy unless the person had been promoted fully into management ranks.

Furthermore, even though most companies do not yet use clusters, they are making considerable use of teamwork in a variety of ways. Hence the experience of having worked in groups is valuable, as are the skills involved in teamwork. Both experience and skills will have been gained by people who have worked in clusters and will look good on their résumés.

In a cluster organization a resource manager should maintain a résumé as part of the career planning and performance evaluation done for each individual. The résumé should be complete not only with position title but also key assignments, contributions, and skills. Should a person look for work elsewhere in a different cluster in the same company or in another company, this résumé would be very helpful in obtaining a good position.

Objection 6
*There will be no effective limit on mistakes made by employees
in a cluster because there is no direct supervision.*

The lack of formally designated supervisors does not mean that there are no standards for performance nor that people are not observing performance. In teams whose members depend on the efforts of others, people will be quick to notice and object to errors.

An individual performance appraisal process also exists in cluster organizations which is different from but probably superior to that centering on the supervisor in a hierarchy. (For more about the appraisal process in cluster organizations see Chapter Nine.)

People who repeatedly make serious errors should not remain with the team. Not everyone is suited for the role of a contributor in a cluster, and when a clear lack of fit is identified, the person should look for something elsewhere. In many instances the team or its leaders will talk with the individual. In some instances a resource manager may have to get involved.

The need to keep in the cluster those who are effective contributors should not obscure the importance of allowing people the leeway to make errors. Mistakes are an important source of learning and will inevitably occur when risks are taken, as they should be in any innovative and aggressive setting.

A hierarchy tends to discourage mistakes, unless individual managers convince their subordinates that it is permissible to take risks. A mistake is permissible when

- It is made in pursuit of the mission of the organization. (However mistakes made in furtherance of a person's ego or own private agenda or solely because of thoughtlessness are not acceptable.)
- The individual who made the mistake learns from it.
- The organization learns from the mistake.
- The mistake is not part of a repetitive pattern of errors.

Objection 7
Clusters will take all the fun out of being a boss.

Whether this is a valid objection depends on the manager. If the fun of being a boss is to push others around, that will be difficult in a cluster organization. If the fun of being a boss is to repay others for one's own ill treatment in the past, a cluster is not the place to do it.

But if you are the kind of boss who would like not to have to get after people, who wants to have time to devote to planning the longer-term future of the organization, and who likes to see people self-motivated and enthusiastic, a cluster organization will make work more fun.

Objection 8
Managers will lose touch with their organizations.

Letting go need not mean losing touch. Remember that managers in a hierarchy have different styles. For the hands-on manager who does most things personally, the increased delegation involved in clusters may cause a feeling of being out of touch. But it frees that person from detail to work on longer-range matters.

For the manager in a hierarchy who likes to set quantitative goals and then step back, intervening only when the targets are unmet, the cluster may act as a device to pull him or her closer to the business. Cluster members may seek help or support and thereby draw a manager in.

Objection 9
There won't be any middle managers left, and those
of us who are middle managers will lose our jobs.

There will be middle managers left—and possibly more of them than now. This may seem paradoxical. After all, one of the great advantages claimed for the cluster organization is that it reduces administrative costs by reducing the number of middle managers.

The paradox encountered here is similar to that which involves productivity increases and employment opportunities generally. For two centuries economists have explained with much justification to workers that technological progress on the whole creates jobs, even though it replaces workers with technology. Why? Because technological progress creates economic growth and growth creates more jobs than those lost to new technology.

The same is true of the cluster organization's impact on middle management. Clusters harness two elements to make progress: organizational innovation and technological advance (especially in computer and communications technology). While the ratio of middle managers to employees in cluster organizations declines, as smaller organizations grow and new organizations are created in an expanding economy, middle management jobs are created.

Data about employment levels in the U.S. economy reveal this process in action. Despite years of corporate downsizing and delayering, the number of middle managers in the economy as a whole has grown.

Objection 10
Companies that have experimented with organizational structures like clusters have failed in business.

People Express Airlines in particular is pointed to as a firm that made highly publicized use of a clusterlike system, lost a lot of money, and was sold just before it went bankrupt.

People Express is an important case. The firm made creative use of an organizational concept much akin to clusters, although never so labeled. Started in 1981, it grew rapidly for several years but then failed. Why?

Because the firm's structure was so unusual and received so much publicity some people ascribe its business failure to its organizational innovations. But most persons who were close to the airline industry do not do so.

In a period when the airline industry was rapidly being consolidated into a few giant carriers, People Express, a start-up company, had to grow rapidly to stay independent. The firm overreached itself in acquisitions and expansion.

Don Burr, who was founder and chief executive officer of People Express, attributes the airline's failure to matters other than its cluster-type organization. From the beginning of the carrier to its end, People Express had the lowest labor costs in the industry and the highest employee productivity. The organizational innovations were what gave the company its opportunity.

"Don Burr was a motivational genius," a United Airlines executive told me, "but he collapsed once the larger carriers applied real competitive pressure." When United, Delta, Eastern, and American cut prices and added flights in direct competition with People Express, the firm lacked the financial and human resources to counter successfully.

Burr acknowledges that he and People Express's other top executives were slow to recognize the crucial role of advanced reservations systems, of the monopolization of traffic in hubs, and of marketing innovations such as frequent flyer programs. Business decisions and omissions made by top executives sunk People Express, not its organizational structure.

Objection 11
The advantages claimed for clusters can also be obtained in a hierarchy.

The response to this objection is yes and no. Yes, most can be obtained in a hierarchy, but only if the managers and executives in it behave much differently from what is ordinary in a hierarchy. It will be difficult for them to do so because the very existence of the hierarchy mitigates against it.

For example, chief executives today seemingly never tire of exhorting their employees to take more initiative in the workplace. But most employees know that should they act without their supervisor's concurrence, they may well be severely disciplined if things don't go well.

Limitations of Clusters

Lest it seem that this defense of the cluster organization against the objections just raised is intended to imply that clusters have no limitations, I will briefly identify three principle shortcomings here and later discuss them at length in Chapter Eleven.

Limitation 1
Clusters won't work with all people.

Clusters require persons with basic skills and a reasonable degree of motivation toward their work.

Limitation 2
They won't work in all situations.

High-volume/low-variance activities are poorly suited to clusters because the work cannot be readily made interesting and because there is little discretion in how it is done. The advantages of a cluster in responsiveness to customers and in lower costs are unachievable in this environment.

There is, however, a tendency for executives to believe that much more of their organization's work is of this repetitive nature than is actually the case.

Limitation 3
*Clusters will fail where managers and employees are
unable or unwilling to let go of the old paradigm.*

As noted, clusters are dependent on the quality of leadership and on the nature of employee attitudes. If managers and employees persist in behaving in ways appropriate to a hierarchy, the cluster will surely fail.

CHAPTER FOUR

"It's Like a Beehive": How Clusters Harness Cooperation and Competition

A manager who had observed a cluster in action said,

> It's like a beehive. When you look in, you see everyone busy and scurrying about, but there is no one in apparent charge and when you ask about it, there is little structure that can be explained to you. Yet, as in a beehive, it is clear that much is getting done. The participants seem to have roles, are accomplishing their tasks, and communicating with each other. There is even a top management team, like a queen bee and her attendants. But they seem to have little to do with the activity in the hive.
>
> Another thing that impressed me is that there is both competition among the members of a beehive organization and mutual cooperation and support. It isn't just consensus and mutuality, as in Asia, or just individuals working separately under direct supervision, as in many American organizations. The beehives seem to have been able to harness both the competitive and the cooperative drives into a very powerful combination.

Fortunately for the reader who wants to move toward a more modern organization, others have already gone through the hard process of thinking out what to do and how to do it. I will draw on their experience to help you understand what the new system is and how to apply it to your situation. You will, of course, have to refine it to fit your circumstances in detail, but you will not have to start from scratch.

Teams, limited hierarchy, delegated decision making, managers acting as information channels and maintaining financial control through budgets and reports, and broad goal setting rather than detailed oversight are all key elements of the cluster form in action. Here is how each of these features exhibits itself in a broader context.

Working in Teams

Individuals are responsible to the cluster for their performance, and the cluster as a whole is responsible for work quality. Tasks may be allocated among members in many different ways, including rotation of assignments. People bring certain competencies to the group and may over time acquire new ones. Conducting meetings and other administrative functions are delegated to members. There is no direct supervision of one person in the group by another except in the context of teaching.

Individuals in clusters often work alone rather than in the close joint activity of an assembly operation. In this situation the cluster operates largely as a support group.

In some firms an individual in a cluster will establish a small group to whom he or she looks for guidance and support. The group may consist of peers, suppliers, internal users of his or her services, and even external customers. In an informal sense the person reports to this group, which may function almost as a personalized board of directors. The committee is responsible for coordinating the activities and support of the individual involved.

A Sales Operation

One of the most ambitious applications of the cluster concept is being made by a sales support division of a Fortune 500 company. The divisional management team, which has the objective of increasing sales threefold in the next five years, appears to have the products and market opportunity to do so. But does the division have the organizational capability?

About a year ago, the division's key manager was concerned that it did not. Several issues had come to his attention.

First, as very rapid growth occurred, managers in different nations would have difficulty keeping pace, especially if the units grew in their current form. They would quickly become so large and cumbersome as to put the sales objectives themselves at risk.

Second, the industry was changing. New products were being introduced at a rapid rate. New customers were less sophisticated technically but wanted more complex applications before they would make large purchases of the company's products. This required the company to field sales teams comprising individuals with different specialties. To field such teams, the different geographic regions would need to be less self-sufficient, drawing on resources from outside their own areas.

As he worked through ways to meet these challenges, the manager saw an opportunity to kill several birds with one stone. By undertaking an imaginative organizational shift, he could deal with changing customer needs and rapid market growth and bring his corporate-level staff functions into closer support of the business itself. The core of the new concept was the creation of cross-functional teams at all levels of the division.

At corporate headquarters, six teams were established; two of them were directed at specific product and service areas. The company's sales managers in key geographic areas abroad were included in these teams. Four others covered administrative areas: marketing, logistics, administration, and finance.

At the geographic or regional level, six more teams were established: technology, logistics, information services, finance, administration, and a service group. Operating managers from subsidiaries in specific countries were included in these teams.

Finally, at the national level, teams that mirrored those at the regional level were started. These teams were intended to permit better mobilization of company resources for interacting with customers.

In summary, the organizational structure consisted of three levels of interdisciplinary teams linked by common membership from one level to the next. To give greater strength to the linkage, a top management team was created at the corporate level, which was then linked to similar teams at the regional level, and each regional level team was linked to teams at the national level.

In principle the corporate teams were to exercise strategic direction, the regional teams were to adapt the strategy to their portion of the globe, and the national teams were to implement the plans. However the organizational structure had other effects on management.

The structure created two separate lines of communications for each team member. The traditional line ran to a member's corporate-level functional manager. The direct line ran through the teams at each level of the division. But would team members receive the same messages from both lines? The key to making the teams work was to see that their members were always receiving the same messages from corporate staff and their own teams.

To ensure that communications were consistent, corporate staff and team leaders would have to pursue the same objectives. One significant way to do so was to measure and reward the performance of functional managers and team members on the same basis. To accomplish this goal, certain changes were necessary in the division's traditional mode of operation.

Team members continued to receive salaries based on their functional areas, but bonuses were based on team results. To make this possible, all bonus reviews had to be scheduled nearly simultaneously, immediately after financial results for each year were determined and available. Also, extensive meetings were scheduled at which the new organizational structure was explained, discussed, and modified as seemed best. Then, approximately nine months after its conception, the new system went into action.

Limited Residual Hierarchy

Neither a cluster nor an informal support group is a new layer of bureaucracy. Nor do clusters and support groups supplement an existing hierarchal structure, for if they were to do so, it would simply add layers to the existing bureaucracy. Clusters are more formal than support groups, but both have a role in enabling work to be done more efficiently and effectively.

Much nonsense has been written about "network" organizations having no hierarchy. This is simply not the case. A residual or limited hierarchy is necessary and exists in all cluster organizations—not in the clusters themselves, which operate with leadership but without formal hierarchy, but in the organization as a whole. It is limited in size, has few levels, and is essential to the functioning of the clusters.

The key functions of the residual hierarchy are (1) communicating with other elements of the organization and among the clusters and (2) serving as a clearing house for suggestions, ideas, new initiatives, and proposals for change.

The hierarchy also represents the organization to the world outside (not necessarily to customers, who are dealt with directly in the clusters), for example, the government, media, and other firms in the industry, and makes such choices as may have to be made on behalf of the organization as a whole. Perhaps someday human society will develop business organizations without any hierarchy at all, but we are not yet at that stage.

Nonetheless, some executives apparently believe that the loss of any of their traditional authority or functions represents a revolution they cannot cope with. As a result some of the most far-reaching plans for clusters have been much resisted by executives, despite the clear business advantages to be gained by the changes.

An Automobile Marketing Operation

When executives try to get closer to customers, they are sometimes shocked at the implications. One marketing division of a large auto company sold its product through dealers, and for years it was very successful. Then, as many foreign firms entered its marketplace, it saw its market share erode substantially. What would be necessary, its managers asked, to turn the slide around and regain share?

The division's management worked hard on a vision statement and developed a new commitment to the customer—at first on paper but also with a determination to make the commitment real. However, the division did not deal directly with its ultimate consumers. Instead it relied on a dealer network to distribute and service its product.

In a sense the dealers were the customers, but the division's executives knew that dealer demand was derived from ultimate consumers. Since advertising, promotion, and product development were functions of the division and not of the dealers, the division knew it had to stay in touch with ultimate consumers. It could not afford to view dealers as its primary customers.

The division stayed in touch with consumers through surveys, focus groups, and personal contact. It also solicited the opinions of its dealers. Finally, of course, it studied its sales figures and those of its competitors. Customer satisfaction surveys indicated that product preference was not the only consideration in auto purchases. The relationship with the dealers, both in buying and servicing the cars, was equally important. The matter was clear: To regain market share customers had to be lured back to the company's products, and thus a closer relationship to dealers had to be forged; there was no other alternative.

Division executives appointed a task force to analyze its dealer relationships. The group soon developed recommendations concerning what dealers could do to attract customers. However, in trying to implement its suggestions, it ran straight into a festering problem—its existing poor relationship with its dealers.

How was the division to get the dealers to take action? Dealers had little confidence in the division's advice. When division representatives visited dealers, the dealers tended to react with all the suspicion of a small businessperson greeting a tax examiner. Closer examination suggested reasons for this negative response.

The field force responsible for representing the division to dealers was supposed to counsel and support them. However, individual field representatives were by and large newly hired and knew little about the business. What training they were given by the division had not yet been supplemented by experience. The dealers generally were personally fond of the field reps but had no confidence in them. Executives in the division were continually receiving complaints from dealers about the ''greenness'' of the reps and said they resented having to educate them.

The problem of inexperience was compounded by turnover. An experienced rep did not stay long in the position. Instead he or she looked for the first opportunity to move further up the division's management ladder, as each step brought higher pay and greater status. The best field reps moved up and away from the dealers quickly; the others remained, but often they were not very good.

To the dealers, the reps were a double source of dissatisfaction. They were always training new ones, and those who turned out to be good left quickly.

Although the reps were a crucial link between division and car buyer, acting through the dealers, they were unable to function as such. Instead, lacking experience and credibility, they became messengers, passing along dealers' requests to higher-ups in the division, and when the division wanted something done, passing messages the other way. When truly important matters came up, major dealers simply went to division executives for answers. The result was a system that did not work very well.

The division's organization was a traditional hierarchy, with six layers of management presiding over some 700 people. The dealers were at the bottom of the diagram, linked to the field reps, and beneath the dealers were the customers.

In their deliberations, the task force reversed this order and put the customers on top. They placed the dealers next to them, and the link between division and dealers—the field reps—next. Beneath the reps in an inverted pyramid came the six management layers. The whole precariously balanced structure stood on a single point, labeled the vice president of marketing.

The task force was looking for a customer-focused organization. They wanted more than lip service, more even than an attitude, no matter how sincere. They wanted a structure to make the new focus a reality and managerial systems to support it.

The consequences of the new vision were dramatic. It required the division to change the nature of the field rep position. It also suggested fundamental changes in the organizational structure.

Rather than being entry-level messengers, field reps had to be the most experienced, capable, and best people in the division. They needed knowledge and experience to appear credible to dealers—to earn their trust and influence them. Because the role was the crucial link between division and ultimate customers, the field reps were to be seen as the key players and supported by others in the division.

The role of the regional staffs and higher-level managers was now seen as servicing the field reps. No longer did managers direct and control. Now they responded to requests from the field staff.

The most significant administrative jobs would be dealing with the

71

reps and were therefore at the regional level, not the corporate level. Dealer sales data would be entered into divisional computers by the dealers themselves, rather than collected by field reps for entry at division headquarters. Field reps were now to be users of the data—professionals, not messengers.

The logic of the changes suggested a new organizational design. Abandoning the inverted pyramid as unstable and improperly suggesting that top management was at the bottom of a hierarchy, the task force developed multidisciplinary teams to support the reps. In the new system, far fewer managers were needed, and the number of levels was reduced to three.

The new concept was exciting. Its costs were lower because of the reduction in middle-management positions; it promised much better dealer relations and also more responsiveness to customers.

But the suggestions encountered great resistance. Many managers feared the loss of jobs and perquisites. Some executives could not accept the idea that they were to support others in the organization. At the core of the resistance was the difficulty that large firms have in accepting the proposition that the customer-relations position is more important than an administrative position.

Other objections appeared. The division's loss of market share, it was said, was inevitable. Alternatively, new products would soon be brought out by the company, which would regain share. Business had been bad before and had always improved.

The division's top executives hesitated. The business need was to get closer to the customer and cut costs. The task force proposal would do both. But the solution was so radical, it upset many comfortable people.

Time passed. The opportunity waited. How long would it remain? No one knew, and yet top management hesitated—and then began only very slowly to implement the changes.

Delegated Decision Making

Members of clusters take a far wider range of responsibilities than is common for employees in more traditional organizations. In cluster organizations groups of employees and even individual employees direct their own work.

Many of the advantages that firms reap from cluster organizations— cost savings, improved flexibility, and employee involvement and commitment—are achieved through reduction of managerial levels, which in other organizations direct the work. Greater responsiveness to customers is generated through the authority employees have to act on the company's behalf with customers.

A Powertrain Plant

At Bay City, Michigan, General Motors (GM) has a powertrain plant making car and truck parts. The facility was projected to lose $3.5 million on a yearly basis through August 1987. Instead, it reported a $2.2 million profit.

The evidence of improvement extends beyond the bottom line. Labor and management have recorded only one grievance in two years, and working time lost is 35 percent less than GM's average. There was a 54 percent reduction in customer-reported problems with Bay City components between 1987 and 1988. Current productivity was up 24 percent over 18 months, the cost of making major components parts was 15 percent lower, and current factory rejects were 10 percent fewer. Inventory balances fell 53 percent in two years.

The wellspring of this improvement has been a new plant manager, Pat Carrigan, and a different approach to management—one typical of a cluster setting. Carrigan's managerial philosophy is to push decision making to lower levels so that ideas for improvements can originate either on the shop floor or from within the ranks of management. She says,

> Typically in this country, management tends to give direction downward, and all the good ideas are thought to belong to management, not the worker. If you stop and think a moment, that's a pretty simplistic view. In a business like ours the precision machining performed by hourly workers is highly technical. The worker who does this kind of activity is the expert. Should I or someone else in my position tell these people how to best do their jobs or what needs to be done?

We've enjoyed success in this plant because we've used the skills and knowledge of all the employees and brought them into the decision-making process. We've opened our books to all our employees and given them a say in what goes on in their workplace.

Carrigan has developed a partnership with plant employees, who are represented by the United Auto Workers (UAW). Her plan has four basic elements.

First, there has been a major effort to improve communications. She has had the company provide basic financial information and training in interpersonal skills. She feels if employees understand the business—costs, profits, waste, and competitors—they will be more involved in it: "If they understand what it takes to be successful—high quality, low cost, and on-time delivery—then about all you have to do is get out of their way."

Information is shared much more widely. A Supervisors' Advisory Council has been created to help supervisors understand their role in a participatively managed system. Management staff meetings were expanded to include the UAW leaders, and the plant's 43 employee participation group leaders also meet monthly with the joint leadership group.

Second, there have been extensive employee training efforts. These include an annual "state of the business" meeting for employees, in which Carrigan and the local union head focus on the auto industry climate both locally and worldwide. Courses in communication, presentation skills, meeting management, decision making, and business understanding are offered to all employees. A special accounting course helps employees with the plant budget. Recently, a course for communication, facilitation, and decision-making skills was added to the offerings to help departments learn self-management and shared management skills.

Third, she has altered managerial practices. Managers do not wear ties. The salaried cafeteria is now a training room, and the former executive dining room now contains offices for the human resource department. The employee cafeteria is the only dining facility.

Hiring has also become more open. When a new personnel director and superintendent were required, both selections were made jointly by the people who would report to the person, the management staff, and the local union leaders. "If we're going to work together as a team, then it makes no sense to put someone in charge of either position whom we can't all work with . . ." said Carrigan.

Fourth, management has created an extensive employee participation program that includes 43 teams, 13 of which have evolved into self-managed or shared management groups. The self-managed groups set their own goals; create schedules; handle absenteeism; set production, quality, and delivery targets; and even sign their own time cards without supervision. The shared management groups still rely on a supervisor for coaching when they are having trouble reaching objectives.

These teams have contributed significantly to the plant's improving profits. For example, one team looked at cost data for making wheel spindles after taking the accounting course and determined that it was losing about five cents on each part made. Over eight months the group turned the loss into a profit. In part it did so through the efforts of one individual, who volunteered to leave the team to cut costs.

This individual joined a special cost-reduction team, which consists of people who have eliminated their previous jobs. In two years, this group has generated savings of $2 million in the plant's operating budget. What does the local union leader say?

> There was some resistance. We thought this was some management ploy. Now we realize that when Pat got here we had the opportunity to be a great plant, not just a good plant.
>
> This is about as simple as ABC—there's nothing complicated about us. When you let responsible adults act their age, you'd be surprised at the results you get. What could be more thrilling than running a multi-million dollar business? People feel good about themselves when they're given the chance to run the business.

Clusters in the U.S. Army

"I was given command only a short time before the invasion of Grenada was to begin," Admiral Joseph Metcalf commented. "There was no time to alter battle plans which had already been prepared by the different services under my command [Navy, Air Force, and Army]. So I relied on what the services had planned. But I held a meeting and made sure of two things: first, that the communications equipment of each service was such that the others could receive and understand what was being transmitted; second, I asked each service commander to explain what he intended to do if things went wrong with the initial plan.''

The invasion of Grenada was a success, largely because of Admiral Metcalf's understanding of how to manage an interdisciplinary force: a cluster, if you will. Metcalf relied on the expertise of the different services, not trying to substitute his own at the last minute. And he correctly understood the importance of adequate communication among the units involved.

The cluster concept has come to the battlefield. It originated during World War II, when field commanders needed to act quickly and had no time to refer to central command. Battles, it appeared, were moving beyond the scope of unified control.

As commanders met rapidly changing and complex conditions, they needed to understand available capabilities, whatever the sources. Informal methods emerged, such as the famed task forces of the Pacific war.

In the aftermath of the war, battlefield needs were forgotten and the system returned to the hierarchical. Then the unsuccessful raid to free the hostages in Iran took place and confusion contributed to failure. Evidently it was necessary to improve coordination.

Today's Army has far more firepower and mobility than ever before. New technology allows soldiers to down fighter aircraft at distances of several miles, successfully challenge tanks in the open field, move hundreds of miles at a time, and fight at night or in fog. However, learning to use this sophisticated material requires specialization in training and deployment.

At the same time, the existence of weapons of mass destruction like bacterial, chemical, and atomic arms means that conventional pitched battles on static fronts will not occur again. Armies will have to remain flexible, responsive, and very light on their feet—able to mass quickly for concentrated attacks or the defense of key positions and then disperse rapidly on disengagement to avoid attracting mass weapons from the enemy.

The Army in particular has responded to these developments by creating specialized units around four main technologies and the regular infantry: the airplane, the helicopter, the tank, the troop transport, and the foot soldier. For maximum flexibility, specialized units are tailored into general task forces by adding and subtracting combinations, depending on objectives. To manage these task forces, the Army has developed a formalized concept for training officers to manage and coordinate in the field.

Its intent is to integrate the different functional units to achieve several purposes: reduce disorder and confusion under fire, enable commanders to make better plans, give commanders exposure to the capabilities of different functions, and generate relationships that will support effective delegation of responsibility under fire.

In the Army the formal concept consists of two parts: a schoolhouse, where officers from specialized units train together for higher commands, and field experience, in which newly commissioned officers participate in field task forces.

At the top level, integration is being driven by congressional mandate. To become generals, colonels must now go through a special intermediate command school with people from other units.

Interservice integration is also being fostered at the operations level. The Army, Navy, and Air Force now are experimenting with officer swaps: "You take my specialist; I take yours; we both gain."

The perceived benefits of the new approach are several. First, there is a faster response to changing conditions on the battlefield, including more imaginative use of resources (e.g., in the desert helicopters without sand screens will no longer be used). Second, there is better morale. The tank soldiers know what the infantry can do and vice versa, and officers do not so readily get into situations in which their units cannot be fully effective.

The military approach correctly relies on training and making cross-functional experience a requirement for advancement. Training and promotion incentives help officers adapt to the new needs, just as they will do for managers in corporations.

Cross-disciplinary clusters at the operational level do not mean that the services are abandoning their hierarchies, of course. But they do show that the military is aware of the limitations of the hierarchical structure on a complex and fast-moving battlefield and is trying to improve its effectiveness by relying on a clusterlike approach.

Managers as Information Channels

Clusters interact with the company through their leaders, usually the most experienced and senior person in them—but not always, as different situations may call for different expertise and data. Data about business activities and group performances are frequently communicated directly by computer data base to other clusters or senior managers in the company. When human communication is necessary among cluster members or between individuals from different clusters, it is the responsibility of the individuals involved to accomplish it.

Clusters in an Airline

The adoption of clusters at Swissair, Switzerland's flag air carrier, brings the new form into close and continual contact with a strongly entrenched hierarchical system. Because the hierarchy was not responsive enough to an accelerating pace of change in the international air travel industry, clusters were devised.

As Swissair's management said in the company's annual report for 1988, '' . . . Airlines are having to take decisions with much shorter lead times than ever before, and [are] become[ing] increasingly market-led in their approach. The situation for Swissair is made more complex by the fact that our production costs as a Swiss-based company are higher than those of rival air transport operators.''

The combination of accelerating change, a need for cost containment—if not reduction—and a push to get ''closer to the customer'' have caused Swissair to adopt a new organizational philosophy and structure. To ensure that the company gets closer to its customers, the operations have been broken down into manageably sized units, each of which is intended to be responsive to market leadership. Each has a clearly defined mission and responsibility for results.

To ensure that situations involving conflict of goals are managed and that marketing gets a more prominent place in the business, direct representation of key functions within executive management has been adopted. Certain managerial levels have been removed from the company, broadening the span of control of those that are left. Division heads will now report directly to the company president, with the level of executive vice president abolished. The group of division heads will include executive management along with the company president.

At the operating levels, the local branch offices are now directed by a new group of 16 route managers, each equipped with wide powers of authority and responsibility for the results obtained in a specific region. Personal titles have been replaced by simple function designations.

In summary the airline is forming largely autonomous work groups wherever possible. Independence of organizational units within an agreed-on framework of goals, strategies, and guidelines is being adopted as the framework of operation.

Maintaining Financial Control

Cluster organizations and clusters are not without control mechanisms. Using the cluster form does not imply losing financial control. However, in deciding what degree of budgetary control to impose, an executive must realize that the tighter the control, the greater the burden of reporting and the greater the risk that cluster members will lose sight of their prime purpose—moving decision making closer to the customer while cutting overhead costs.

A Cluster at the CEO Level

At a diversified company a transition was taking place at the level of the chief executive officer (CEO). The company had experienced considerable difficulty in recent years and had been downsized rigorously by the outgoing CEO. Now with lower costs and facing an upturn in its most important markets, the company was poised for renewed growth and profitability. But whether the opportunity could be grasped depended greatly on the continued adaptation of the company to a changing business environment.

In trying to accomplish that adaptation, the outgoing CEO had developed a new set of managers at the divisional and top staff levels drawn both from inside the corporation and, in some few instances, from outside.

In one particular case a division vice president from a totally different business had been made president of a key but underperforming subsidiary to try to turn it around. Hence when the top management of the corporation—12 persons in all—gathered for a week-long meeting, the newly designated CEO faced a situation of remarkable fluidity.

Privately, the outgoing CEO had complained bitterly about the lack of initiative in the organization and the failure of his subordinates to adjust to the changing business world. He was concerned with how to manage change in the organization and was disappointed at the inflexibility of his top officers. He expressed his disillusionment graphically by pointing out that just 20 years ago, a time when he and most of his top officers were already with the firm, their company had been the same size as IBM, which had neighboring headquarters. Today, IBM was roughly 20 times the size of his company. By that standard, a very personal one, the organization of which he was a part had failed to seize the opportunities offered by technological advancement and economic growth. He was dissatisfied with the record, and his subordinates knew it. Slowly over the past few years he had released most of the executives who had been running the company upon his accession to the CEO position. Now, with high hopes for what the future would hold for the company, he was handing over to his successor a new management group.

On the second day of the management meeting, discussion turned, hesitantly at first but with increasing candor, to the manner in which the corporation had been and was to be managed. Although encouraging his executives to think broadly about opportunities and to take risks for long-term advantage, the outgoing CEO had spent his meetings with the same executives, going over their budgets and the income statements of their organizations in great detail. He had a brilliant mind for numbers and enjoyed demonstrating his detailed grasp of the businesses of the company. While satisfying himself about the numbers in each of the businesses, the CEO was perceived by his subordinate as being nit-picking and uninterested in the long-term future of their units.

The outgoing CEO had met with his division and subsidiary chiefs individually on an ongoing basis and infrequently called the group as a whole together. When there was a group meeting it consisted primarily of reports by each executive and of statements by the CEO about the company's progress, or lack of it, and targets for the near future. There was no real discussion in these meetings, the executives complained. As a result, none of the division and subsidiary top executives felt as though they knew anything about how areas of the company other than their own were managed and what problems and opportunities they faced.

The company has been a collection of separate baronies, they complained. Decisions about each business have been taken privately by the CEO and the division or subsidiary chief without involvement of the others, and very often the decisions, even when made, have not been shared. Rather than being informative and useful, from the point of view of the business managers, the top management group meetings have been a waste of time.

When the new CEO announced his intention to continue to manage the company in much the way his predecessor had done, there was an outpouring of dissent. If the top executives of the company were to be knowledgeable of the company as a whole, as the former and new CEO both said they wanted, and if synergies were to occur, the managerial structure and process had to be changed.

Instead of a focus on one-to-one meetings with the CEO, there had to be more frequent group meetings. The division and subsidiary chief executives and the three key corporate staff officers (international business, human resources, and technology) needed to meet regularly with the CEO.

The meeting agendas ought to include, it was suggested to the new CEO, three types of items: those for information, those for gaining input or developing options, and those for decision making. Executives in the company just below the top level wanted real input in running the company as a whole. They argued,

> It will be a far better system. We will be able to understand the company as a whole; we'll be able to contribute to better decisions, to take over for each other if that's necessary. The company will benefit from a broader review of its businesses. We will understand why things are being done, such as the direction of the company's investment budget, and be both more accepting and more supportive of the whole effort. By listening to the others talk about their businesses, we'll get ideas for our own. As for the CEO, he'll be freed of much of the mass of detail for which he now holds himself

responsible, and better able to lead us in the direction of growing the company.

In essence the new CEO was being asked by his subordinates to convert the company's managerial structure at the top from a one-to-one hierarchy to a cluster concept, in which the group of top executives would manage the company as a whole. Each would retain his or her specific assignments, and the CEO would have overall and undivided responsibility for the entire company. But the management meetings would become real exercises in management, not just a series of formal reports, and practical responsibility for the company would be shared among top management.

As part of the attempt to persuade the new CEO to embark on the cluster course, one of the division presidents pointed out that the cluster concept closely resembled the way IBM has long been managed: by a committee of top officers of the corporation in which there is shared responsibility for the corporation's performance among a group of managers whose individual positions are also separately identified on a formal organization chart. In effect the new CEO was being told not to let the formal hierarchy dictate a too-narrow structure of management. The top management of the company should operate as a team, if the company is to succeed, not as a boss and a group of subordinates.

Surprised by the careful thought that had gone into the suggestion and by the vehemence with which it was pushed by his executives, the new CEO asked for time to consider the proposal and to discuss it with his predecessor, for whom all the company's managers retained both respect and admiration. The outgoing CEO approved, and at the time of this writing, the new CEO was beginning to accept as his partners in the firm the executives who ran the corporation's businesses.

Broader Goals Are a Key Element

Typically, a cluster organization subordinates detailed budgets and reporting in favor of broader goals, which are communicated to the organization as a whole. Members of the clusters are expected to understand the broader objectives of the company and to use their imagination and initiative to help accomplish them. The old "you're not paid to think but to carry out orders" syndrome of traditional management is explicitly abandoned.

Self-Directing Work Groups

The 400-person plant of the Square D Company, located in Columbia, Missouri, makes circuit breakers for residential and commercial use and has recently adopted the idea of self-directed work groups. Its management team was looking for a way to lower product cost, reduce managerial layers, increase worker morale, and push decision making down into the ranks. "We want to move the point of manufacturing as close to our [in-house] customers as possible and eliminate layers of management in the process," noted one manager.

By reorganizing and making workers responsible for productivity measurement, costs, quality, performance appraisal, work assignment, and interaction between departments, managers hoped to eliminate the need for first-level supervision. The work teams also manage their own attendance and time-keeping records, pass out paychecks, schedule overtime, screen applicants, and set promotions.

Management decided to try self-management after adopting other new manufacturing techniques such as just-in-time inventory and *Kanban* (Japanese-style production scheduling). These techniques provided what used to be purely managerial and supervisory information to workers. Each employee has access through computer terminals to a material-resource-planning system telling what ought to be produced, what inputs are on hand, and when the finished output is due. As employees showed more interest, management decided to move more data into their hands.

When these systems were working well, self-management was introduced in the punch-press production team, which had ten highly skilled machine-tool operators. The group was asked to get more involved in day-to-day decision making. Members were trained in interpersonal skills, the tasks of supervision, and the details of self-management in order to be self-directing.

The team of punch-press "associates" now talk directly with their in-house customers (the assembly group) and interact with all support functions—engineering, accounting, purchasing, and human resources—without supervisory intervention.

The payoffs have been substantial. Punch-press overtime fell by 70 percent after the concept was introduced. "The set-up operators themselves are better able to manipulate work and in a more productive way than a supervisor could ever dictate," noted the plant's product manager for fabricated parts. The ratio of production workers to supervisors has gone up substantially and made the business more profitable.

Thus in productivity and profits the company has reaped the rewards of involving its employees much more deeply in the goals of the corporation. To do so the company was prepared to alter substantially the way it conducted its business. Only by such dramatic actions could employees be freed to contribute all they might to the success of the enterprise.

Clusters in Action

Clusters and clusterlike organizational units can be found in both service and manufacturing settings. Consider the following examples of each.

Professional Service Settings

Although such organizations have hierarchies, the levels are limited and the freedom given to most professionals is much greater than in many other hierarchies. *Collegial* is the common term for such organizations and is a quality much desired by employees, whether in traditional professions or not. Professional service firms have many of the characteristics of cluster organizations and therefore merit attention.

To develop some insight into how a cluster organization works, let us imagine a discussion with a professional about his or her work. A description might go as follows:

> I don't really have a boss or a specifically defined job. I have a range of competencies and experience that I put to work wherever the organization needs. I am always involved in a group of projects. Sometimes I initiate projects; sometimes I sign on to projects others have initiated. I have a certain assignment or group of assignments at any time, and I can go to a

manager or an officer of the firm when I think I should communicate something or when I need help. Otherwise, I rarely see a person who would be considered a superior in the firm.

I am the judge of the quality of my work—but the company checks on it with our clients and customers and with my peers when appropriate. If my work is substandard, I would be asked to see someone, and I might find myself with a boss. I could even be edged out, if I really don't perform, but only in an extreme situation.

I am responsible for keeping myself effective and up to date, but I may ask for leave and for financial assistance if necessary.

I have a network of contacts on the inside of our firm and on the outside, which I use to get my work done, to get ideas for new projects, and to keep up with what's going on generally. I also use my network to hire new people when we need them and to place people outside if that becomes necessary. I presume that if I do well, I'm employed here for life.

There are several types of service firms and units where such a description of the work environment is appropriate, including investment banks and other money and asset management houses, consulting firms, law firms, group medical and dental practices, selected religious organizations, engineering service firms, architectural practices, accounting firms, some scientific research institutions and foundations, and actuarial practices. University faculties and other educational institutions might also be incorporated into this group.

For the future, the most important observation is that all types of firms in many industries are becoming more like the professional service firms. The legions of the hourly—production and clerical workers alike—are giving way to automation. Salespersons become consultants to customers; production workers become monitors of automated processes; clerical workers become troubleshooters. Work itself becomes a professional and quasi-professional matter well suited to the clustertype organizations that many professional service firms already utilize.

On the Manufacturing Floor

One of the areas in which organizations have experimented with a form closely akin to clusters is the factory floor. In the 1960s, thinkers and managers began to see the disadvantages for motivation and product quality in traditional forms of work organization and began, both in Europe and in North America, to experiment with alternatives.

In the decades since, experimentation has progressed, and being closer to the plant's customers and cost control are now both objectives as well. Today most large manufacturing corporations on both sides of the Atlantic have some plants that are using a cluster format. In many instances the productivity and quality performance in these plants are markedly superior to those in more traditional plants.

A.O. Smith Corporation The Milwaukee automotive plant of A.O. Smith had many of the typical problems of U.S. manufacturing plants during the late 1970s and early 1980s. Union leaders and supervisors clashed repeatedly over work rules. Workers were expected to behave like robots, doing a few limited tasks over and over throughout the day. Quality was no one's concern; with wages based partly on piecework, the philosophy was "get it out the door." In 1981, some 20 percent of the frames produced for a major truck line had to be repaired before being shipped.

A.O. Smith's plant managers, trying to reverse these trends, began a quality circle program as part of an employee involvement (EI) effort. After three years, they had seen some improvement in quality but noted that their program suffered from lack of union involvement.

During 1984, the managers tried to get the union involved by forming joint union-management problem-solving committees. Quality improved again, but not enough. Finally, in 1987, A.O. Smith took the big step: The managers reorganized their workers into production teams that "for all practical purposes, manage themselves."

These teams have five to seven members who rotate production jobs among themselves. A team elects its leader, who assumes managerial responsibility for scheduling production and overtime, ordering maintenance, and stopping the line to correct defects.

The work teams enjoy considerable power. They are even allowed to revise work standards set by engineers. (This allows them to influence the production rates that underpin any piecerate pay system.)

With hourly workers taking over managerial tasks, A.O. Smith was able to reduce its first-line supervisory ranks. The ratio of supervisors to workers dropped from 1 in 10 in 1987 to 1 in 34 by 1989. This amounted to a tremendous reduction in overhead but also undermined the morale of the remaining supervisors. The company then belatedly embarked on a training program to help them adjust to the new work environment and culture.

The participative culture is not all-pervasive yet. Union and management are still locked in battle over abolition of seniority rights, with the union insisting on lifetime employment in return. Quality measures, although improving significantly, are still not first rate on all dimensions. However, the workers did receive a profit-sharing check in mid-April 1989. Moreover the defect rates in the plant dropped to 3 percent from 20 percent in 1981, and productivity doubled in 1988 over 1987 levels.

How was A.O. Smith able to make such a shift? For a start, the Milwaukee employees wanted to save their jobs. Fears of closure began to dog the plant in the early 1980s as Detroit started to reel under the pressure from Japanese imports. Pushed by its Big Three customers, A.O. Smith had to come up with quality improvements in a hurry. This prompted the quality circle drive from 1981 through 1984, which began to fail for lack of union involvement.

In 1984 GM in particular began to switch away from the traditional products it purchased from A.O. Smith. At this point, the unions, alarmed at potential job losses, agreed to join in the cooperative problem-solving framework, aimed at boosting quality to retain A.O. Smith's position with GM. As a part of the process, the union local leaders gained a voice in the company's strategic decision-making process and began to share power. However, the production floor remained locked in the 20-second cycle (very limited autonomy in the way jobs could be performed) and absenteeism still ranged at 20 percent on some days.

In 1986 the Big Three automakers forced major price cuts on their suppliers and then cut orders. A.O. Smith was faced with a layoff of 1,300 of its 3,200 hourly workers. Although A.O. Smith never threatened complete closure at Milwaukee, the local union president, who was involved in the strategic planning at this point, could see that there might be a closure in the near future if practices did not change.

When the new contracts were negotiated in 1987, the two sides eliminated the piecerate pay system. Rather than push through the resulting three-dollar pay cut immediately, the company agreed to freeze earnings for four years. At this point, the union leaders and members softened. The local union leader persuaded the company to install the work-team concept: "I was anxious for our people to take control so we could get all the people involved in building a quality product." As an outside participant in the process noted, "You need a cultural change that can't be legislated by contract or law. . . . The people have to want to make the transformation, and it must evolve from their own experience."

Volvo Uddevalia Experiment For the Swedish automaker Volvo, the Uddevalia plant that opened in August 1988 represents an ongoing commitment to innovation. It functions without assembly lines and with workers who are treated like craftsmen and craftswomen instead of interchangeable bodies. In a further break with current practice, the use of robots and other mechanization is restricted to operations supporting the factory floor. Roger Holtback, car division president, said, "I hope that one day in the future somebody will be able to stand here and say 'Henry Ford invented the assembly line but Volvo did away with it—in a profitable way.'"

Traditionally, automobiles have been assembled on long production lines. Workers were trained to perform relatively unskilled tasks (e.g., fitting bolts to car doors) repetitively on subassemblies and assemblies as they moved down the line. General Motors and other automakers moved away from this philosophy on an experimental basis in some plants during the late 1970s to counter absenteeism and other psychological effects of monotony on their workers, switching to a concept known as "stall build." In stall build, cars are not assembled on a line but rather in decentralized and stationary stalls. Workers are grouped in teams around a particular stall and are cross-trained to handle a variety of assembly tasks.

Volvo, a comparative latecomer to production lines, had the same difficulties with it as other automakers. However, being less wedded to the concept, the firm decided in the early 1970s to switch to stall build at its Kalmar plant. Kalmar has been consistently profitable, producing the low turnover and absenteeism rates Volvo was looking for.

Given this success, Volvo seized the opportunity presented at Uddevalia to experiment further with nontraditional assembly, when the Swedish government decided to phase out an uneconomic, state-owned shipyard. After negotiations with the state and the metalworkers union, Volvo embarked on the Uddevalia experiment, deciding to improve on stall build by adopting still more hand-built tasks and work autonomy rather than automation. As Holtback described it, ''Before 1914 auto workers were all-around, skilful mechanics who worked in small groups of six or seven and together they built an entire car in one and the same place . . . most of them were well-trained and experienced craftsmen, who felt professional pride and dignity and identified deeply with their work.'' Uddevalia is an attempt to return to this style of production, with enhancements from engineering and computer science breakthroughs that have occurred since it was last used.

Uddevalia workers are organized in autonomous teams of eight to ten members in six production areas. The teams are responsible for complete vehicle assembly, the volume of output, and quality control. If a particular stage of assembly requires an hour, in the judgment of the team, then it takes an hour, or more if necessary.

There are no supervisors on the teams. A team picks a coordinator for itself in rotation, and although there is a manager in ultimate charge of the operations, with a second tier of managers in place, the workers are expected to perform a wide variety of functions for their teams and themselves.

As a production incentive, each team member may earn a bonus of SKr 6 per hour, on a base salary of SKr 2,132 per week. (If the work week is 35 hours, the bonus amounts to about 10 percent of base pay.) The bonus is earnable only if the teams meet the quality, delivery, and productivity targets *they themselves set* each week to meet the company's monthly target figure.

The actual number of cars assembled each day is decided at the start of the work week by the individual team. Although Volvo sets monthly and annual production targets, and eventually hopes to get up to 40,000 cars per year from the plant by 1991, the teams decide where and how to meet these targets.

Volvo is making a tremendous investment in its work force. Each new employee goes through a 16-week initiation course, which is the first stage of a 16-month development cycle, during which it is hoped the newcomers will learn how to do about one-quarter of the tasks required to complete an assembly. Since 40 percent of the teams' membership on average are women, special tools ergonomically engineered for women have been introduced.

The level of mechanization in the plant is very low, but what is there is state of the art. As much as 80 percent of the work is done standing upright because of a device that allows the platform on which the cars are assembled to rotate and tilt at different angles, up to 90 percent. Although no robots are involved in production as such, the parts transfer and inventory management systems are highly automated. An observer is immediately struck by the low level of noise, the lack of dirt, and the use of natural light on the production floor.

The financial success of Uddevalia will turn in large measure on how efficiently the material supply process can be run to meet the needs of the production teams. Parts from 400 outside companies and painted and finished car bodies from Volvo's Gothenburg plant are brought to the materials distribution center on a "just-in-time" basis, to minimize inventory levels. There work teams do some preassembly work on axles, steering columns, and exhausts and put together kits of parts and pieces for the work assembly teams. These kits are ordered by the production teams as needed through a computer system and loaded onto special automatic carriers running on magnetic tracks in the production area to the appropriate team site.

Another critical variable will be the level of absenteeism and turnover in the work force. The cost of training multiskilled workers requires the work force to be more stable than is the case in a traditional assembly plant. So far Uddevalia's absenteeism is running at about 8 percent, the same as Kalmar, while in the more traditional plant in Gothenburg, absenteeism is running at 17 percent—and as high as 25 percent in its paint shop.

CHAPTER FIVE

"Keeping Tight Control Is Out of Date": The Revolution at British Petroleum

Several years ago, Julian Darley became managing director of the London-based Engineering Technical Centre (ETC) at British Petroleum Corporation (BP). Although he had worked for 26 years in various BP Group subsidiaries and had held numerous engineering and managerial positions, this was his first assignment at ETC.

His advantage in the position was that he knew BP, or at least what one could learn of a company that employed 126,000 people worldwide and was the world's third-largest oil company. He had seen ETC as a customer or client sees it and so had some familiarity with what outsiders thought needed to be done to help it make a greater contribution to the corporation.

"How," he wondered, "does a chief executive cut administrative costs, improve customer responsiveness, and help his staff keep up with a rapidly evolving engineering technology?" Darley's idea was to meet these objectives largely through a major change in how ETC operated.

On his desk sat a copy of *Insight*, ETC's newsletter, which told the 1,800 or so employees that Darley was now making large waves in ETC's pond. Read *Insight's* lead article:

> BP Engineering is to be the new name for the Engineering Technical Centre. The name change, which will take affect August 1, 1989, will mark the introduction of radical changes in the way we operate and the organizational structure of our business. . . .
>
> The new strategy will impact considerably upon the management structure and on working relationships. Customers will have direct access to our expertise and routine [of] working through a management hierarchy will be widely removed. . . .

ETC had emerged during a 1981 corporate reorganization. Its mission was to supply technological, engineering, procurement, and contractual services to BP and its partners, serving as a "critical core" for technology development and application. It worked closely with BP's Sunbury Research Centre to commercialize new technical applications at BP Group businesses and held a group-wide mandate to enforce the BP Code of Engineering Practices—the vehicle through which safety and equipment operating performance standards were maintained in BP's operating installations.

ETC prided itself on being BP's engineering heart. With roughly half of its engineers scattered around the world on BP project sites and the rest concentrated in London, it was a global operation. Besides providing engineering services, it also served as a stepping-stone for managers being trained for higher executive positions in the BP Group, and it was recognized far beyond the company for its expertise.

Operating Problems

Several concerns had immediately caught Darley's eye when he arrived at ETC in March 1986. Among them were difficulties in getting a good price for ETC's services and in defining "quality" in the services provided to clients.

Although ETC did not have a profit measure and target per se, it was asked to recover costs through charges to its BP Group clients. These costs had been rising faster than inflation for some time, and the client organizations were balking at the increases.

Before 1981, engineering costs had been handled by the central budget of BP Group. Other BP Group units had simply been charged enough money to cover ETC expenses. This had been a favorable setting for the engineers. They had been insulated from fiscal pressures, enabling them to design as they saw fit. Their tendency had been to go for the best technology and take considerable time to "get it right." This was seen as good practice when oil prices were high and BP was pioneering in the great oil fields of the North Sea.

But then in 1981, efficiency became the watchword. BP units were given permission to bypass internal services if doing so reduced costs without impairing performance. ETC's superior engineering resources and established relationships with others in BP had discouraged outside engineering firms from winning BP business. But after four years of accelerating prices, ETC's advantage was eroding. Declining oil prices had cut into industry activity, forcing independent firms to reduce their rates, thereby making them even more attractive.

As ETC's prices rose, it also began losing touch with the service needs of its clients. Big projects—those with long lead times, cost insensitivity, and new technology—were drying up. Tie-ons—smaller projects with short lead times—were drawing attention as oil prices fell. These tie-ons required speed and simplicity of design rather than costly technology. However, many at ETC still equated quality with the most up-to-date technology. They were caught up in technical perfectionism despite ETC's slogan: "engineering for purpose."

Initial Solution: Cost-Cutting

Soon after he arrived at ETC, Darley decided to take direct action on costs. He cancelled a planned recruiting drive and initiated indirect cost-cutting programs to slow the rise in billing rates. Reviews of paperwork and office costs were started.

ETC's internal department structure was consolidated to reduce overhead and overlapping responsibilities. Management hoped that integration would diminish the internal rivalry that had emerged from the overlaps while also cutting administrative costs.

Sections of ETC were moved out of London, with its high and rising rents. This move had implications that went beyond cost savings. ETC had always been geographically close to BP Group headquarters, but this proximity might have to be discontinued.

Finally, Darley started direct cost cuts. Because the largest budget items at ETC were for salaries, management was led to consider staff redundancy and lower pay raises. A 10 percent cut in engineering staff through resignation and redundancy was decreed. Managers assessed and ranked staff by performance level, and those not measuring up were asked to leave. ETC had never done this before, and although it offered relocation assistance and followed British labor law, the process was not popular.

As 1986 drew to a close, it was clear that cost cutting was putting the organization back on track but that the goal of improving client service was not being met. Morale was poor in the wake of the layoffs.

From his reading of management literature, Darley was aware of the opportunities that team-building efforts might create, and he asked Richard Mindel, group training advisor in the BP personnel office, to begin team-building sessions for ETC staff assigned to a key BP project team at Wytch Farm.

Concerns were raised during these meetings by ETC engineers, not about their own working relationships per se, but about ETC's ability to work effectively with its clients. These comments led Mindel to propose, and Darley to commission, a more detailed study on ETC's role at Wytch Farm. The proposal noted,

> ETC is in the process of re-evaluating its mission as a front-line service organization alongside key clients and market segments. This is to ensure that it provides the best possible service to meet the needs of its customers. . . .
>
> The past 18 months have witnessed considerable change and fluctuation in the demand for ETC's skills and services. ETC client markets have also been subject to important changes. . . . A thorough appreciation of ETC's relationship with its market—including both in-company and third party customers and contracts—is crucial. . . .

The study's conclusions were striking: ETC's specialists and the project team members from the client organization were not communicating well. In the words of one team member, "You would get the idea that [ETC's] people are sitting back and watching you [mess] it up." On the other hand, the ETC specialist's view of the clients' attitudes was "They don't want us to call them; they will call us."

Mindel noted that clients appeared to be seeking ad hoc advice from ETC engineers who could be briefed quickly and asked to solve problems with "no frills and fast response." These were demands ETC engineers felt uncomfortable fulfilling.

The clients' staffs were blunt. One said, "What the project needs from ETC is experts in the field who recognize that projects want good quality decisions or advice based on limited information—quickly." Said another, "What we want is expert advice on an ad hoc basis—at the end of a telephone, say for 15 minutes or so. I don't mind being billed for a few hours work at the end of it." Noted a third, "Getting the project up and running is what it's all about. There are massive benefits in cost savings. There's no prize for producing a perfect design, or for being a world-leading specialist."

Some ETC engineers also recognized that this was a major change in what clients wanted. Said one, "Businesses are seeking a professional consultancy service from ETC—not a detailed design service." Said another, "Engineers need to probe much more into what the client actually needs." A third noted, "We are becoming a confederacy of consultant engineers, not an engineering office as . . . in the past."

For Darley, this study of the clients' perceptions was an eye-opener. It was clear to him that ETC's key people were aware of these changes. But ETC was not adapting its systems, structures, and attitudes to match the change occurring in its role. Something significant had to be done. Others felt the same way. Said one ETC staff member, "Individual responsibility of engineers will be paramount. People need to be clear about what they know and what they don't know, and be up front about it." Said another, "the culture at present is uncomfortable about delegating authority." Noted a third, "the idea of the Centre's management having to keep tight control over everything that is happening in the Centre on behalf of a client is out of date."

Now Darley and ETC faced a dilemma. Becoming consultants would require a new operating philosophy and vision. After considerable discussion with his key staff, Darley decided an offsite meeting was required to sort things out.

The Offsite Meeting

After the Wytch Farm report was formally delivered, Darley convened a two-day meeting in London's Tower Hotel to develop a new concept of ETC and securing commitment to it from senior executives. Ten key executives, Mindel, another senior personnel officer, and an external consultant attended.

Among the attendees from ETC was a new face. While the Wytch Farm study was still in progress, Darley had brought in additional outside perspective in the form of Paul Pearson, a management information systems specialist with a leading British computer consulting company. Pearson was not an engineer, but he brought the perspective of an open market service firm to ETC. Darley was betting that Pearson's different perspective and his skills in high-tech communications and computing would make a valuable contribution.

The meeting at the Tower Hotel was neither easy nor smooth. Multiple points of view about ETC's role and direction quickly surfaced.

Some attendees felt ETC had to remain a center of specialist engineers. They saw specialization to support technology development and commercialization as critical to ETC's survival. In their view, if ETC became a consultant and ceased to be the guardian of technology, it would lose its technical edge. If this happened, those BP operating units that were currently ETC clients could justify expanding their own engineering groups to speed up design and procurement work; ETC could no longer offer them anything different.

Others felt that although technology development was important, it should not be ETC's key purpose. Instead of being experts at designing projects in a relative vacuum, with clients often becoming upset with the high cost and length of time required for results, ETC needed to become more willing to accept its clients' actual needs. If this meant making engineers look like consultants instead of scientists, that was what was necessary, they argued.

The vision that emerged from the Tower Hotel meeting was a synthesis of views. It recognized ETC's technological edge but shifted the driving force. ETC would try to be client-driven but maintain a technology focus.

The session also sparked debate on organizational issues. If vision changed, then skills, structures, and systems also might need to change.

From Vision to Model

ETC developed a three-pronged plan to push the vision process forward and grapple with organizational issues. One committee made up of those who had been at the Tower Hotel was charged with repeating the vision process for ETC's middle management. A second committee was given the task of reducing the elements of vision to their essentials and formulating a short statement that could easily be shared with others. A third committee was charged with devising a program of documents and speakers, to get the results of the vision-setting process to the rank-and-file engineers.

Two senior ETC managers—Paul Pearson and Peter Carr—led the involvement team. They developed a series of four workshops for middle-level managers during January and February 1988 to share, or as they put it, to "cascade down," the Tower Hotel material and solicit additional input. People who had attended the offsite meeting led these four sessions. Output from these meetings was given to the "vision synthesis" committee, as it worked on distilling various views into a short vision statement:

> Our aim [they ultimately wrote of ETC] is to contribute to BP's success by harnessing technology for competitive advantage. We will: be responsive to our customers, provide services that have distinct value and are fit for purpose, be committed to the development of our staff and encourage their effective deployment throughout the BP Group, be available to BP's senior management as engineering consultants, [and] be prepared to initiate the exploitation of opportunities that we find.

The communication committee decided to rely on Darley and the ETC newsletter to get the new vision to the rank and file. In four meetings held in the main BP building, Darley addressed the London staff in groups of 100 to 150 and answered their questions.

The ETC newsletter was used to get the same message to engineers in the field. It published a special edition to call attention to the revolution going on at ETC, with articles outlining the need for change, Darley's signed statement, and verbatim transcripts of important questions asked by the London staff and Darley's responses to them.

A Working Model Emerges

As the middle-management vision sessions were finishing, a team under Paul Pearson's leadership began reviewing operations and work methods. This team addressed three themes: client marketing and responsiveness, methods for deploying and managing staff, and work accountability. It reviewed data from clients, vision meetings, and interviews with senior staff. Then it developed a model linking vision, role, and strategy.

To act on the emerging vision, client interaction, engineer assignments and roles, work accountability, and technology and development processes had to change. Each presented a particular challenge.

As the team talked over the needed adjustments, a radical revision of ETC's organization began to take shape. The traditional role of management would be very much altered. Engineers would come into much closer contact with clients. But how else could ETC both cut costs and deliver what customers were now demanding?

Perhaps it was because Paul Pearson was new to ETC that he was prepared to think seriously about a revolution in the organization. Coming from an independent consulting house, he had a different view of how a professional group providing services to a business could operate. Having an information systems background, he was comfortable with rapid change and understood the potential being created by new communications technology.

He had ideas about both of the forces impinging on ETC. His experience had taught him about a different way to interact with clients and about how an organization could be run. He now employed both of these perspectives to help shape a new organizational design for ETC.

Darley had brought Pearson to ETC in the hope he would contribute to a reformulation of its approach. Now Darley was going to see the result. Would it go too far?

Pearson's team decided that ETC needed explicitly to recognize customer primacy. This meant not just having engineers work to client schedules instead of their own but also creating a new role in the organization to facilitate interaction. A person in this role would actively seek out engineering work opportunities, gauge client satisfaction with work in progress, and act as a contact point for clients seeking ETC help. Those holding this role would be called "business managers" and would be vital to ETC's future.

ETC could also make more effective use of engineers, Pearson thought, by reducing their degree of specialization and enhancing the working relationships and flexibility among them. This could be accomplished by changing ETC's internal structure.

Reduced specialization implied fewer and broader working groups. With this change at the base would come reduction of existing group, branch, division, and department levels in the managerial hierarchy. Enhanced flexibility implied an expanded role for engineers and a reduced one for managers. Engineers would have to assume more accountability for their own work and for managing communications across their groups, while the specialist managers would be assigned different and less supervisory-oriented roles.

To make this arrangement work it would be necessary for ETC to embrace a new type of career development for its workers. This responsibility would be assigned to "resource managers," who would manage the interaction between engineers and assignments to ensure the effective development of self-standing professionals in each broad grouping of engineers. By using performance appraisal data obtained from talking to clients and project leaders, career aspiration data obtained directly from engineers, and available opportunity data obtained from "business managers," the resource managers could "make markets" in engineers, matching assignments to staff in a way that maximized both client and engineer satisfaction.

Resource managers could "create markets" for engineers to assess project needs against available ETC skills and bring in temporary help as required to balance work teams. ETC could then contract for skills it did not have rather than trying to be all things to all people.

To ensure that accountability and quality assurance for individual projects were maintained, a third new role was established, that of project leader. Existing ETC supervisors and managers had held this responsibility for the engineers in their particular areas, but Pearson felt that this role needed to be concentrated in the hands of one individual per project. Project leaders would hold oversight authority on projects assigned to them by business managers and would seek out the resources necessary to do the work from the resource managers.

Finally, ETC would continue to pursue technological development under the auspices of a centralized technology group. (This responsibility had also been handled on a decentralized basis by existing managers in the hierarchy.) By gathering technology development into one group, rather than leaving it decentralized, it was hoped that ETC could focus more closely on projected client needs rather than having diffuse groups working on many ideas at once. This approach would also shield development efforts from the pressure to do client work to meet budget requirements that would be sure to emerge in the new environment.

Pearson's group finished its work and brought Julian Darley a proposal for a radically revised organization that was intended to resolve the two critical issues facing ETC: its costs and relationships with clients. But the change envisioned was so dramatic that it would take courage for Darley to sponsor it himself. BP was a large and traditionally minded company. Could a part of the company make so substantial a change in how it operated?

Darley decided to go a step further. He asked Pearson's team to spell out in greater detail what the new organization would be like.

The New Organizational Model

The proposed elements were gathered into an organizational model that was neither a hierarchy nor a matrix. It was something new.

Each function—Engineering Resources (which housed resource managers), Technology Development (the research and development group), and Business Services (which housed business managers and project leaders)—would report directly to the chief executive. Each consisted of a general manager, a small team of subordinates, and staff. In form the functions looked like project teams. These functions were arranged on the organization chart in a doughnut-shaped ring.

Inside the ring lay 16 clusters of engineers. These clusters were to be self-standing units with no formal reporting link to any functional leader.

(For client purposes they were placed next to Engineering Resources in the organization chart, but no lines were drawn to the managers located here.)

Each cluster had one "senior consultant," who was responsible for coordinating the interaction between functions and cluster members. For example, this person might help the resource managers assigned to the cluster evaluate trainees' progress toward journeyman status. He or she might help the business manager, project leaders, and resource managers assigned to a cluster find free engineers for specific jobs or pick out the right engineer for a specific task.

Senior consultants were not to be responsible for work supervision. That was in the hands of the engineers themselves. Engineers within a cluster would be expected to be more or less self-managing on the basis of their experience and qualifications.

Each functional group in turn had individuals assigned to service the clusters. For example, Engineering Resources had resource managers, whose job was to review assignments and career progress for the 45 to 50 or so engineers in each cluster. Business Services and Technology Development each designated key people to handle contacts, solicit business, and manage technology issues for particular clients being served by a cluster's engineers.

Implementation Issues

After the new ideas had been fully spelled out by Pearson's team, Darley reviewed them carefully. He discussed them with some of his key managers, and finding a certain receptivity, decided to take yet another step on the road to revolution.

A group under Roy Fletcher's leadership picked up the Pearson team report and examined implementation issues. (Fletcher was another of ETC's general managers with a direct reporting relationship to Darley.) Fletcher's team saw a need to define how ETC would manage client requests to maximize client satisfaction with the new organization. It defined key resource groups (clusters) in a way that recognized complementary engineering disciplines but also sharply reduced the formal specialization of the old structure. It addressed the critical issue of managing quality assurance and setting up specific responsibilities for Technology Development. Finally, it set out specific duties for the three functional leaders, the senior consultants, and the project leaders, to prevent overlap and confusion among them in the new structure.

Client Considerations

Keeping clients happy would require several measures: titles that clarified what people did, more on-site work by ETC engineers, and careful management of work requests inside ETC.

Even though developing new titles that would convey clear meaning to clients might be desirable from an ETC perspective, some members of the team felt it could cause client confusion. Relatively junior engineers might end up managing work relationships with senior client staff in the new arrangement. It was uncertain whether outsiders would accept such mismatches. Clear titles might reinforce this problem.

The team felt this issue should be addressed by refining the Business Service's charter to give business managers a specific client focus, and also specified in the relevant job description that ETC's most senior staff should hold these positions so they could back up junior colleagues. They left the specific engineering titles somewhat vague. The team assigned greater accountability to the project leader role to allow leaders and engineers to locate closer to clients—even in client offices. This meant reducing to a modest degree the authority assigned to business managers by Pearson, but this was felt to be worthwhile to put the engineers in direct physical contact with clients.

To prevent confusion over management of work requests, the team developed a special set of accountabilities for this process. Business managers were to be the source of most client requests for service. If others at ETC spotted a market opportunity, they were to inform the business manager with responsibility for that client before pursuing it further. Business managers in turn would pass on refined requests to specific project leaders and senior consultants. These individuals would be responsible for backing up the specific engineers whom the resource managers found.

Business managers would be informed about quality of service issues from the field, so that they could raise them with clients. In this way, resource managers would be prevented from offering inexperienced or inappropriate engineers to clients to find work for them.

The Fletcher team also incorporated work done by ETC's management information systems staff to support implementation of better client service. The most important of these innovations were work request forms and engineering timesheets, which together would serve as the heart of an enhanced budgeting and monitoring system.

Clients requesting work from ETC would negotiate the work to be done and the hours budgeted to it at ETC's rates. This information would be described and filed under a unique identifier—a "job number." Engineers or teams picking up the request would be asked to report time spent against that number on timesheets. These could then be fed to the computer, allowing management to track utilization of engineering resources by different aggregations. Some categories were BP businesses, centrally funded development programs, and overhead.

This information could also be used to examine individual utilization rates. Since client billing also contained job numbers, it would be easy to match timesheets against client billings to see who was contributing to which clients or who was requiring excessive amounts of help to be "independent" since other engineers would turn up on jobs assigned to them.

Reducing Specialization

A key problem the team encountered in reducing specialization while recognizing engineering disciplines was that civil, mechanical, electrical, and other engineers did not speak the same technical language and could not communicate directly on engineering issues without further training or help. The team tackled this problem by putting together clusters of engineers with somewhat related backgrounds.

This proved to be a difficult task. The team wound up with a compromise solution of six broad resource groups, each having limited subdivision along discipline and functional specialties to produce the 16 clusters.

Developing Accountabilities

The team tried to define leadership roles and status for each of the three new functions: Technology Development, Engineering Resources, and Business Management. Each was to be led by a general manager with equal power and authority and a direct reporting relationship to the chief executive. Although Engineering Resources was a bigger and more complex group, the Fletcher team felt it should not be allowed to dominate the other functions.

The team also felt existing branch and division manager roles from the old hierarchy would have to change substantially. Branch managers had held responsibility for work supervision, client service, quality assurance, human resource management, and technology development.

Most of these duties would shift elsewhere. Work supervision would be held by the engineers themselves, with oversight and support provided by project leaders; human resource management (assignment, performance appraisal, and career development) would be held mainly by resource managers; and technology development and quality assurance would move to Technology Development.

The service aspects of the branch manager role—some client contact, advice to engineers, and more informal mentoring—would remain. Responsibility for coordination between engineers and the various functions would be added. These changes eventually led to the new title of "senior consultant."

Defining a Role for Technology Managers

Last, the team took on the task of establishing a place for technology development. This was perhaps its most sensitive task as the debate over technology versus client service had been at the root of the tension over the initial vision statement.

Generally, the team agreed that the qualities required for promoting and managing technical innovation were not the same as those needed for leading specialists in a field. Those managing innovation required coordinating skills, whereas technical authorities required state of the art knowledge and theoretical insights. Thus, managers in Technology Development could not be the ultimate authorities on particular technical issues and would not, therefore, have automatic right of review on work issues. (This, the team hoped, would reduce the obsession with new technology over client service among the engineers.)

Instead, the team recommended that project leaders feed technical issues requiring innovation to the technology function through agreed-on formal channels, while relying on direct communication with experts among the various clusters to get specific technical details sorted out.

Technology Development would then concern itself with both technological quality and relevance of deliverables. These aspects could be enforced by maintaining written guidelines or codes dealing with new technology as it was made available to the working engineers.

Quality assurance was critical to ETC's service, and the team felt it deserved chief executive attention, with oversight provided by Technology Development. The real quality need was seen as early assessment of the fit among what ETC engineers were developing, what the client thought was necessary, and what the client really needed to get the job done. This fit had to be managed at the client interaction by the engineers, and they required the cooperative involvement and support of both business managers and technology people to get it right.

Comments and Concerns

Initial reactions to the suggested structure and its explicit self-management concept were varied. Many younger engineers were eager to try it, but some expressed concern about the impending loss of guidance and access to knowledge of branch managers on key procedures used to maintain BP's Code of Engineering Practices. Older and more experienced engineers, who knew the standards well, were also willing to "have a go," but because they were steeped in the old culture, they were hesitant to assert their independence. Such concerns were neatly expressed by a junior engineer:

> I'll try to take responsibility, but a lot of what we do here is procedure and much of that is really learned only through doing. If I don't know

procedure I waste my time and the time of others who have to redesign my stuff. . . . The older engineers here have the knowledge they need to set their own agendas but they don't know how—they have been here so long they've forgotten what independence is all about.

Those in senior consultant roles were far more positive about the changes. Noted one in particular; "The new organization makes me responsible for the things I need to be responsible for in getting things done. No more waiting for approvals. . . . It's like I'm in my own business. Now I can get on with it!"

Seizing the Opportunity

The Fletcher team reported on April 6, 1988. All existing information and plans were then condensed into a strategy report. In part it read,

> The context of the review is set by our strategic themes [of client responsiveness, human resource development, and technology], our external business environment and the demand for our services.
> Our business strategy has major implications for the way we work and represents a radical shift towards an information-based business organization, networking internally and with both our clients and suppliers. It will offer to self-standing professionals delegated authority for responding directly to clients. Customers will have direct access to our expertise. The need to work through a management hierarchy will be removed. Adoption of this working style has significant information system and training implications and will involve substantial internal investment.
> Technological development will be drawn together under separate management to give a new focus to this area of investment.
> The "centre" concept is no longer appropriate to our business and does not convey the new mode of operation nor the right image. . . .

Darley had discussed the changes envisioned for ETC with his superiors in BP. They recognized the need for ETC to alter its operations, and they grasped the thinking behind the proposals. Darley was given the approval to implement the new structure if he wished, knowing that he would have the responsibility for its success or failure. He decided that only the new system gave hope for the ultimate success of what was to be BPE. He decided to seize the opportunity.

"When I became a professional engineer many years ago," Darley commented, "I thought I'd have some say in what I did. But years of work showed me that wasn't so. When I didn't get any say, I was very disappointed. Now I'm offering my junior engineers that opportunity."

CHAPTER SIX

Linking Strategy, Structure, and Attitudes: The Corporation of the Future

In complex corporations, what will be the future role of the corporate office versus that of the operating subsidiaries or business units? How should the corporation be structured? Should the corporate level direct operations in detail or function more like a holding company? Should it be large or small? Where should top-level staff functions be placed—in the corporate office or in the operating units? The cluster concept has a key role in answering these questions, indicating both the generality and great utility of the cluster as a mechanism for business organization.

Many companies have recognized that they are actually in several different businesses. For some companies, being in several businesses is a new development, which occurred because of acquisitions. For others it is a consequence of the establishment of entrepreneurial ventures. Whatever the reason, the result is a group of business units that seem to call for separation. Because they are different businesses, they need to operate independently and be measured separately for success or failure. Hence many firms are separating businesses in order to improve the focus of each.

The Role of the Corporate Office

However, separation of businesses raises in a dramatic fashion the question of the corporate office. Should it become more like a holding company? If so, what functions should it retain and to what degree?

At the extreme, the corporate offices of large companies such as Sears, IBM, GE, Exxon, AT&T, and BP have been shrinking even as their businesses have grown in number, size, and complexity. Sears, for example, operates with a corporate office of some 300 professionals (i.e., people who are managers and not support staff), who have responsibility for four major companies—retailing, insurance, stock brokerage, and real estate—and several smaller initiatives.

IBM long considered itself one business and therefore was managed centrally from corporate headquarters. In recent years the increasing complexity of its lines of business have led to the separation of its U.S. operations from the corporate office, which has shrunk accordingly. IBM itself has not yet transformed its management at the corporate level into clusters, but we shall see in the next section that at least one of its subsidiaries abroad—IBM Canada—has taken a long step in that direction.

In these companies and others in similar situations, the entire corporate office is increasingly acting as if it were an enhanced office of the chairperson. It oversees the successes and failures of the operating units through financial reporting from the units to the corporate office and through a schedule of review meetings between the chairperson and the top executives of the various businesses. Staff in the corporate office support each of these functions. An accounting and control unit—often containing most of the professional employees at the corporate level—reviews financial results. Other units, including planning, human resources, and finance, assist the chairperson in reviewing the performance of the business units.

Broadly speaking, the corporate office performs three key functions: external relations (particularly with the investor community), strategic planning for the corporation as a whole (including the establishment of

109

new ventures, which may later be assigned to one of the operating units), and review of the operating units.

The human resources office at the corporate level, for example, develops compensation programs for top executives, conducts the planning process for succession to key management positions, oversees the performance of the human resource departments in the operating units, and periodically undertakes special assignments. In today's climate such a special effort might involve coordinating the health insurance buying of all the operating units to achieve economies of scale in dealing with providers. Another might be to help develop the capacity to plan for the capability of the organization as a whole, not just through individual performance reviews in the operating units.

By having the corporate office perform certain functions, the company also frees the business units to concentrate more fully on operations. Top officers of the units have more time to devote to their businesses, and the units themselves can be streamlined administratively for greater efficiency.

How does the interaction between the corporate office and the operating units actually work? There are different ways, of course, and some are better than others. There are opportunities to be grasped and pitfalls to be avoided.

Consider, for example, the strategic planner in the corporate office, who both plans for the corporation as a whole and oversees the planning activity in each business unit. In providing oversight, the corporate planner asks the operating units to prepare strategic plans of their own in accordance with templates the corporate planner provides.

What is the primary purpose? Does the corporate planner want the business unit's plans to ensure that the unit is looking ahead as it should— that is, as part of the corporate planner's oversight function—or does the corporate planner want the unit's plans to help create an overall corporate plan? This is a key question, for on it turns both the size of the corporate planning office and the relationship between the corporate staff and the business units.

The best answer for today is probably that the corporate planner should be dealing with the business unit's operating plans only as part of his or her oversight capacity. To do the planning for the units would require a much larger staff in the corporate planning office than is desirable and would risk considerable duplication of effort with the business units.

The specific objectives of the corporate planning office are therefore to ensure uniformity of plans across the operating units of the company, to make cross-plan comparisons to identify opportunities or weaknesses, and to create an overall corporate plan from the operating units' plans. But will the corporate planner be able to restrain himself or herself from doing more for individual units, especially if one is in difficulty? How can the corporate level be involved with the operating companies without doing their jobs for them? The problem is to meet key purposes without falling into certain traps.

A dangerous trap is to duplicate costs of the staff functions across the several business entities and the corporate office itself. If each unit has its own staff functions, substantial costs have been loaded on what are probably highly competitive and cost-conscious businesses.

To avoid duplication, functions could be centered in the corporate office, but this solution falls into another trap: It creates a process that is often far too slow. The operating units would have to transmit information, then wait for instructions.

To avoid delay, the functions must be decentralized to the business units, but there are important reasons to coordinate. A fully integrated structure could be designed, but that would probably create a large and unwieldy process involving many people at great expense.

Hence the dilemma of relationships between the corporate office and operating unit in the modern complex corporation: Too much centralization in the corporate office results in a process too slow for today's economic situation, whereas too much decentralization in the operating units creates costly duplication and loses the advantages of coordination.

How is this dilemma to be resolved? One answer is through the establishment of clusters that include both corporate office staff and those of the operating units. The cluster modifies the role of the holding company's professionals. They act as central points or coordinators in the clusters, which are made up of the key professionals from the operating units. Further, the operating units are tied together by a formal communication network supported on PCs or mainframe terminals.

The cluster strips away vertical reporting relationships, allowing people from the corporate office and the operating units to work together without the complexities of supervision and evaluation. It permits coordination and learning without imposing a ponderous bureaucratic structure.

For example, linking the human resources of an organization to its business plan is an important way to prepare for needed changes in skills, organizational structure, and personnel policies. Furthermore, different businesses often confront similar problems and so can benefit by learning from and working with each other. Bringing together representatives from different businesses is a key opportunity for corporate staffers. Most desirable is an open exchange of views among the employees from the different businesses and support for each other. Those involved would be strategic planners from the various businesses, human resources executives, line officials from the businesses, and corporate staff from planning and personnel.

There is likely to be a temptation to include only staff professionals in a cluster of this type—that is, only human resources and planning people. A cluster so constituted would do an excellent job of preparing and coordinating plans, but it would be deficient in trying to get them implemented. Without the perspective and active involvement of line managers in preparing an operating plan, the business unit is unlikely to see it as directly relevant to line needs. The result will be lack of enthusiasm in implementation, which may well undercut the plan's effectiveness.

Clusters at the Corporate Level

BP Builds on Its Success

"What I'm trying to do," Robert Horton, chairman of British Petroleum told a reporter for the *Financial Times* in March 1990, only one week after becoming chief executive officer of the company, "is to simplify, refocus, and make it clear that we don't need any longer to have hierarchies. We don't need any longer to have baronial head office departments. This is fundamentally a different way of looking at the way that you run the centre of the corporation."

To design the posthierarchical firm, Horton turned to a task force of young executives, who searched widely for a model, including an in-depth look at Julian Darley's success in British Petroleum Engineering. They proposed to simplify the role of the corporate center by delegating authority and responsibility down a corporate hierarchy, which was flattened by eliminating layers of control and planning.

Some 70 percent of corporate-level committees were eliminated, their functions delegated to individuals. Hierarchical departments were eliminated, their roles taken over by small, flexible teams. "To whom do I report?" no longer has an answer for many at BP headquarters. Instead people have accountabilities and are expected to create their own patterns of communication by networking.

The new organization chart lacks boxes and lines. Instead there are ovals—representing such units as Finance and Tax Policy, Chief of Staff and Private Office, Group Accounting, Human Resource Support, and Educational Affairs—placed inside an all-encompassing oval referred to as "the Egg."

Each oval is to operate essentially as a cluster. Groups of professionals across the firm with a common interest will link informally, avoiding the bureaucracy and rigidity of traditional departmental and committee structures. The teams are to be small, some permanent and some temporary, and will be activity-oriented (rather than turf-protective) and fully interconnected internally. Electronic networking will be a critical component of the new approach.

BP's organizational design team recognized that a new set of attitudes would have to accompany the new managerial system if it were to succeed. Hence, the announcement of the cluster organization was accompanied with programs for top managers and support staff that were aimed directly at changing attitudes and behavior to fit with the new working relationships. Robert Horton estimated for the *Financial Times* that the process of education and attitude change would take two to three years.

IBM Canada Takes a Long Step in the Direction of Clusters

At virtually the same time that the BP task force was redesigning the corporate center, a similar group at IBM Canada was embarked on a simliar effort. A vision of the firm in the 1990s was developed. It would provide not just hardware or softwear but also total solutions to customers, it would empower the work force so that each person saw that he or she was making a solid contribution to the company, and it would provide a responsive management support system.

To get closer to its customers, IBM redeployed its people so that more than 60 percent functioned in roles designing, building, selling, and installing or servicing IBM offerings. In the early 1980s only 40 percent had been so engaged.

To empower the work force, decision-making power was delegated downward and reasonable risks encouraged. For empowerment to be more than a platitude it must consist of clear direction and context; necessary skills and education; and proper tools, information, procedures, and authority. IBM worked to provide it all.

The business was simultaneously delayered. The number of managerial levels was reduced from nine to five. The span of control was almost doubled. Also, automated plants shifted to different production, and productivity was virtually tripled.

But IBM was not prepared to go as far as BP. The flattened hierarchy was retained, and clusters were created as an overlay, that is, an additional element of the structure. Fifteen cross-functional teams were made responsible for identifying key areas of needed change and tackling them. Members of the teams were to spend 20 percent of their time in the team efforts.

"We've ended up with a flexible, interfunctional team-based structure sitting on top of our previous hierarchical structure," Tom Corcoran told Lynda Applegate of Harvard. "While this new structure resembles a matrix, it does not perform like one since the teams are less static than typical matrix organizations."

There was some danger in adding complexity to the organization, Corcoran acknowledged, but IBM was unwilling at this stage to go further in the direction of a fully clustered organization. Why go to clusters at all? Couldn't the traditional organization do all that was necessary? Corcoran thought not. The business environment is dramatic and changing, and cross-functional teams with a delayered bureacracy are crucial to meeting its demands.

Tackling the Central Problem of Corporate Management

The central problem of managing a large corporation is getting the business units to align on the corporate mission. If the firm is made up of clusters, what holds the separate clusters together?

The response begins traditionally, with top management direction. I am aware of no large corporation that is managed without a hierarchical component at the top. Probably today our level of human and systems development does not permit it. Even in a company that uses clusters at the operating and staff levels, both the corporate office and the top executive levels of each division will have a hierarchy of command and control in the traditional manner. In efficient firms the hierarchical elements have few layers and there is considerable delegation of authority, but reporting relationships exist in the traditional manner. Thus alignment of divisions on the corporate mission and intervention in the operations of a stumbling unit occur in the traditional manner. To say that alignment is pursued in the traditional manner at this level is not to say that achieving it is automatic.

In fact clusters operating across unit boundaries between divisions and the corporate office are an excellent method of coordinating the activities of the various businesses. In the place of today's complex, expensive, and formal interacting mechanisms is a much more flexible unit. Therefore, the cost of complexity is reduced without sacrificing communication and coordination.

But the foregoing is about clusters within the corporate office itself. To whom does the chairperson of a Fortune 500 company, which may have hundreds of clusters in its operating units, go to improve performance?

The answer: either to the executive in charge of the division involved or, if appropriate, to the group of executives in charge of all the units of the corporation. Some top executives work with their division executives in a team format—that is, as a cluster group, with open discussion about the role of each division in the company as a whole. Other top executives prefer to deal one on one with their divisional subordinates.

It is within divisions that clusters become a primary form of organization. Questions of alignment, coordination, and control arise principally at this level.

Alignment of clusters within a division is the responsibility, in a traditional sense, of the division's management. Division management accomplishes this task through frequent meetings with representatives of the clusters and sometimes with groups of employees. Management explains divisional missions and articulates the corporate vision. The vision is communicated to cluster members as the principle unifying device of the division. Employees are then expected to utilize their own discretion in pursuing the vision, but close networklike communications and frequent meetings help to keep each person aware of what others are doing.

There must be in a cluster organization a series of committees on which the various clusters are represented and through which they communicate with management and with one another. Does this mean there will be too many meetings? Not if the meetings are well run and the people are knowledgeable, are well intentioned, and share the same vision of the business and information about its situation.

Let me emphasize that by empowering individuals to serve the customer better, clusters serve the larger corporate goals effectively. However, it is likely that there will be some competition among clusters for the same customers.

That is what happens, for example, in British Petroleum Engineering when a potential client contacts two or more clusters about a single project. A business manager may have to step in to mediate if the two units cannot split the work appropriately. To a degree this internal competition is good and is welcomed by management. It is an advantage of the cluster format that internal competition can flower. In a traditional hierarchy, managers would allocate assignments among elements of the organization, and thus the striving for excellence that healthy competition engenders would usually be lost.

But internal competition can also be destructive. This can occur when prices to a customer are cut below reasonable levels, when promises are made that cannot be kept, when resources are pirated to fulfill unwarranted commitments, and when animosity develops between people in different clusters because of competition among them.

Whose responsibility is it to avoid such difficulties? The cluster leaders and the managers have that obligation. Cluster leaders understand the difficulties that negative competition can create for the organization as a whole, and they meet frequently enough to identify problems and resolve them. Division managers, although few in number, have relationships among the clusters as their principal responsibility, and they will call problems to the attention of cluster leaders if necessary. In an extreme case management has the authority to allocate work among clusters, or even within them. But in a cluster organization, intervention by management based on authority represents a failure of understanding and performance by all involved.

To whom does a cluster report? It is answerable to division management for its results. Each cluster has goals, subordinate objectives, budgets, and measurements, which are prepared in conjunction with management. The performance of the cluster is monitored by management but not the performance of detailed work instructions nor that of individuals within the cluster (except through the performance evaluation process). The work performance of individuals on a day-to-day basis is evaluated by peers and by the cluster leaders or project leaders.

Who notices when a cluster needs fixing? Cluster members notice first of all and try to rectify the situation. Leadership may be changed internally or work processes altered. If additional people are needed, the cluster will seek them through resource managers. Managers may also notice a cluster in difficulty, either by direct measurements or by hearing about it from others in the organization.

When a cluster's performance lags, management intervenes to determine the cause and to help set the matter right. Managers may persuade a cluster to replace its leaders, to add expertise that is lacking, to restructure work teams, to meet to work out internal problems, or even in extreme cases to dissolve. If persuasion fails, management may act on its own authority. But this can be done only when the remainder of the organization fully comprehends the necessity, lest the autonomy and initiative of the cluster be compromised to the detriment of the division's performance. As a practical matter, a cluster that is performing well experiences limited managerial intervention.

Refocused Business Strategy

In recognizing and adopting clusters, firms gain a new competitive advantage—true marketplace flexibility. Decisions are made more quickly and as close to the customer as possible. Because of this, organizational capability becomes an independent variable in setting overall strategy. Executives must thus rethink the way they make corporate strategy.

The generally accepted doctrine is that a chosen business strategy determines the organizational structure. In essence the prescription is for a company to establish its business strategy by selecting the most profitable opportunities available to it. Then, choices are made between a centralized or decentralized operation, cost or profit centers, divisional or unitary structure, and types of incentives for managers to carry out the strategy.

As described by the "Seven S" model widely used by business consultants, the strategy process is as follows:

Strategy

determines what the organization needs as

Skills,

which then dictate

Structure   Staff   Systems   Style   Shared Values

Thus, after determining a business strategy by an analytic process, which identifies and chooses among alternatives on the basis of expected profitability, a company turns its attention to implementation. It determines by deduction from the business strategy what skills are needed in the organization (e.g., the ability to schedule for the optimal use of transportation equipment) and then proceeds to decide what is needed in the structure of jobs, staff (or types of people with particular job-related skills), management systems (e.g., computers or personnel policies), style of management or leadership, and the shared values (or the culture) of the firm.

The basic notion is that any organization can be shaped to carry through a chosen strategy successfully. In this thinking strategy is clearly the senior partner, with organizational matters merely secondary and derivative considerations. Although this approach may make sense in establishing a new company where nothing is already in place, it is close to absurd when applied to an established organization with years of history and methods of doing business that are already firmly set. An existing organization, especially a large one, cannot be altered easily to fit a shifting business strategy.

This is not to say that an existing firm cannot be modified, even substantially, over time. Transformations can be accomplished. But the somewhat cavalier reshaping of an organization and its people, which is often attempted in pursuit of a shift in business strategy, more often leads to frustration and disaster than to success. In consequence the naive approach is now being superceded.

Today the notion that "strategy determines structure" is not so much wrong as outdated. Business strategy is now only one of a triad of factors that taken as a group determine the corporate direction, and which is recognized to be of broader importance than business strategy alone. Fortunately, the new concept is already emerging in some corporations so that its early characteristics can be identified.

Specifically, executives must weigh separately and then align with one another the company's business strategy, its organizational structure, and the behavior of its employees (including themselves). Today, American business has available, and often utilizes, soft technologies for modifying each element. In fact there are consulting companies that specialize in each of these areas, and some large firms already employ three different consultants when attempting to revitalize or reorient the company.

Figure 2 shows the three factors in a triangle. None dominates; each has an impact on the others and on the organization itself. Aligning them requires careful judgment. For example, creative tension may exist when structural capability is outgrowing business objectives and the attitudes and behavior of employees. This, of course, is what happens when new technology makes wider spans of control possible.

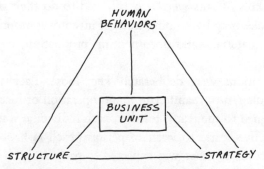

Figure 2 Aligning Behavior, Structure, and Strategy

Consider the following example (A Green-Field Plant), which has been analyzed with this model.

A Green-Field Plant

Strategy Faced with the aftermath of a lengthy and bitter strike, a well-known manufacturing company decided to improve productivity in its engine-making facilities. Some executives felt that the only real alternative was to locate operations overseas, where cheaper and more "eager to work" employees could be found to boost output and productivity. Other executives felt that new work practices and structures might shift the attitudes of enough U.S. employees to make such a costly move unnecessary. However, until the senior executives could see how much improvement would result from a new structure and attitudes, no long-term corporate direction could be chosen.

To test one alternative structure, the company chose a "green-field site." Local plant management was given the opportunity to try to create a different kind of culture than that which existed in any other company operation. The goal was to create a situation in which four words—*excellence, trust, growth,* and *equity*—would describe the culture. Working from this base, they hoped to raise productivity and cut costs.

Structure The basic unit local management chose to work with was the team. Within each team, emphasis would be placed on self-management, learning new skills, and performance. Teams were to be trusted to regulate themselves, track their own performance, and encourage members to acquire new skills. Teams were also expected to do their own administration and housekeeping by keeping track of inventory; ordering and inspecting necessary materials; and documenting production, costs, attendance, and performance.

Job descriptions were deliberately kept loose. Each worker was expected to handle setup, maintenance, and operation of machines or assembly tasks assigned to the team. Further, each individual was expected, over the course of five years, to learn to perform each task on each machine. Finally, each team member was expected to perform both production and administration tasks.

Teams were to sort out who was going to do which task at any given time. Once an assignment was made, however, it would last for a calendar year.

Rather than supervisors, each team had an "advisor," who was expected to work with the team, not manage it. Advisors were to facilitate the acquisition of new skills and performance and had to be technically proficient with the work and able to communicate with people in a nonauthoritarian, nonthreatening manner. They were expected to share performance appraisal, discipline, and compensation decisions with their team members. Members of individual teams were also expected to oversee safety practices and participate in budgeting and forecasting with their advisors.

Groups of three or four teams were arranged into what were called "businesses." A key assumption in planning was that the maximum number of people in any "business" would be between 200 and 300. This number would allow the business manager to get to know everybody in his or her area. Each of the 40 manufacturing teams was thus clustered around a business manager, reporting to that manager through its own team advisor.

Attitudes Plant management planned to allow a maximum amount of freedom, responsibility, and flexibility for employees in the hope that they would respond with dedication and high levels of performance in their work. Management also designed various attitude influences with employee participation in mind.

For example, the compensation system was designed to limit the gulf between management and workers. All employees were salaried. Everyone was expected to work 40 hours per week and make up any missed time. To reinforce cooperation and communication in the teams, promotion and pay increases were based not on seniority but on the acquisition of new skills and the willingness to perform varied tasks. Wages in the plant would be relatively high compared with Green-Field's surrounding area but low in relation to the company's other operations.

Performance was appraised on "cost-per-piece" measures. The reports assembled by the teams were simple yet complete. Costs were given for variable manufacturing items (broken down to elements like scrap, rework, operating supplies, tools, and freight), semivariable expenses (salary, gas, travel, etc.), and total team costs. These figures were then compared to those of the previous month and previous year as a "base." At the same time, the plant manager and directors set plant-wide goals for cost reduction on specific items (direct materials and team expenses). The idea was to give the teams the data they needed to make their own decisions on how to save money and measure their own productivity.

The physical space and manufacturing process also reflected the new philosophy. The south end of the plant held the self-contained production units that made various components of diesel engines (e.g., pistons, liners, camshafts, and camboxes). The north end of the plant held the assembly stations. These were arranged in lines designed to allow teams to build up a surplus of between eight and ten engines (roughly half a day's production). Management hoped that whenever a surplus developed at any one station, workers could shift up and down the line either to help out or to provide motivational support.

The entire plant floor of 930,000 square feet was open from top to bottom, except for a core of offices dividing it down the middle. In an effort to link support staff to the manufacturing teams, these offices were later enlarged to put even more of these workers right in the middle of the plant.

Results

The Green-Field plant managers attained many of the initial goals over the five-year span of the experiment. Absenteeism was running at 3 percent versus 6 percent elsewhere in the company. The safety record, although poor at first, was improving. Warranty data on the plant's products were extremely favorable. Plant-wide utilization rates were running at 60 to 70 percent, as opposed to 50 percent at the company's other engine plants. Team members were performing major and minor machine overhauls and maintenance themselves. Indirect labor costs were projected to be 20 percent lower than elsewhere since this plant had only half the supervisors of the other facilities.

Some of the goals were not so clearly attained. As the teams jelled into effective work groups, management hoped that they would be largely self-managing. This was somewhat of a hit-and-miss situation. Roughly 25 percent of the teams became self-managing. However, when teams did become self-managing the effect was powerful.

One team—the cambox team—found itself assuming significant managerial authority. As plant production grew, the cambox team had 80 members spread over three shifts with only one advisor. Although the advisor felt things were going well, the team members felt otherwise. Communications between shifts had broken down, and morale and performance dropped. Product quality soon followed. However, the team advisor refused to admit he had problems.

Finally several members decided to take action. They rallied the teams from all three shifts in a meeting without the advisor, called in the plant manager, and vented their feelings. He encouraged the team to plan its own reorganization. The original rebels then called for a group of two representatives from each shift to look at the situation. Meeting each night after work, over a five-week period, this group eventually concluded that 80 people in a team were too many.

They decided to break the team into four subassembly groups; and to ensure better communication between shifts, they appointed a coordinator for the second and third shifts of each team. Productivity immediately shot back up. Said the plant manager of this experience, "It seems that whenever we have a chaotic situation, and a team is able to deal with that chaos, the productivity rises. I'm not sure why that is, but it always happens."

Other teams were not so effective at managing themselves and had to rely more heavily on their advisors. The determining factors on effectiveness seemed to be length of time the team had been together, the willingness of the adviser to encourage self-help, and the size of the team.

The Structural Emergence

The Green-Field plant example shows how the linkages among strategy, structure, and human attitudes must be considered when structure is a true organizational variable. Previous models, such as the Seven S model assumed implicitly that structure was largely "fixed." Although the boxes and lines could be rearranged at will, virtually all firms used hierarchy in its assorted forms (e.g., centralized or divisionalized), a few using matrices at key levels with hierarchy above and below. Under these conditions, strategy is the dominant variable simply because it is variable, whereas structure is not.

The emergence of a new structural option—clusters—as a competitive weapon for mobilizing employees, enabling technology to work more efficiently, and meeting economic challenges, introduces a fundamental change to the business environment. Executives and others must be prepared to consider structure as the coequal of strategy in their longer-term thinking.

Today, we are in an era equivalent to that of American football as the forward pass was introduced. With four downs to make 10 yards, the game was rush, rush, rush. Every team had the same offensive and defensive set (structures) on the field—designed to execute handoffs and pitches and to block against them.

Then came the forward pass—a structural revolution. Suddenly, the old emphasis on ground strategy took a back seat. Coaches swore that the forward pass would ruin the game. But fans demanded the excitement of the 30-, or 40-, or even 80-yard gain; the explosive scoring drive; the grace of the ball in the air; and the one-on-one all-or-nothing struggle between cornerback and pass receiver.

The forward pass remained legal. Coaches had to design entirely new structural alignments for offense and defense. Through practices and games, new strategies began to evolve to exploit the power inherent in a flexible formation that could both run and pass with the same personnel on the field.

Today, with the forward pass, the Jim Kellys and Dan Marinos of the world could destroy the run and lateral-only teams of the previous era. The best ground-based strategy in the world (the "wishbone") seldom is effective against the air and ground structures in this era of the professional mixed offense. In the same way businesses with inflexible structures that try to change strategy will find limited success against those prepared to use new structures—particularly clusters—as the business equivalent of the forward pass.

PART II

What Managers Can Do

CHAPTER SEVEN

Seven Steps:
How to Set Up Clusters

Suppose you should want to move in the direction of clusters at your own workplace. How should you go about it?

Businesses adopt clusters by two routes: unconscious and planned. Some firms embrace clusters without being aware of doing so. One industrial concern did so through cost cutting: Fiscal pressure caused the firm to prune managerial layers, forcing those remaining to adopt cluster-type middle-management roles and less direct mechanisms for influencing employees, and thereby implicitly reducing hierarchy. A bank brought in powerful new computer technology to enhance its responsiveness to customers. The new systems gave front-line employees access to much more data, and as customers discovered this development, they began to demand more service and advice. As employees took on decision-making and advising duties, middle managers were stripped of influence. The result was that the hierarchy declined in importance.

Unconscious approaches can lead to structural change, as seen by these examples. But this approach can also be highly destructive of morale since employees do not understand what is happening and resist the changes. Also, backing into clusters, as it were, is usually very inefficient and may produce serious losses if competitors use ongoing organizational confusion and turmoil to lure away staff and customers.

Other organizations explicitly set out to change managerial structures—defining new roles for managers, training staff to take on more duties, and working out new work organizations—before embarking on the systematic cost reduction that the cluster form allows. These planned approaches are usually more efficient and minimize the disorder and confusion that often accompany change.

The Seven Steps

The first and most critical rule in exploring a cluster format is not to think about organization. Instead, think about customers, relationships, and information.

Why not think about organization? Because for most executives that means thinking about titles, functions, and reporting relationships. You have been trained to live and breathe hierarchy, so despite good intentions you will fall back into hierarchical modes of thought. Instead, put the business together in a way that makes sense for its basic purpose; then see where that leads in organizational terms. Think about how best to serve the customer. Then put people into the concept.

Clusters are flexible and can be adapted to a variety of needs. The essence of moving to clusters is to determine the enterprise's mission and translate that mission into customer contact, communications, and work relationships. Include key employees in the discussion and planning.

Moving from hierarchy to cluster entails seven steps. These are listed in Figure 3 and explored in the accompanying discussion.

Start at the Top

An important actor is on top. The leader—whether a CEO, division executive, or field manager—must be committed to the new approach or it will not work. Radical delegation and hands-off management must take its signals from the leader's behavior.

However, this does not mean that to embark on a cluster approach, a company unit requires the CEO of the parent company to be a firm support. In fact, the CEO need not be a supporter at all. A great deal can be done by a responsible unit manager as long as two conditions are met.

- Start at the Top
- Take Initial Dramatic Actions
- Talk to the "Front-Line" Troops
- Refine Your Vision
- Review Organization Practices in Light of Your Vision
- Define the Clusters and Deal with Organization Constraints
- Communicate with the Ranks

Figure 3   The Seven Steps to a Cluster Organization

First, the top executives of the parent organization must not be hostile to the effort. If they strongly oppose the initiative, it is unlikely to succeed. Second, personnel and the controller's office must permit enough leeway from the hierarchy's standard practices for the clusters to function. Where these two conditions are met, much can be done by a business unit on its own.

Typically, those unit leaders who adopt clusters have several distinguishing attributes. First, they are new to their positions. Second, they have less personal prestige invested in the existing scheme and are more open to different ideas. Third, they have come to consider the cluster format as a desirable alternative after reviewing organizational performance and discovering a lack of customer sensitivity (noncompetitive pricing and slow response times to customers), excessive overhead (high management-to-staff ratios), and loss of innovative drive among employees (complaints about too many rules or too much paperwork).

Experience shows that an outside perspective on such matters is critical. The leader should ask, "What do customers really want from us?" Answers can come directly from customers through surveys, focus groups, or complaint channels. The field sales force and second-line managers often have valuable information to contribute as well. Sometimes consultants or internal thinking at top staff levels are useful, although the leaders may already be getting back what they want to hear from those sources.

Take Initial Dramatic Actions

Organizations have their own internal momentum and culture based on years of accumulated incidents and events. This momentum is hard to break with gentle means. Case histories suggest that leaders must be prepared to take some dramatic actions, even if only symbolic, to signal that old ways cannot continue.

One approach is to start selective and high-profile cost cutting. Several leaders I observed cancelled and changed their recruiting patterns, initiated job cuts, and slashed overhead.

Another approach is to hold off-site meetings, where people are forced to explore new ways of doing things. The idea is not to get instant change but rather to signal that change is expected to emerge.

Whatever the means, the natural resistance to change must be broken for clusters to be installed successfully. Memos and directives are not the way to proceed.

Talk to the Front-Line Troops

A key step in adopting clusters is delegating both authority and responsibility in the organization to operating levels. This ought to begin with the initial process of change itself. A leader contemplating change must remember that although employees have fewer chances to think about and express company concerns than he or she does, they do think and, for the most part, will want to participate in change. Their jobs and lifestyle are on the same line as the CEO's. If this is not true, the change effort will fail. Employees' participation can be generated through initial dramatic actions, if these are taken correctly.

Involvement with change efforts will enhance the employees' commitment to the new order. It will also help overcome roadblocks thrown up by any middle managers afraid of losing power and responsibility.

There are several points to be noted about tapping front-line employees' ideas. These have to do with both content and process.

First, concerning content, front-line employees do not tend to think strategically but rather operationally. This has the advantage of focusing their attention on day-to-day realities; front-line employees are unlikely to wander from such issues as customer service or the support they need to do a better job. It also has the disadvantage of necessitating translation, analysis, and interpretation of views into executive language before they can be understood and incorporated into the change process.

I have seen these views translated by internal human resource professionals, outside consultants, and management task forces. It requires patience and time. If the organization has been plagued with poor vertical communications, leaders may be forced to rely on outside consultants.

Second, concerning process, the ideas of employees may be at wide variance with those of the middle managers and supervisors whose staff they are on. For this reason, employees' views must be assembled in ways that will preserve confidentiality to ensure honest responses. It does little good to hold meetings and invite comments when trying to gather data that will disturb the hierarchy. For the same reason, it may be difficult to involve managers in data collection, although they can help in the analysis and interpretation role after the initial collection is completed.

Refine Your Vision

Once ideas are in, top-level work can begin. Several organizational variables are affected by a move to clusters, and these should be considered at some length. Once the die is cast, there is limited ability to return to another hierarchy.

Observation shows that leaders who invest time and energy in analyzing and debating their vision of the future with their top subordinates usually go on to implement clusters successfully. The process of communicating helps executives build consensus and commitment as much as it helps employees. Although the temptation can be very great, executives who impose their will in such matters generally do not do as well as they otherwise might.

The idea is not to obtain 100 percent commitment. Universal acceptance is not desirable, as differences can lead to healthy and creative tension; "complete" commitment usually indicates submerged conflict that will later emerge to hamper implementation. A leader is best served by those who express differences and reservations but pledge their loyalty to the concept of change.

After management's acceptance is achieved, the vision-building process can be moved down to the middle-management ranks in a cascading process. The message communicated will have to change as the concerns of the managers change. I have seen both external consultants and internal senior managers lead such efforts to obtain alignment with the new vision.

Review Organizational Practices in Light of Your Vision

Success requires alignment and balance among strategy, structure, and behavior. But it is possible to start in one place rather than another. At British Petroleum, Julian Darley came to clusters through structure. Du Pont's Andy Harriss, whose clusterlike units I will discuss in Chapter Thirteen, began from the attitudes and behavior of people. Both leaders sought to cut operating costs as a business objective.

For Darley to be successful, he had to help his workers develop the attitudes that drive a cluster organization. For Harriss to utilize the new energy of his workers, he had to move toward a cluster organization.

To try to obtain a new organization without the requisite attitudes will result in failure. Similarly, to develop the new attitudes without changing the organization so that people can express them will yield only frustration and bitterness.

The process of alignment is illustrated by the effort made at a large chemical company. This company had established a new division to market its products to a particular consuming industry. The target industry was growing very slowly, and the company already had a large share of the available market. Yet the new division was given rapid growth targets.

"Where is the growth to come from?" its executives asked. It could not come from competitors because the firm already had most of the market. It could not come from internal growth because there was very little. Searching for an answer, the division looked to innovation in products, marketing, and management skills.

Quickly, its executives identified the patterns of thought and behavior that had developed in the large organization as a major barrier to success. So it put key managers through programs designed to change their attitudes and behavior. The results were positive.

New initiatives sprouted everywhere in the division. Thus executives were faced with the need to devise business plans accommodating innovation and to develop a new structure encouraging initiatives rather than hindering them.

Define the Clusters and Deal with Organizational Constraints

In some ways this is the most important step in the entire process. Most of the people in an organization—those who actually do the work as opposed to thinking how it is to be done—will be critically affected. Thus the clusters must be defined correctly for the new approach to work.

In hierarchies work units are largely ordered by function, and various specialists are grouped together to maximize their common specialist knowledge. In clusters groups are set up to be largely self-contained operating units. They should hold all the necessary specialist knowledge to enable them to carry out their chosen tasks effectively; they are multi-skilled.

Throwing people of highly varied backgrounds together in an ill-defined way, and then removing experienced supervisors overnight to create autonomy, is not the way to proceed. This will create anarchy—as various specialists struggle to work out a common language in which to do business with one another—and tremendous pressure to return to the old hierarchical style.

Nor should clusters be designed by placing together on an organization chart several narrowly defined jobs. In the cluster each person will have to take broader duties than are encompassed in the old job structure.

A manager ought to work in a participative fashion with employees to assemble clusters around key corporate missions; activities; and if possible, concrete production or service tasks. This step will reduce the amount of specialization that needs to be overcome initially and also establish early a common framework of goals and objectives that all of the diverse cluster members can see.

For example, clusters might be established to link the activities required to service a key client or a key geographic market or to make and distribute a key product. One company—Swissair—is building clusters around routes in its schedule. Manufacturers like Volvo are building clusters around machining stations, parts facilities, and assembly stations. These are concrete and stable business anchors from which to build a flexible organization to reach business objectives.

Darley had a team of experienced BPE managers sit down and review different engineering disciplines (e.g., civil, mechanical, and electrical) and different services (process control, facilities, and contract management) that BPE provided to the BP Group. The end results of the clustering process were 16 independent units, each without direct reporting relationships to the top, holding the appropriate combination of specialist engineers needed to meet one particular business objective or to serve one key client group. More or fewer clusters could have been established had there been more or fewer continuing missions to be performed.

One thing to remember in defining clusters is that they are highly flexible. Once in place, their skills and memberships can be altered easily. Sometimes, through external education or skill-based training, existing members may even transform a cluster themselves in pursuit of an established corporate mission.

To ensure that empowerment and flexibility do not cause confusion or lose sight of business objectives, the basic mission, goals, and financial or other reporting systems established for an individual cluster ought to remain reasonably constant once they are established. It is through these means that cluster members retain their alignment to corporate objectives while using their individual initiative.

If corporate objectives are changed, the changes should be widely distributed and discussed so that the cluster members can realign themselves. The members cannot be directly ordered to do so since direct orders as such no longer exist. Indeed, eliminating "looking over one's shoulder" is a basic reason for establishing the cluster format in the first place.

A clear and coherent link must be established between vision and the three organizational variables. For example, speed of service is not encouraged by a performance appraisal or compensation system that requires multiple sign-offs on work performed by professionals. Employee behavior and attitudes will be affected negatively when the vision of faster service confronts the reality of rewards handed out for delay and review. Similarly, teamwork will not be encouraged by physical space that encourages isolated individual efforts or by a company culture that argues for supervisory control.

A realistic assessment of the organizational constraints and available levers must be made. For example, Harriss did not have control over most of the standard managerial instruments for encouraging behavior change. Du Pont set his staff salaries, directed how and when he could make promotions, and set corporate directives and the culture in which he had to operate.

He did have control over his physical office space, and so it was altered to facilitate a cluster structure. He did have control over his training budget, and so money was invested in helping people become more team-oriented and trusting of each other. He did have control over his organizational structure, and so team leaders were installed.

Similarly, the speed and pace of change must not exceed the tolerance of the broader corporation. Darley, for example, had to deal with the quality concerns of BPE's major customers, and their occasional reluctance to rely on the sole effort of a junior engineer, by installing a business manager as an intermediary and other checkpoints on critical work.

Communicate with the Ranks

Leaders who want to make a successful transition to clusters communicate extensively with their rank and file. As noted, Julian Darley held multiple question-and-answer sessions with all of his London-based engineering staff and arranged for those in the field to be informed as well. Harriss met all Fibers I/S (Du Pont) recruits to his organization at Pecos River and his managers and supervisors in formal forum meetings and informal hallway and other social gatherings.

The cluster form is a communication-driven approach to organization. It thrives where communication is free and open. It is designed to augment and replace the limited communication channels based on a chain of command.

Microcomputers and cellular telephone connections should be made available to most personnel to establish an interconnected network. Individuals should be trained so that they become comfortable with these instruments and use them well. Newsletters and documents ought to be available to all.

The communication system should include a complete data base about the business and its activities, including both financial and nonfinancial elements. It should include a message capability faster and more widely shared than at present. This capability will help free professionals, managers, and others from the time-consuming task of preparing and distributing paper. It will also increase the accessibility of reports to the organization as a whole.

Figure 4 presents in greater detail an outline of the seven steps to setting up a cluster organization. It should be useful as a guide and checklist to the organization of the future.

1. Starting at the Top
   —acquire outside perspective of the organization
     • from own thinking as previous outsider
     • from bringing in an outsider as senior manager
     • from bringing in consultants for further perspective
   —perspectives usually include
     • price and quality of service to customer
       ○ what does the customer really want?
       ○ how does the customer really want it?
     • how to motivate work force
       ○ why do people work?
       ○ how can they be encouraged to be more productive?
2. Taking Initial Dramatic Actions
   —grabbing middle management's attention
     • cost cutting via layoffs and budget reviews
     • consolidation of overhead centers
     • some delayering (increase supervisory span of control)
   —informing them that the old order has to go
     • create steering committee to push change
     • hold off-site management/training meetings
     • set up management teams to define a "new order"
3. Talking to the "Front-Line" Troops
   —talk to them via internal consultants
     • they deal directly with customers
     • they can tell consultant why customer is not happy
   —get interpretation of what they say from consultant
     • generally not strategic, but operational
       ○ so you have to translate for them
       ○ (remember, they cannot translate for you)
     • need flexibility, self-management to deliver service
       ○ delegation of authority
       ○ less coordination by supervisors
       ○ more independent initiative
     • also need to enhance communications across specialties
       ○ fewer specialist managers
       ○ broader work teams
       ○ new communications systems

Figure 4   Setting Up Clusters

4. Refining Your Vision
   —secure commitment of top-level management team
   - get significant share through "visioning" process
     o off-site of top 10 to 20 people
     o with process consulting person to break barriers
     o may take a long time (one to two weeks in some cases)
   —push visioning process down into the management team
   - get people from first session to lead
     o reinforce commitment obtained in initial meeting
     o get middle management buy-in and momentum
   - have people from subsequent sessions work with their reports
     o further reinforcement of change
     o feed ideas back to the troops to let them know they've been heard
   —come out of the process with simple statement of new vision
   - key words that people *believe*
     o we will be more flexible
     o we will deliver more quickly
     o we will listen to our customers
5. Reviewing Organization Practices
   —launch review of operations
   - have internal team look at organization practices
     o top people plus one who understands organization models
     o cross-functional to ensure multiple perspectives
     o multilevel to ensure operational/strategic concerns addressed
   —introduce or develop from scratch the cluster model
6. Defining the Clusters and Dealing with Organization Constraints
   —have teams of senior managers work on parts of the model
   - don't attempt to change without a plan
     o work has to go on
     o many people will see problems in the approach
   - have managers spend the necessary time on planning detail
     o communications with clients/customers a key issue
       —they're hierarchy, we're not—how can we bridge that?
       —we must remain credible to them
     o communication across specializations may be a problem
       —different specialists speak different lingo
       —how to coordinate without experienced leaders in place?
     o ensuring that all tasks are covered can be a problem
       —if everyone consults, who keeps up with the technology?
       —how can we ensure technology development is a valued assignment while rewarding heavily for client service?
     o how should we promote old specialists to make them useful?
       —teams need seniors with client experience as leaders
       —specialists know technology—not clients

Figure 4 (*Continued*)

137

—flesh out new responsibilities for clusters
- strip down the first-level management role
  - take out job supervision, human resource management
  - put in customer management and coordination
  - leave in job assignment (who goes where)
  - create senior consultant/team leader role
- augment employee's role so that people become self-managing
  - require person to plan own work
  - interact directly with client
  - provide high signing authority limits
- create broad managerial functions
  - resource management (handle human resource issues)
  - business management (handle major client relationships)
  - technology/product management (handle technology development)
  - no formal promotion ladders in or out of these positions
    —assistant managers act as understudies (apprentices)

—alter supporting systems
- new performance appraisal system and measurement criteria
  - staff evaluated on planning/client skills
  - managers on delegation
  - engineers on technology
- new compensation system
  - pay based on performance
  - considerable variance allowed in single grade

7. Communicating with the Ranks
- objective is to share new vision with all employees
  - allow question-and-answer sessions
    —reinforces feeling that staff has been heard
  - utilize senior managers
    —they have great credibility
    —clusters are leader-dependent
  - off-site culture change meetings
  - extensive training sessions
  - newsletters and meetings

Figure 4   (*Continued*)

CHAPTER EIGHT

"What Would You Like to Do Here?" Surviving and Prospering in a Cluster Organization

As the boss, are you trying to create a cluster organization? Are your employees confused and disturbed because it seems so different? Are they worried about how to cope with the changes?

Among the key skills they need are the ability to work well with others, to communicate effectively, to see the broad picture, and to learn continually. But managers, like employees, must learn different attitudes and behavior. Consider the following example.

Monica James heard about a rapidly growing firm that was looking for additional people. She already had a sales position in a large company but was bored, so she decided to investigate. A meeting with some personnel representatives followed, then a meeting with the new firm's president. There were several other interviews and finally a call with an offer of employment, which she accepted.

On her first day, James met a second time with the company president. "We hired you," he told her, "because we are impressed with your experience and your abilities. Now, what would you like to do here?"

The question crystallized in an instant a number of concerns James had about the interviewing process she had been through. There had been many questions about her background, skills, and interests, but she had never been told what she was being hired to do—apparently because the company did not have a specific spot for her. She became anxious about the situation.

"I don't know," she answered. "Don't you know what job I'm supposed to have?" The president smiled. "Not yet," he answered. "Why don't you hang around the company for a few weeks. Get to know our people. Find out what's going on. Decide where you can make a contribution. Then, come back and we'll talk about it. Meanwhile, I'd like you to meet the staff person who will be your sponsor. He'll help you to meet people and show you the ropes. Just call on him whenever you want to know something or get an introduction, or need something."

"He's my boss?" James asked.

"No," the president replied. "You don't have a boss. But there are many people you can go to if you need assistance. You can start with your sponsor or come to me or to other people you'll soon meet. Later, when you decide what you want to do, you'll probably be attached to a group of other people, and they may have a manager for you to work with." He paused. "But then they may not."

In her first few days at the company, James felt insecure without a specific job. But soon she began to enjoy the opportunity to look into whatever aspects of the company's operations interested her. To feel useful, she carried some messages and did some data entry and some typing. No one asked her to do these things, but the people whom she assisted were grateful and she felt better for having made some small contribution. In her second week she discovered that the company was expanding its operations and was contemplating opening a new facility on the West Coast. That was the opening for which she had been waiting.

She concentrated her next several days' efforts on the group that was planning the new facilities. At the end of the third week, she was ready to see the president. She explained to him what she had learned about the new expansion effort. "I've had some experience opening new offices," she told him, "though I have to admit it isn't much. But I've always enjoyed it. I think I can be good at it, but I've never had a chance to try it really on my own. That's what I'd like to do here for starters, if you think it's okay."

The president was pleased. "That's an important initiative for us," he told her, "and I'm delighted that you want to be a part of it. Sam Johnson is running the effort at this time. Go see him and work out where you'll fit in. I'm sure you'll do a great job for us."

James was also very pleased. She had an assignment that interested her and the opportunity to learn and grow. In addition, because the company paid attention to her desires in making assignments, she had the promise of further interesting projects.

The skills Monica James needed to survive and prosper in a cluster organization were indicated in her first weeks at the company. She received only general directions from the few managers in the firm. She was expected to show considerable initiative in deciding what to do and where to do it.

She was also expected to be able to work with others and to demonstrate to them her ability so that they would want to work with her. Her role was to contribute to the overall effort of her team, not simply to perform certain narrowly defined tasks. In addition, she was asked to have a broad view of the company and its objectives so that she could find where she best fitted in.

Energy, ambition, and teamwork were the key qualities that made her successful. These are the attributes that employees will need to have as they move into cluster organizations.

Will I Get Lost in a Team?

Many people enjoy working in a cluster. For them, having others with whom to talk and to share accountability makes work more interesting. They may experience the world as overly complex and threatening, so that the cluster appears to be a safe haven.

Others have reservations. They are not looking for a refuge and instead fear that they will lose their own identity in the group. "How will I get recognition for myself if I'm part of a cluster?'' someone may ask. ''I want to climb the ladder, not be stuck somewhere as part of a team.''

These are legitimate concerns, made more significant because it is often the more ambitious and hard-working people who express them. A cluster need not, however, spell the end of individual recognition. The individual need not get lost in the group.

Think of a professional sports team. The group plays as a unit. Whether in baseball, football, or basketball, the team comprises persons who have different specialties: pitchers, catchers, first basemen; quarterbacks, tackles, linebackers; forwards, centers, guards. Often, too, some team members are stars, whereas others are not. Some get paid much more money than others. Some have the public limelight. Some have opportunities for lucrative product endorsements. Others have none of these things. Clearly some individuals stand out in the group, yet the team still functions as a unit.

So it is with a cluster. There is opportunity for outstanding performance by an individual and the recognition that accompanies it. Some will advance out of the cluster and into management ranks, perhaps into the limited hierarchy that remains even in a cluster organization. Someone must be the coach, the manager, the club president, or the director of player operations. Although the roles carry less power and authority than in a hierarchy, they still exist.

So that individuals are able to gain recognition for their contributions, it is important that a cluster organization have a well-functioning performance appraisal system. Since there are no direct supervisors, performance must be appraised on a different basis than in a traditional structure. As we will see in the next chapter, not only is a system of individual performance appraisal perfectly feasible in a cluster organization, but also it can be a better system than that ordinarily functioning in a hierarchy.

How Will Senior Managers Adapt?

Clusters require managers to delegate greater responsibility. This can be difficult for managers at all levels in the organization. It is perhaps especially difficult for senior executives because of the temptation to be intimately involved in the activities of the organization.

New information technology is a powerful support to delegation because, by permitting closer review of results from decentralized units, it reduces the risks of decentralization. It is not a derogation of management's decision-making responsibility to delegate, for choosing not to make a decision is also a decision-making activity.

Executives wishing to delegate can rely on the increasing capability of information systems to provide support for the choices and actions taken by their middle managers and workers. For example, cluster leaders in a multicluster office might use a key-stroke tracking system to identify the one among them with the best productivity record and call its leader for tips to improve their own productivity, without involving a manager at all.

The new technology also has the capability to provide communications on a far more complete basis than previously. For executives who want to delegate, enhanced communications permit employees at any level to gain access to the information necessary to perform higher-level tasks than in the past without unduly high overhead costs. Electronic mail and on-line file storage allow direct access to relevant data from any point on the system.

Such capability breaks the link between centralization and control. Until recently, an executive team that wanted tight control was required to centralize decision making. Communications and information reporting were too slow for executives to monitor operations at arm's length and yet preserve the ability to intervene in a timely fashion. Today's information systems have advanced to a point where operations can be monitored very closely, but at a distance, allowing an executive team to step in on an as-needed basis. No longer does delegation have to imply a loss of managerial control.

Instead of focusing their attention on closely directing and controlling the activities of people, top executives in cluster organizations have a better outlet for their energies. They are intent on finding challenges for the organization and on creating the sense of adventure that can be so highly motivating. Thus they can set the pace of work and point the direction in which the organization should go. Done well, these tasks create the environment in which both people and the firm can prosper.

Changing Roles

If you are a middle manager or on your way to becoming one, what do you need to know about managing in a cluster organization that is different from managing in a traditional company? Although there are many specific differences, the most important challenge will be to rethink your role. Instead of being a boss, you will be more like a coach.

Clusters operate on a different base than hierarchies. In clusters, various disciplines relevant to a business process and their support functions are assembled. The internal logic of the organization is driven by the objective to be accomplished. Clusters are mission-centered and employees take greater responsibility for work and its quality. They are not "controlled." Managers do not supervise; they find the right person to fit the culture and task, then step back. They rely on reporting systems to provide data to senior executives instead of analyzing the data themselves.

As I pointed out in the previous chapter, analysis, decision, direction, supervision, and reporting have traditionally been middle-management duties. In hierarchies these elements are what defines middle management. Without them, the position would lose its meaning. But there is more to middle management—even in hierarchies—and in clusters the additional elements are the dominant ones.

When firms trim layers, middle-management survivors have to decide how to perform their functions in the new setting. Some keep the same degree of control as they had exercised historically, usually by running twice as hard. Others have realized that a new setting requires new methods.

They relinquish supervisory functions to subordinates, permitting clusters to form and implicitly recognizing that radical decentralization is the best route in the new environment. Their realization applies up—as well as down—the hierarchy.

Freed from supervision of others and reporting to the top, middle managers can focus instead on facilitating work, maintaining communication channels, and obtaining and coordinating resources for their clusters. Clusters thus give middle management a "support" rather than a "control" orientation. Currently, middle managers do both. But in many cases they focus on the former instead of the latter.

OVERALL ORIENTATION	HIERARCHY "control"	CLUSTER "support"
More significant tasks	Supervise	Facilitate
	Monitor	Communicate
	Organize	Coordinate
to	Report	Report
	Coordinate	Organize
Less significant tasks	Communicate	Monitor
	Facilitate	Supervise

Figure 5 Middle-Management Functions

Moving from hierarchy to cluster requires middle managers to rethink their work priorities. Although the tasks remain largely the same, the priorities are reversed, as shown in Figure 5.

What Cluster Managers Do

Executives often forget that the natural composition of organization is a leader and people who do the work. Middle managers will continue to help the interaction of these players by translating strategic visions, ideas, concepts, or goals into more specific objectives for cluster members and relaying cluster concerns back to those who create strategy. Eliminating all middle managers, or supervisors in a plant, for that matter, would lead to serious problems. As one observer has noted,

> It has been demonstrated over and over and over again that the more and better supervision you have in a shop, the higher the level of productivity. This is not to say or even imply that people do not work when there is no supervisor around. The vast majority of factory workers are eager to work, to produce, and to protect their company and their jobs by high productivity. A foreman is not a policeman placed on the floor to keep people working. . . .

I'm sorry, friends, but laying off another foreman will not reduce costs. Payroll expenses may go down momentarily but in the long run production costs will increase. The secret to increased productivity is how efficiently factories are run, not how few foremen or supervisors there are.

Facilitate Work

Middle managers in cluster organizations are responsible for facilitating work flows and transitions that must be made in the course of changing business situations. The role of intermediary between top managers, who determine overall strategy, and employees, who carry it out, will not disappear, only change.

Clusters require more supportive behaviors of their leaders in facilitating work—leading by example, a willingness to counsel without judgment those who ask for help, a readiness to provide information from experience, and a tolerance for different but still effective approaches to work.

Consider the situation of a professional baseball coach. He is in the middle between his manager—who has a key role in hiring and firing the players with whom he works and who makes the strategic decisions, such as who will play and who will not—and the players, who are generally paid far more than any coach, attain more public recognition, and must play the game the coach cannot.

The players are generally far younger and less mature than the coach. They require guidance in dealing with the stress of performing consistently throughout the course of a season—both on the field and off. Yet they have substantial egos and may or may not accept the direction a coach chooses to give. How can he facilitate winning behavior?

Because he usually has extensive experience—probably as a player—he can "feel" what the players are feeling. He can lead by example in the hotel, on the bus or airplane, and in dealing with the general public and fans. He provides a "book" or scouting report on opposing players, about what to look for and ways to counter it. He spends endless hours going over pitching or batting mechanics. When players go into a slump, he tries to motivate them out of it, yelling if yelling is appropriate and just being there if yelling is not appropriate. A coach is a combination of father figure, mentor, and friend.

At BPE, the senior consultants and project leaders are expected to act as mentors and reference points for their cluster members. They have a unique body of practical knowledge gleaned from years of working with clients to pass on to their less experienced colleagues, and so they lead by experience and example. This knowledge may involve everything from explaining the tricks of effective presentation, to providing a "living memory" of BP's engineering practices and standards, to pointing out quirks in the client's approach to business. As the junior members of the cluster acquire their own body of practical experience, they will gain in the estimation of their senior colleagues until they are treated as equals, whereupon they can be "advanced" to senior consultant status themselves and be given junior engineers to coach.

At a more general level, one study reported that leaders who exhibited supportive behaviors did so by collaborating on problems with employees, providing help in terms of training and resources, expressing concern for employee needs and objectives, and expressing empathy for employees and attention to obstacles. These individuals were the most effective coaches or facilitators.

Maintain Communication Channels

Since a cluster organization has fewer layers of management and wider spans of control than a hierarchy of equivalent scope, the middle manager of the future will deal with many more persons than in the past. By today's standards, the span of control will seem quite large indeed. Already it is not unusual to find managers with 40 or more direct reports.

However, the terms *control* and *direct reports* are anachronisms, which reflect old hierarchical assumptions that will be misleading in the new environment. A manager can have a great number of persons to interact with because she or he is not dependent on them for information and does not direct their activities.

In a cluster environment middle managers assume responsibility for supporting communications, which involves less control over the content of communication and more management of the communication channels. Since these channels are largely made up of people, the responsibility

147

actually becomes one of managing the quality of relationships between persons so that communication proceeds smoothly.

It is important to remember that there are two types of channels at work: intracluster and intercluster. An intercluster channel includes the one that links a cluster to senior managers, who are still setting goals and visions and monitoring performance in the organization, as well as those that link other operating clusters.

On the one hand, a middle manager will have limited dealings with intracluster communications. Most cluster members will know each other and are expected to interact directly. This freedom is one of the form's greatest strengths. However, there will be employee turnover, and the manager must be prepared to "plug" new members into the internal network as a necessary part of their orientation.

On the other hand, the middle manager will have greater dealings with intercluster communications. Although employee freedom to communicate with anyone in the organization extends to other clusters, and even to top management if necessary, limits will inevitably appear. If an employee does not know anyone in another cluster, for example, he or she must have a point of reference—someone who knows whom to call and, more important, how to call—to extract relevant data. It is at this point that a middle manager can step in and smooth the way.

Someone must also serve as the external contact point for a cluster. That person must have both credibility with outsiders—specifically customers, suppliers, and members of higher management in the firm itself—and enough influence in the cluster to help get things done. Again, this is a natural role for a middle manager, who has connections in both the industry and the company.

Remember also that being a contact point means neither supervising the group nor being the exclusive source of external information in the cluster. Senior management, for example, may contact anybody in a cluster when looking for relevant data. The middle-management role is one of information distribution—ensuring that those who need to know something get the information accurately and in time to work with it—not hoarding information as a source of power. This is a hierarchy dysfunction that clusters seek to eliminate.

Coordinate Resources

Middle managers will continue to have considerable impact on personnel decisions and resourcing issues. Their function is to select, hire, and arrange for the training of new cluster members. They will be aided in these duties by existing members, but someone must also be able to look at the cluster from an outside perspective as well.

Although many cluster members have multiple skills, they may not have the general management skills needed to analyze purchase decisions or inventory control problems or other business-related matters. These will also be picked up by the middle manager, who will be in position to call the appropriate expert or solve the problem in the cluster itself.

Middle managers will also continue to be involved in the evaluation of individual and cluster performance through performance appraisal and may remain involved in administering reward systems as a neutral umpire for a cluster team. The development of the capabilities of individuals and the organization as a whole will be their concern.

Prospering as a Middle Manager in a Cluster Organization

A study conducted at the Harvard Business School of senior and middle managers found four major elements of managerial style. One was administrative: the ability to organize work. A second was controlling others: holding people to rules, procedures, and established ways of doing things. A third was relating to people: the ability to understand and persuade others. And the fourth was visioning: being far-sighted and willing to take risks to accomplish important goals.

Most middle managers today would score high on administrative and control elements, which are the province of management in hierarchical organizations. Relating to others and visioning are less highly developed skills.

A cluster organization is ill served by the administrative and control elements of managerial style. For managers whose self-image is tied up in dominating others, the cluster will be a difficult format. Those unable to outgrow these elements in their styles will clash with, and probably fail, in a cluster organization. When such situations occurred at BPE and Du Pont, those involved were transferred out, often at their own request.

In hierarchies managers ordinarily must push employees to motivate them. The manager sets the pace of the organization by how hard he or she pushes.

In clusters energy and motivation spring out of the work force. Thus in a sense managers lose the ability to set the pace in a process that moves with or without them.

Managing with clusters requires empathy and vision. Since these are key components of leadership, as opposed to bureaucratic behavior, it is fair to say that clusters require greater managerial leadership. In a cluster organization the leader must work to bring order in what is a potentially chaotic setting, but he or she must be careful not to formalize, for fear of losing the creativity involved.

In a way this mimics the situation in professional service firms, where management is expected to find customers and resources for those who work there. Returning to the BPE example, you will recall that the managerial role in the new structure resolved itself into finding customers, providing resources, and creating vision and goals for working engineers.

Managers become servants, in a sense, of those who do the work. For many executives, this involves a major shift in perspective. Henry Rosovsky, for several years dean of Harvard's Faculty of Arts and Sciences, was wont to comment that "at Harvard, a dean is to the faculty as a fire hydrant is to a dog." Though an exaggeration, Rosovsky was merely reflecting the willingness of faculty members to complain bitterly to a dean when things did not meet their expectations. They complained because they felt they had a right to an environment conducive to doing their best professional work.

A cluster organization is similar. Middle managers become less involved in the work being done and more involved in providing necessary support to those doing it.

The ultimate implications of this process were well set forth by Walt Burdick, IBM's sr. vice president for personnel. "The key to success," he said, "is to hire the most talented and adaptable people and give them good communicative managers."

FEAR	RATIONALE
Mediocrity predominates	All opinions count nearly equally
Rule by the uneducated and unskilled	Workers do not have the experience of managers
Lack of accountability	When power is shared, no one person is responsible for it
Instability	Supervisory role will rotate frequently
Flattery versus objective decision making	Charismatic people rise in democratic situations
Bureaucratization	Managers seek to cover for unskilled workers in leadership roles

Figure 6   Managerial Concerns

Some managers have expressed their apprehensions about operating in an "employee involvement" environment like the cluster setting. Figure 6 lists some of these concerns.

These objections have mostly been discounted by evidence. By having cluster leaders set a high performance standard for the group through example and by skillfully hiring good performers, high output can be maintained and even enhanced in a cluster.

As I pointed out previously, workers can be just as skilled—if not more so—in key managerial tasks, even though they do not have the title of "manager." This fact makes lack of supervisory experience on the part of workers a red herring when considering arguments against using clusters.

Cluster output can be measured just as easily as individual output when clusters are properly formed around clear business objectives. In accounting terms, if clusters are seen as profit centers, their performance can be charted as profit centers.

Instability is not a vice—but a virtue—in a business environment that demands constant innovation and creativity to stay ahead of the competition. Stability is frequently the handmaiden of stagnation.

Finally, no one has ever said that a cluster organization is a democracy; senior management retains, and may explicitly choose to exploit, its role as hiring and promoting agent to put capable people in cluster leadership slots. A cluster organization is delegative; it does not coddle poor performers.

The greatest resistance to clusters never comes from employees but from managers who fear a loss of control. However, managers who have worked in clusters are generally delighted with the greater freedom it gives them to watch the business, and not the employees.

CHAPTER NINE

New Visions versus Old Habits: Managerial Practices for Clusters

What changes have to be made to enable clusters to operate effectively in an organization? That is, what muscles have to be put on the cluster skeleton for the whole body to function well?

This question is especially important because in most instances clusters will operate in only a part of a firm. In the remainder, traditional hierarchical practices will continue. Can a firm endure half traditional and half cluster?

The answer is yes. Proponents of clusters believe that much potential is sacrificed by leaving traditional managerial practices in place in much of the firm, but that is today's reality. Clusters are new in businesses and cannot be expected to dominate.

Can clusters persevere in a largely traditional organization in which managerial systems and personnel practices in particular are attuned to hierarchies? The evidence clearly indicates yes. It may not be comfortable, but it is possible. And over time practices can be adapted more closely to the needs of clusters.

When changes can be made in existing policies and practices, where is it most important that they occur? The critical area involves managerial practices: in particular, administrative controls. This area is significant because budding clusters can be strangled if managers interfere too much with the units' autonomy. Hence the first topic here will be managerial controls. Thereafter, the discussion will examine personnel practices including hiring, education and vision setting, compensation, career management, and performance appraisal.

Measurement and Control

It is inappropriate to speak of executives controlling clusters, for the concept of control is hierarchical. But executives must stay in touch with clusters and be aware of their performance.

How do executives stay in touch with what may appear to be a formless or even amoebalike organization? How can they influence what occurs when people aspire to independence and the chain of command has largely disappeared? Although systems used by managers to influence behavior are a source of concern in any organization, in a cluster they are basic.

In a hierarchy managers ask, "What are the mechanisms by which we retain control?" However, utilizing the term *control* in connection with clusters sets expectations that are at variance with the cluster ethos of removing rigidities, cutting costs, and loosening bureaucracy.

How, then, do executives ensure that a cluster organization follows the path they set for it in terms of goals and budgets? The answer lies in examining the mechanisms available for influencing employee behavior that do not depend on a supervisory hierarchy to retain control. These range from direct technology-based mechanisms to less direct results-based mechanisms to relatively indirect personnel-based approaches.

Technology-based mechanisms are the most direct; they allow executives to track specific employee actions. For example, computer data-entry systems can count keypunching errors by entry clerks, video cameras can monitor access to key facilities, and time clocks can track employee attendance.

Results-based systems are less direct and typically revolve around numbers rather than actions. For example, a firm that produces profit-and-loss statements by product lines can also measure unit profitability by product line. Employees may also file a monthly time report, as in some professional firms.

Personnel-based systems exert the most indirect influence. For example, a firm may use training, rigid hiring practices, novel compensation forms, or a corporate vision in motivating and channeling employee behavior.

Technology-Based Systems

The new computer technology brings not only hard choices but new problems as well. As "decisions" move inside software and expert systems, concern about global control over organizations is being expressed by executives and employees alike. The paradox of simultaneous decentralization and recentralization is upon us.

On the one hand, executives complain about losing control over self-managed or decentralized organizations. They would like to see more detail about operations, not only because they can get it from their systems but also because they are held accountable for its use or misuse.

The consequences of not maintaining close control were illustrated dramatically in the program trading that helped trigger the 1987 stock market crash. Computer models, watching the spreads between options and equity prices at predetermined and programmed points, issued substantial sell orders. So quick were the responses to opportunities, and so rapidly were orders executed, that human involvement was cut out of the loop and a downward spiral ensued. In the aftermath, top executives on Wall Street and at the Securities and Exchange Commission wrung their hands over technology that appeared to be out of control.

On the other hand, employees increasingly complain about "big brother," who can monitor virtually all phases of operations, right down to the average time a telephone operator spends answering customers' questions. As noted earlier, when executives make too many decisions or control too closely, they lose the initiative, ambition, and drive of their employees.

More than 30 years ago scholars Harold Leavitt and Thomas Whistler speculated on the future impact of computers on management. They focused attention on the expectation of improved decision making. Questions of managerial control—excessive or otherwise—did not arise. Today, the promise of improved decision making is compromised by fear of excessive control.

A company requires both an organizational form and a computer network that remain in close touch with the external world, especially with customers, and that are able to react quickly to changes. Executives must be careful not to smother the cluster with overly tight monitoring through their computer network.

Results-Based Systems

The cluster form encourages use of financial data to influence employees. Demanding profit goals and targets can be set and monitored. Budgets and resource policies can be developed and transmitted to cluster members. In many organizations computer technology allows powerful inventory and accounting information to be generated on a daily basis for local operating units, and such information is transmitted simultaneously to senior executives as well. If clusters are built on product lines, plant lines, or even customer lines, financial measures can be used in the same way as they would be if a company created divisions in its hierarchy.

At Brunswick—a $3 billion per year sporting goods company—for example, CEO John Reichert decided product development was taking too long. "Product development was like elephant intercourse. It was accompanied by much hooting, hollering, and throwing of dirt, and then nothing would happen for a year." To spur the process, Reichert cut the layers of management between him and the shop floor from ten to five and adopted a clusterlike approach to structure. "If you want to know how to do a job right, ask the people who are doing it," he said. "Don't have some corporate bureaucracy tell them how to do it."

As these cuts took place, Reichert adjusted his financial reporting mechanism by increasing spending authority limits for division heads from $25,000 to $250,000 and by eliminating all but a weekly, one-page report from his division managers. "Those reports," Reichert said, "tell me what *they* need." Reichert estimates Brunswick can now develop new products 25 percent to 30 percent faster than it could before.

A slash in reporting levels at Adca Bank, a subsidiary of West Germany's Rabobank, had similar effects. Before the change, loan approvals wound their way through many layers of management. Said Hans Van der Velde, managing director, "Someone at the branch sent loan papers to someone at headquarters who was looking and changing them. Then his boss was looking and changing them. All those layers were useless." When the bank cut five layers out of its management hierarchy and gave officers in all branches more authority, the employee hours required to approve a loan dropped from 24 to 12—a 50 percent cut. The effectiveness of clusters precludes the use of detailed results data collected on people, as opposed to the work they do. Executives must be prepared to delegate heavily to cluster members if they want the new form to boost performance. Strangling clusters with performance measurement paperwork will not help them.

In traditional hierarchies the process of collecting such data strongly influences work, too. Supervisors end up using the collection process as a source of power to enforce their commands, not as a means to measure work quality or quantity.

At BPE, for example, supervisors and senior managers had to delegate many project sign-off rights to working engineers when BPE adopted the cluster form. Documents that required four signatures became documents with two—one from a business manager and the other from an engineer. Closer contact between engineer and customer, with the oversight of a business manager, replaced multiple work reviews inside a hierarchy. The results: The time required to complete work decreased, client satisfaction rose, overhead costs of review dropped, and billing rates fell to reflect cost reductions.

BPE did not give up on quality control, which was the original purpose of multiple signatures. It simply recognized that engineers had as great a professional incentive to do the work correctly when they had a client and one observer—instead of three, intent on exercising control.

157

Personnel-Based Systems

Today, organizational analysts have given us new approaches for guiding employees that do not rely on the intervention of supervisors and managers. In a cluster organization rigorous hiring, education, performance appraisal, compensation, and other managerial practices can be used in place of results-based or technology-based guidance mechanisms. By finding the right people, instilling the right values, and offering rewards in the right fashion, executives can loosen their grip on budgets, goals, and timetables and focus on broader performance measures like profit-and-loss statements. The following discussion explores each of these personnel-based influence mechanisms.

Hiring

The first and most important personnel mechanism is the hiring process—recruiting, selecting, and orienting new employees. People who want to do the job right often do not need extensive supervision.

In traditional hierarchies recruiting, selecting, and orientation are carried out by a supervisor, a personnel office, or both, with limited involvement from the work group. This system may lead to mismatches between work group environment and individual personality. What pleases a supervisor may not please the group or vice versa. There are several ways organizations deal with this problem.

One is to refine the hiring process with complicated tests and highly trained interviewers. Often this is an expensive and time-consuming process that simply misses the point.

Another is to put recruits through what John Wanous has described as "realistic job previewing." By exposing a recruit to the job and work mates over a period of several hours or even days, the chances of a better fit are greatly increased. Those people unhappy with the environment will drop out of the selection process. The extra cost is often outweighed by the savings in reduced recruitment, although it does require time on the part of the work group to make the process work.

A third is the assessment center. In such a program professional observers watch recruits as they move through a set of simulation exercises to determine their likely potential for success or failure. These processes do not have to be elaborate or expensive, although when new managerial employees are involved, their costs can be heavy.

Cluster organizations move a step beyond assessment centers by delegating selection to a cluster itself. Managers retain influence through the resource management function, which can continue to develop recruiting programs and test candidates for technical skills. Once the candidates arrive for interviews, however, the cluster members take over. This direct involvement allows individuals to be tested on the basis of their ability to "fit" into the group and perform in that environment immediately. However, there are issues to be dealt with when using this approach.

First, there is the issue of cost. When teams hire, many people must interview a candidate and then meet for discussion. This takes time, and time is money—particularly when production schedules must be met. The benefit of reducing turnover or improving productivity through work group harmony must outweigh the cost for it to be effective—and generally speaking, companies do not spend enough on selection.

Second, there is the issue of discrimination. When a team does the hiring, criteria such as sex, race, or ability to play baseball after work may enter into the equation. These problems also exist with manager-based hiring, but because the decisions can be traced to an individual, it is easier to find and prove discrimination. A team may hide behind a group decision. This problem can be addressed through interviewer training or by setting initial membership. If teams are established on a nondiscriminatory basis, the interaction of their members will reduce the opportunity for direct bias.

Third, there is the more subtle issue of assessment. The work group will naturally assess social skills and interaction ability. It may not assess technical work skills. However, this assessment can be done through more objective testing in the case of knowledge-based skills and by actual demonstration in the case of physical skills. With several observers on hand, the chances of an individual getting through to a group-based interview without having the technical qualifications are slight.

Instilling the Right Values

It is not common to think of education and dialogue as alternative control systems, but they are. Competence and professionalism at all organizational levels constitute an assurance to top management that activities are being conducted properly. This is, after all, the purpose of reporting relationships and tight supervision.

Hierarchies rely on the willingness of workers to carry out directives as the basis for confidence in their performance. Clusters rely on the knowledge and professionalism of workers as their basis for confidence in the firm's performance. It is thus possible to use the corporate culture as a means of communicating and influencing behavioral standards of employees in a cluster setting.

The actions of some chemical firms after the Bhopal (India) disaster provide an instructive example. To minimize the possibility of plant leaks, one firm sent out streams of directives to its staff: This was to be checked; that was to be done; this form was to be filed. Managers began to complain about paperwork and to ask for staff to cope with it. It then occurred to top management that supervisory directives might not be the way to go. After all, an accident might have any of a thousand causes, some of which they could not foresee and warn plants about. Yet the last thing executives wanted was an accident, with plant management defending themselves on the grounds that they had complied with all directives. The firm's president recalled the situation:

> It occurred to us that we had never brought the plant managers together to discuss what we are worried about and how to avoid an accident. Instead of sending them directives, we needed to discuss the matter with them and then rely on their good judgment to take the steps necessary to protect employees and the communities in which they operate. By providing training to staff in the best safety techniques, and conducting a forum about how to use the techniques, we would probably be more effective than what we were doing, and could avoid a costly expansion of overhead.

A shift like this would fit a cluster organization well. It substitutes education about a problem and opportunities to discuss it, instead of an increase in reporting or rules and regulations. It involves some costs in training and bringing people together but avoids expanding overhead and stifling flexibility. It recognizes people's aspiration for professional treatment by involving them with peers in solving the problem, without reducing their responsibility for achieving the desired result.

Honda deliberately set out to educate its employees about spirit as part of its culture when it entered Formula 1 auto racing a number of years ago. By rotating its young engineers through its Formula 1 team, Honda teaches them about the racing spirit—which means thinking about minutes, not hours—when making decisions. The hope is they will take this spirit back to the factory with them. As a Honda managing director pointed out, "When a problem arises, you have to find the solution now. And if it is a problem you have never seen before, you have to have the flexibility to create a new solution on the spot."

At Domino's Pizza, a firm that recently became the second largest in the home-delivery pizza market, CEO Tom Monaghan educates his workers about the importance of speed in fast food by modeling Domino's along the lines of a professional sports league. Each regional division competes to make the best pizza, deliver it faster, and sell more than the next region. Like Monday-morning quarterbacks, Domino teams watch films of their fastest colleagues in action. The sports metaphor extends further: The delivery persons must run from the truck to the house— carrying pizzas like footballs. Says Monaghan, "Our whole business is built on speed."

Offering Rewards in the Right Fashion

Compensation is an important influence on people and has more elements than money. In fact there are several kinds of currency. Among the nonmonetary types are opportunity, growth, and involvement. The cluster itself is a form of compensation. To be able to work in this organizational form is a benefit to many people and one that they ardently desire. It is work without the hassle of a boss and a bureaucracy. For a cluster organization, the company's culture helps to attract and retain people.

But culture is not a substitute for money, and financial compensation must be dealt with in a careful and imaginative way. Cluster organizations tend to use pay as a way of motivating people, not just as an entitlement for showing up for work. The compensation scheme in a typical cluster organization sets base pay rates in broad categories and then uses performance incentives and profit-sharing arrangements to add to it.

This system can be complex and may result in workers in clusters

161

getting different amounts of compensation. But the objective is to minimize any leveling down of individual performance to the lowest common denominator in the group, a process that could otherwise destroy the productivity advantages of the cluster format.

In most hierarchies, compensation is fixed by rank and determined largely by length of service (often equated with experience). Pay levels or grades are based on carefully defined "comparison jobs," both inside and outside a firm. In theory this system should work well, but in practice, people who have been around build up compensation based on length of service, not performance.

Since employees increasingly view base compensation as a form of entitlement, more is necessary to bring forth extraordinary effort. In some instances the "more" may be incentive pay. In others it may be individual recognition.

One CEO of a large organization found this to be so when he met with a group of younger employees. "Top executives don't really care about us," insisted one employee with some heat.

"Don't care about you!" protested the CEO. "We pay the highest salaries and offer the best benefits of any organization in our industry."

The employee was struck dumb by this answer. His eyes widened in astonishment. Finally, he said quietly, "It would never occur to me to think of pay and benefits as evidence of caring. Those are things you owe us for doing our work. We're entitled to those things. Caring is about things that go beyond what is owed us."

Pay beyond what is simply owed and personal attention are necessary to generate real commitment in today's work force. Variable bonus schemes designed to augment salary based on performance implicitly recognize this fact. They typically take three forms: the standard lump-sum bonus, profit sharing, and gain sharing. Many firms invest huge sums in them (for example, a Sibson & Company study noted that in 1988, variable pay in the United States would exceed $125 billion).

However, the motivational effects of variable bonuses are largely lost because of a failure to establish links between individual or small-group performance and payment. Individuals must know exactly what they have to do to receive bonuses. They must feel that they are measured fairly, that they can influence the measure used to reward them, and that the payments received will vary among recipients. Otherwise bonuses will not motivate.

The lack of impact can be demonstrated by statistics. A survey by the Public Agenda Foundation of 845 blue- and white-collar workers showed that 45 percent believed there was no link between pay and performance.

The problems are legion. For example, the traditional lump-sum bonus, based on management's good will and given at Christmas, bears no relationship to productivity. People at the same level receive the same amount, which may be withheld at the whim of a supervisor. It is given at a fixed time, not after a good performance period.

A profit-sharing plan to generate bonuses requires employees to influence profits. In an environment in which there are thousands of employees and dozens of costs that also influence profits, an individual's share of influence is very low, as is the motivating effect of the bonus.

Gain sharing addresses some problems of profit sharing but also requires employees to trust explicitly management's motives. If management pushes up the standards, so that last year's gain becomes this year's base, the plan will end up demotivating people. If the base on which gains are made stays constant, the bonuses quickly acquire an "automatic" component and lose their initial motivating effect.

Clusters allow executives to reestablish the link between pay and performance, which is often lost in a hierarchy. In a cluster people cannot argue, "I've been here 15 years, I'm a manager, so I deserve X amount of base and merit pay." There is no hierarchy of jobs; no defined comparison standard; and above all, limited supervision of individuals by others.

Rewards can be given on the basis of knowledge, performance, quality, teamwork, or productivity. Being able to do so is going to be an increasingly important consideration for firms in the near future.

In GE Canada's financial services group (the subject of Chapter Sixteen), two of the managers—Bev Davids and Marie Percival—described their efforts to alter the salary plan to fit a cluster organization:

Currently, we have two salary plans—Management and Professional, and Technical and Administrative (called Administrative Support). We no longer feel that this distinction makes sense in our organization structure. As we redesign the compensation system we need to analyze the compensation and benefit structure corporate-wide and ensure that anything we adopt allows the flexibility for movement within the GE Canada organization. We also must keep in mind labor legislation that can influence how we design our compensation system.

Finally, we would like our compensation and reward systems to be tied more closely to our evaluation systems, to consider both team and individual contributions, and to support the goals of the Pooled Financial Services organization. As a result, we expect that in the future, compensation systems will reward work quality, productivity, risk-taking, management skills, initiative, group cooperation, and teamwork. Progression and career advancement should reflect the acquisition of more advanced skills and responsibilities in the three areas of job design—Technical, Team administration, and Team process.

An interesting base for compensation in clusters is the concept of "pay-for-knowledge." Several firms going to the cluster form have chosen not to reward on productive output but on the potential output implicit in demonstrating new work skills. The idea is that more skills improve employee usefulness in a team environment, where job descriptions are vague and task rotation is a key motivator. Pay-for-knowledge has a number of benefits.

First, it allows staff members to demonstrate to themselves and others why they received raises. When an individual steps up to a new machine and does the work, it shows all observers that he or she earned the raise. This eliminates the subjectivity around raises inherent in many work settings.

Second, pay-for-knowledge makes horizontal as well as vertical career moves both legitimate and possible. By building skills, it is possible to cover a broader job. This is a key point for organizations trying to reduce vertical hierarchy or to reward many employees without having open slots higher up on the job ladder.

Third, since new techniques and processes are constantly appearing in the workplace, a pay-for-knowledge system is self-renewing. As old skills become obsolete, they can be replaced with new ones. Where knowledge is key to running sophisticated machinery or dealing with complex processes, it makes sense to reward people for acquiring it.

These systems are not without problems. These include such issues as who does the measuring, what happens when all available skills are learned, and what behavior is actually being rewarded.

First, there is the issue of evaluating skill proficiency. Some firms rely on the work group itself to measure proficiency. If defect rates rise, productivity will fall, and all members will be affected, so cheating is minimized. Others use the cluster leader or even an outside supervisor.

Second, there is the issue of "topping out"—that is, having employees reach the peak of the pay system by learning all available skills. This can be addressed in part by adding new skills or moving people into available management slots. Also, with topping out comes the issue of cost. By their very nature, these systems tend initially to boost labor costs, although increases are often made up for by low turnover in the longer term.

Third, there is the problem of what is being rewarded. If the learning behavior is being rewarded, that is what employees will do, rather than practice their new skills. To deal with this situation, firms can install a "pay-back period," in which employees either use the new skill they have learned before they go on to the next one or lose the pay increment.

After the Shenandoah Life Insurance Company in Roanoke, Virginia, implemented pay-for-knowledge in conjunction with autonomous work groups, the number of people in its teams decreased almost 16 percent while work volume increased 28.5 percent. The supervisor-employee ratio dropped from 1 in 7 to 1 in 37.

Northern Telecom (NT) adopted pay-for-knowledge at its switch plant in Santa Clara, California. In 1987, half the plant was upgraded from assembly, in which workers repeated the same step, to a team-based system, in which workers were expected to understand the manufacturing process and were rewarded with raises only after they demonstrated new skills. Said Dick Dauphinais, compensation director at NT, "To have flexible manufacturing, you must have flexible compensation."

Career Management

Since cluster organizations are flat, there are few rungs on the management ladder, which limits promotion opportunities. To ambitious people this is a serious limitation of clusters.

Certainly, clusters do offer less likelihood of managerial advancement than do traditional hierarchies. But this does not mean that opportunities are completely missing.

As I mentioned earlier, there is a residual hierarchy in a cluster organization (though not in an individual cluster) some workers can climb. Also, in a cluster organization within a larger hierarchical company, there are opportunities for advancement by leaving the unit. For example, Julian Darley recognizes that a key career path for his BPE engineers is promotion into managerial positions in line units of the global BP corporation.

Nor should we accept without critical examination the assertion that there are substantial opportunities for promotion in traditional hierarchies. Many have been downsized and delayered, with consequent reductions in promotion opportunities. Thus, as the average length of service increases and the baby boom generation plugs up the hierarchy, more and more people recognize that they are effectively stalled.

In fact the vaunted promotion opportunities of traditional hierarchies are in today's world much less significant than is claimed. Hence the disadvantage of cluster organizations in practice is far less than might be imagined.

Without promotions as a major incentive, cluster organizations have developed other rewards. Among these are the broadened scope of work itself, the greater opportunity for diversion and challenge, and the wider range of people with whom a worker can interact. Each constitutes a significant reward in a cluster organization. As one engineer in a high-tech company put it, "It's the pinball theory: The reward for winning one game is that you get to play another."

Seen in this way, a career is a succession of interesting projects rather than a lengthy, difficult, unpleasant climb to the top. The reward is in the doing, rather than at the end. A career in a cluster is typically an interesting, challenging, and enjoyable progress through different assignments.

Performance Appraisal

The final personnel mechanism available for influencing clusters is performance appraisal. Although cluster members have considerable say in administering appraisals, senior executives and cluster leaders still control the development of performance criteria and can use this lever to influence employees by setting the standards to which the cluster members will measure themselves for compensation purposes.

Since job descriptions in a cluster are deliberately vague, appraisal criteria must include measures that are not job-specific. It must be possible to earn a good rating in several different ways in the same cluster; otherwise multiple skill usage will be discouraged.

The success of a cluster depends on the ability of people to work together. As well as work output, appraisal criteria must also include some measures for social skills, interaction, and communications.

Sources of appraisal information are varied in a cluster. External feedback from clients or customers is key. Cluster leaders are often unable to see every one all of the time because of the wide span of control, nor do they have specific task or behavior descriptions to use as baselines for measuring performance. Instead such detail must come from clients. This fits in well with the autonomy of a supervisor-free environment. If the client says you are not doing well, you are not doing well, regardless of how you feel about it. If the person paying the bill is happy, then generally speaking, things are going well.

Since all cluster members may not be in contact with customers and reliance on any one source of data is suspect, other internal standards may have to be set as well. In industrial settings the production process yields some natural measures (e.g., scrap rates, defect rates, or output per hours worked) along with the setting for testing individuals in a pay-for-knowledge format. These are standard factory measures that remain unchanged when a cluster arrangement is set up.

Service settings are more problematical, but practical measures still exist. BPE's appraisal system uses two three-part scales to review engineer performance, as shown in Figure 7.

A number is assigned to each part of both scales based on a 1 to 10 rating. The results are summed to produce a score on each dimension and then an overall score, which can be translated into a performance level and converted to a pay bracket. The maximum score of 60 (6 items × 10 points) would produce the perfect consulting engineer.

Should engineers acquire more skill and experience and demonstrate their abilities with clients and elsewhere, the resource managers at BPE will

A. Professional Technical Skills
  1. *Versatility:* The degree to which the individual can apply technical competence and productivity outside the area of current employment
  2. *Productivity:* An assessment of output. How long does it take to achieve a quality job?
  3. *Technical Competence:* Applied level, in terms of quality, of technological experience and expertise

B. Personal and People Skills
  1. *Consultancy Skills:* The degree to which the individual can persuade and influence clients and others to cooperate with the processes of analysis and to support the recommended actions on the basis of value added
  2. *Client Acceptability:* The degree to which the individual is accepted and in demand from those he or she is servicing, both internal to BPE, BP Group, and the outside world where relevant
  3. *Self-Standing:* The ability of an individual to organize his or her own time, take responsibility, and work without line management supervision

Figure 7 Evaluating Contributions of BPE Engineers

move their ratings upward, producing pay increases. Should performance fall off, pay can be adjusted downward or bonuses can be withheld.

As the system is presently configured, those engineers being paid above their current performance level are held to zero increases. Those being paid at their performance level receive minimal increases. And those being paid well below their performance level are receiving large increases. Over time, BPE hopes to bring pay and performance into line for its entire engineering work force.

In the performance appraisal system of a cluster organization the resource manager serves as a clearinghouse for appraisals offered by an employee's peers, clients, and suppliers. Is the direct knowledge that a supervisor brings to an appraisal a better method? In fact does the importance of performance appraisal argue against the decoupling of managerial functions that a cluster requires—that is, separation of analysis, decision, and direction from planning, coaching, assessment, and communication? Does a manager need to be closely involved in the work to evaluate individuals properly? Does supervisory appraisal constitute a strong argument in favor of a hierarchy?

The answer in each case is no. In practice things do not work out well for supervisor-based performance appraisals. This is a crucial point. Many managers romanticize the operation of performance appraisals and other supervisory-based practices in hierarchies. They talk about these practices as if they worked perfectly, when in fact they are deeply flawed.

Hierarchies are much better in theory than in practice. For example, in a recent survey by Carnegie Mellon's Robert Kelley, 400 professionals and managers in technical and other highly skilled white-collar jobs in hierarchically structured firms gave poor ratings to their bosses. An amazing 95 percent believed they could be more productive on the job but were not being challenged or rewarded for doing more. Nearly two-thirds said their bosses failed to use their ideas at least half the time. Almost half said conformity, not creativity, was encouraged. They admired fewer than 15 percent of the bosses they had encountered in their careers. About 40 percent ascribed ineffectiveness to the overdeveloped egos of many managers and their inability to deal effectively with people. Perhaps there do not have to be such poor results, but there are strong reasons for them. Hierarchies operate by direct supervision, but firms continually promote into management individuals whose "people skills" are awful. No wonder subordinates chafe under control.

Also, the obligations of close supervision keep managers tied up in detail and leave little time for the empathy and caring that employees so value from their bosses. The result is a cynicism and bitterness that undercuts motivation and makes things worse than they would otherwise be without any supervisor at all.

Nowhere is the gap greater between the idealized functioning of a hierarchy and its reality than in the crucial area of performance appraisal. For almost 40 years companies have been trying to perfect supervisory-based performance appraisal.

Practice is still far behind the ideal. Most appraisal systems are beset with exaggerated ratings given by supervisors. In fact in many companies the appraisal system is not considered a source of reliable data about people. In frustration, top executives and personnel offices blame the perverse unwillingness of managers and supervisors to do appraisals well.

Why, after decades of effort by top management and personnel executives, is the record so dismal? Because performance appraisal by supervisors in hierarchies violates basic aspects of human nature. First, it forces a supervisor to make invidious distinctions between people with whom he or she must keep a good working relationship. Poor appraisals create animosity.

Second, differences in performance appraisals create jealousies among those receiving them. An element of teamwork is often desired, and appraisals undercut the mutual liking and respect that are important in forging a team.

The cluster approach in practice is better than that of the hierarchy because there are no direct supervisors whose relationship with the teams require preservation. To the extent that a resource manager needs good relationships, he or she is placed in the position not of an evaluator but of a data processor and communicator. Hence even bad news can be delivered while personal relationships are preserved.

CHAPTER TEN

The Fourth Form:
From Mob to Hierarchy
to Matrix to Cluster

Clusters are actually the fourth entry in the catalogue of organizational structures. The first and most ancient form of human organization is the mob. It is a large aggregation of people with shifting leadership, dominated by the emotions of the moment.

The least structured of human organizations, the mob is capable of great exertions and accomplishments but is always unpredictable and unreliable. Many large armies of antiquity were primarily mobs, loosely held together by the hope of gain and by the leadership of an individual. With the death or flight of the leader from a battlefield, these armies simply melted away, as did the Persian hosts before the Macedonians of Alexander the Great.

The hierarchical organization is of superior structure and performance to the mob. The hierarchy establishes direction throughout the organization, imposes discipline, and provides continuity of leadership as individuals disappear. It is today's most familiar organizational format.

In the aftermath of World War II a third form of organization was introduced: the matrix. It is a distinct form because it violates two basic assumptions of the hierarchy.

First, the hierarchy requires that each person have only one direct superior or boss. The matrix relaxes this assumption by permitting an individual to have at least two direct bosses.

Second, the hierarchy requires executives to maintain a balance between responsibilities and resources. Thus a manager given a certain task to perform expects to have reporting to him or her the people and other resources necessary to accomplish the task. If resources do not correspond closely to responsibility, tasks will not be accomplished. If resources are excessive, the organization will be inefficient.

The matrix also violates this assumption. Project managers commonly have greater responsibilities than they have direct control over resources. To accomplish projects, they must assemble resources from functional managers. Even then, they must often share scarce resources with other project managers.

Matrices have been used in a number of different settings. Thus an aeronautical designer in an aircraft company reports not only to the executive in charge of the design function at the plant but also to the manager in charge of the particular project on which he or she is employed at the time. In a consulting firm, a physicist reports to the director of the physical sciences and also to the managers of one or more projects on which he or she is currently engaged.

The matrix was the subject of experimentation and gradual development for years before it was given a generally accepted label. This occurred in the 1960s and was accompanied by a theory of the form. Successful applications were made, but there was also considerable disappointment. Although it has proved useful in some projects, there are apparently an insufficient number of these to make the matrix common.

The fourth and newest structure of human organization is the cluster. That it is truly a new form is demonstrated by the variation of certain basic assumptions common to both the hierarchy and matrix. Figure 8 presents a brief outline of some key differences among the three modern organizational forms, which I will expand on through the bulk of this chapter.

Three basic principles of the older forms are violated by the new cluster format. The locus of decision making shifts, jobs are broadly instead of narrowly defined, and managerial control is separated from direct reporting.

	HIERARCHY	MATRIX	CLUSTER
ORIGINS	Military	High-tech industry	Professional service firms
Why?	Limited communications technology available; need close span of control	Coordinate many complex resources in a single project setting	Manage networks to speed data flow and respond to rapid market change
ATTRIBUTES			
Management Levels	Many	Several	Few
Span of Control	Limited	Partial	Very wide
Reporting Relationships	To supervisor	Split	None direct
Communications	Guarded; need to know, vertical and horizontal	Limited; focus on conflict resolution	Open, direct, network of fax and computers
Performance Appraisal	Supervisor alone	Project mgr, Functional mgr	Peers, customers, supervisor
Compensation	Job scales, pay grades, people managed	Conflict managed	Skills mastered; individual performance
Management Focus	Coordination	Cooperation	Collaboration
Goal Setting (organizational and individual)	Key management activity	Less significant	Goals self-established; based on vision
Decision Making	Issues passed up to boss with information and perspective	Issues resolved as functional and project bosses meet	Issues delegated to level closest to customer; team based
LEADERSHIP	Boss/bosses anoint "top down"	Project managers, functional managers "negotiate"	Leadership rotates to task competent

Figure 8   Clusters and Other Forms

	HIERARCHY	MATRIX	CLUSTER
RESPONSIBILITY	Supervisors hold	Project managers hold	Cluster members accept accountability
RESOURCE ALLOCATION	Done by managers	Done by managers and project leaders	Done by negotiation between cluster leaders and central management

Figure 8 (*Continued*)

Shifts Locus of Decision Making

In a hierarchy, the locus of decision-making authority is as close to the top of an organization as time and communications allow. The motivation for this rule is that executives high in the organization have more information and a wider perspective from which to make correct choices.

In a matrix organization decisions must be made at the level where the shared reporting relationship exists. Here, conflicts and resource sharing must be worked out between functional and project bosses and their common subordinate.

In a cluster organization the locus of decision making is as close to the point at which action is to be taken as possible. The motivation for this principle is the belief that those nearest to the action have the clearest understanding of what needs to be done. Thus the advantage of clusters in giving better and quicker service to customers is partially the result of putting decision making close to the customer.

Defines Jobs Broadly

Both hierarchy and matrix structures depend on well-ordered layers of narrowly defined jobs. These jobs—when combined into work units, departments, and divisions—establish appropriate spans of control and supervision for different managerial levels. Clusters largely abandon narrow job descriptions in favor of much broader team assignments—where an individual is capable of doing several "traditional" jobs—and in the process explicitly drop the notion of a limited span of control and supervision.

In practice this does not mean that everybody does everything. Instead people utilize the competencies they possess and often specialize. However, each individual also has a "general duty clause" to do whatever needs to be done at the time, to rotate among tasks, and to develop skills as need and interest suggest.

Abandons Reporting Relationships

The cluster form separates top management control of the organization from direct reporting relationships. Both the hierarchy and the matrix involve boss-subordinate relationships. As noted earlier, the hierarchy posits a one-to-one relationship, whereas the matrix permits an individual to have more than a single boss. The new form eliminates the reporting relationship, at least as it is generally understood to exist.

For example, the resource managers in the BPE organization, who may seem at first glance to be bosses in the traditional sense, are not. There is no reporting relationship on work issues from the cluster members to the resource managers.

In a hierarchy and matrix, leadership goes to those with authority: the bosses. In a cluster, leadership goes to those best able to perform the task. In place of boss-subordinate relationships there are communication interactions and the transfer of information between individuals in the organization.

What is gained by abandoning reporting relationships is a lean organization with fewer levels of middle management, fewer specialized jobs in report preparation, and much less overhead. Generally, in place of layers of managers and of employees with carefully defined jobs and reporting relationships, the new form places multifunctional teams without formal reporting responsibilities.

Certain other assumptions of the hierarchical model are also altered in the new form. With hierarchy severely circumscribed and its significance reduced, compensation no longer has to rise step by step with the reporting chain. Hence contribution to the firm may be compensated for more independently of a formal position. This is an advantage in today's competitive economy because it permits firms to reward key employees without having to ratchet upward the compensation of the entire managerial hierarchy above those employees.

Clusters in Operation

It is easier to understand the new form if one thinks about how a hierarchy actually operates. Years ago, researchers observed that when a hierarchy functioned as a communication device, it was a bottleneck. That is, with several people all reporting to a single individual, information had to flow upward to the manager before going to other persons. The manager became a communications bottleneck, and the capacity of the unit was limited to his or her own capacity.

No effective organization works in this way. Instead, there is an informal organization in which people communicate laterally with others, regardless of the organization chart. It is through informal channels that much of what is accomplished by an organization occurs.

The informal organization is characterized by freedom of contact across organizational lines and by a lack of rigidity in what individuals do. People get in touch with those who have the competencies to assist in a task and do not depend on formal job definitions in helping a colleague. This network is a supplement to the formal organization in accomplishing objectives.

From one perspective, the cluster organization is an attempt to make the informal organization the only one by dispensing with the formal organization almost entirely. I say "almost" because some rudiments of hierarchy—in particular top officers and middle managers—remain. Clusters are often described as flat organizations because they have few layers of management. But they are not entirely flat—a limited hierarchy remains.

Cluster Processes

A number of the operational features of clusters are quite different from their hierarchical and matrix counterparts. Let us briefly explore these differences.

Leadership

This process is not ordinarily associated with formal authority. Instead, cluster leadership tends to flow to persons with the greatest competence in the particular tasks or projects at hand. Nor do clusters encounter the problems of the matrix, where project managers lack direct control over those who make up their teams and so have to negotiate to obtain resources. In fact the cluster is a simpler form than the matrix, and many people who are confused by the multiple reporting in the matrix are pleased by this simplicity.

Resource Allocation

A key aspect of a business organization is resource allocation. Some persons have expressed concern that a cluster organization cannot have a logical resource allocation process. This is incorrect.

In a hierarchy, allocation tends to be done through a budgeting process, which may be initiated in a bottom-up form but ultimately assumes a top-down configuration. In a matrix, resources are allocated through negotiations among three sets of managers: resource managers, project managers, and top management.

In a cluster organization, resources are allocated through processes similar to those of the hierarchy or of the matrix. The clusters may initiate requests for support that are reviewed and decided by top management, but the process most consistent with the spirit of clusters is one that involves negotiations between management and clusters.

Power of Direction

Cluster organizations minimize managerial authority but do not dispense with it entirely. The residual hierarchy retains power that can be used by managers if they decide to do so. In ordinary functioning, however, cluster managers forego the power of direction that is common in a hierarchy.

Instead, cluster executives rely on incentives and leadership. They negotiate targets with clusters, measure results, and reward accordingly.

Managers in hierarchies also rely on incentives, of course, but they generally rely more on the authority of their positions.

What a Cluster Is Not

So far, I have been discussing what a cluster is. At this point, it is important to make clear what it is not. Several organizational devices bear some resemblance to clusters but, in one way or another, do not go as far or have as much potential.

A cluster organization is neither a self-managed work team nor a quality circle. Self-managed teams and quality circles are incremental changes to traditional hierarchies. Although they are attempts to loosen up a hierarchy to get better performance, they do not go as far as the cluster.

A cluster organization is nonincremental. It is revolutionary. As said in Chapter Two, it is a one-way ticket to the future. If a company establishes clusters and then tries to eliminate them, the good employees will leave.

At high-tech firms, which initially operated as clusters and then were acquired by larger companies, the imposition of hierarchical models has often led to an exodus of the most talented people. Many times, the acquiring firms have been left with mere shells of the acquired company. Similarly, when managers from larger firms have been hired by smaller companies and have brought their hierarchical practices with them, they have often strangled the smaller companies. A notable exception occurred at Apple Computer when John Sculley adapted himself to the different setting and was able to preserve the company's strengths while adding his own.

Clusters versus Self-Managed Work Teams

A self-managed work team is closer to a cluster than is a matrix to a cluster organization. But even in the self-managed team there are strong managerial functions performed by team leaders that separate it from the cluster's looser approach.

At the extreme, however, self-managed teams that interrelate without significant hierarchical control become much like a cluster organization.

An excellent example of such an approach—the effort at GE Canada—is described in Chapter Sixteen.

Clusters versus Quality Circles

Ordinarily a supplement to hierarchy, a quality circle permits employees to meet and discuss work problems outside the direct work environment. This is a very limited, though often useful, concept that does not go anywhere near as far toward a different organizational concept as does the cluster.

The Japanese are, of course, major users of the quality circle device. After having studied a cluster organization one Japanese executive told me, ''We have never gone that far in our thinking.''

Clusters versus Task Forces

Some firms use multidisciplinary teams on an ad hoc basis to do special cross-functional tasks. Such a team is very close to a cluster. However, the cluster is not formed for a one-time specific purpose but to be a permanent component of the organization. Also, most multidisciplinary teams are overlays on the hierarchical and functionally structured organization; clusters replace the hierarchy.

Clusters versus Participative Management

To loosen a hierarchy, many managers use participative management in which subordinates are deliberately given some freedom of action within the system. Participative management in a hierarchy is a step in the direction of a cluster organization, but it does not go very far. The authority of the executive remains, and employee participation more or less depends on the personality of the individual manager and the stress of the moment.

Clusters are by their nature so free of authority and close supervision that to speak of participative management is a misnomer. Clusters are participative, which is all that can properly be said.

Cluster Strengths

What are the strengths of clusters versus hierarchy and matrix? Consider

- Low administrative overhead
- More entrepreneurial behavior
- Greater flexibility and adaptability
- More openness to new technology
- Better utilization of new technology
- Better retention of workers
- Less risk of promoting those who aren't ready

Low Administrative Overhead

Compared to hierarchical and matrix organizations, clusters have lower administrative overhead—fewer managers to be supported—and are therefore cheaper to operate. In today's fiercely competitive business environment, this is a major advantage.

More Entrepreneurial Behavior

Lacking the bureaucratic structure of the alternative formats, the cluster permits more entrepreneurial and innovative behavior. People are freer to pursue ideas and to gather support for them. The degree to which the hierarchical structures of large organizations inhibit innovation is not even today fully appreciated. The record of successful U.S. companies is full of examples of employees whose basic idea behind a new business was offered first to their firm's founders, who told them to stick to their knitting. The entrepreneurs then set up their own successful venture, which cost former employers considerable profits.

Greater Flexibility and Adaptability

Many bureaucracies are unable to adapt quickly to market opportunities. I once heard an aggressive middle manager of a large firm in difficulty tell top management that the company's problem was not foreign competition or unfavorable economic trends but that its headquarters was a graveyard for opportunities sent in from the field. "By the time you give us approval," he said, "the opportunity is gone." Given this background, the informality and potential speed of action of the cluster seem tremendous advantages.

Openness and Utilization of New Technology

The cluster organization had early supporters among the high-tech community, partly to keep a company more open to outside technology. Reliance is placed on professionals in the clusters to help keep the organization up to date in technology.

Better Retention of Workers

The customer's informality also helps to attract and retain top employees. Many hierarchical organizations rely on promotion up a corporate ladder to reward and provide challenge to top performers. Unfortunately, if business growth slows or if layers of management are removed to cut costs, formal promotions may be few and far between. This fact may make it difficult to attract or retain top people by customary methods.

The cluster form permits successful companies to fashion assignments that are challenging, often varied, fun, involved with other workers, and financially rewarding. Work in this sort of environment, with the independence from close supervision that clusters foster, presents an alternative to rapid advancement up a hierarchy.

Less Promotion Risk

With less reliance on advancement up a hierarchy in the progress of managers' careers, the cluster organization lessens the risk of placing people in positions for which they are poorly suited. This phenomenon, often referred to as the Peter Principle, has two different causes: people who are promoted beyond their level of competence and people who are promoted into jobs in which they are uninterested.

John Cooke described a circumstance of the latter type to Larry Reibstein of the *Wall Street Journal*. His "mentor and friend at Bendix . . . was promoted once too often, to a senior position in which he had little interest. As more people felt the executive was doing his job poorly, he lost stature and credibility with peers and superiors." Further, the lack of respect for Mr. Cooke's predecessor was displaced to him and resulted in disrespect for the function he performed.

The lesson is that when the boss in a hierarchy is out of place, his whole part of the organization suffers. The cluster organization, with its deemphasis of hierarchy, minimizes this problem.

Cluster Limitations

What are the weaknesses of cluster organizations versus hierarchy and matrix structures. Again, consider

- Dependent on quality of leadership
- Motivation possibly fragile
- Loss of some managerial control
- More volatile earnings
- Loss of some specialization and expertise
- Shift in loyalty from boss to cluster

Dependent on Quality of Leadership

Cluster organizations are very dependent on the quality of leadership exerted in them. Clusters elicit from their members a higher level of commitment to work than is common in other firms and, with it, a greater emotional intensity. Top executives must be alert to the quality of leadership and manage it most carefully.

Motivation Possibly Fragile

Relying on influence and suggestion as much as authority and direction, cluster organizations are vulnerable to shifting opinions about top management among cluster members, who are subject to swings of optimism or pessimism. In this sense motivation and performance are fragile in a cluster organization.

Loss of Some Managerial Control

Top management relinquishes traditional forms of control over operations in a cluster organization. The hierarchy necessary to issue formal directives is sharply limited. But how great a limitation of the cluster form this constitutes is arguable.

Managers experienced with the cluster insist that control is actually greater because there is far more acceptance of responsibility among employees for what occurs at work. Traditional managers may feel at sea in this environment.

Volatility of Earnings Possibly Increased

Probably a cluster organization will have more volatile earnings than a hierarchy. Since clusters are less able to be fine-tuned, they may turn in spectacular performances for a while and poor ones at other times. They are more emotional, less machinelike in their characteristics. Where predictability is at a premium, lessened direct control may constitute a disadvantage.

Loss of Some Formal Specialization and Expertise

A cluster organization relinquishes expertise. People who are specialized may tire of their specialty and insist on doing other things. The organization thus becomes a learning vehicle for its members.

To many managers, this situation represents an inefficient use of skills and a waste of the investment that a firm has made in training an employee to do a few things well. Whether inefficiency is a result depends on a number of factors. Companies ordinarily employ people for long periods, usually many years. During that time a person's expertise may increase because of experience.

Conversely, however, the skills people possess may become obsolete. Obsolescence is ordinarily thought of in terms of technical knowledge, which is important, but it also occurs in less technical areas. For example, sales expertise may erode as society evolves and as customers change lifestyles, attitudes, or aspirations. Such changes occur continually. An experienced salesperson complains that she does not seem to understand the consumer anymore or that his contacts at a retail distributor have all moved on and he is lost with the new generation that has replaced them.

There is also social obsolescence in a changing society, just as there is technical obsolescence. When companies insist on keeping people in their specialties long after the individuals have lost the ability or interest in keeping abreast of the times, a great inefficiency results.

Also, the transfer of a person into a different area of activity can often be handled to allow for quick effectiveness, so that inefficiency because of inexperience is minimized. Use of education and training facilitate transitions in careers.

A company reported to me that it tried for years to get some of its managers to move to new jobs, believing that they were ineffective in their current assignments. Those involved refused to make the change, apparently fearing that they would be ineffective in the new positions as well. Finally, when the firm gave them the option of moving or resigning, they chose to accept the new assignments. Two years later, according to the company, the results were very favorable. In particular the man who had most resisted reassignment was doing very well in his new position and enjoying it a great deal.

Also, a cluster organization develops extensive secondary expertise in others that can provide significant support for the people with the primary expertise. As a result, the organization's total expertise is enhanced, not reduced. Hence loss of expertise in a cluster organization may actually be more apparent than real.

Finally, in today's world, in which change is rapid and people are more independent than in the past, an organization often suffers from overspecialization. It becomes rigid and unable to adapt. The cross-utilization of workers provides a breadth of knowledge that gives the organization greater flexibility than otherwise.

In general, firms have pushed too far down the human learning curve. Overspecialization has given us bureaucratic rigidity in the utilization of people, caused overstaffing as specialists of every type are assembled, and resulted in cumbersome organizations that are slow to react to marketplace changes. Bored employees allow themselves to become outdated and emerge as less than peak performers. The cluster organization with its flexibility in the use of its members becomes an efficient response to today's environment.

Shift in Loyalty from Boss to Cluster

Decades ago, the organization man in U.S. business was fiercely loyal to the company for which he worked. But over the years two great forces have eroded corporate loyalty.

First, the men and women in today's corporation are less prepared to subordinate self to organization. Second, companies, by massive downsizing, have forfeited in the hearts and minds of many any right to loyalty from those they employ. "The firm isn't loyal to me," middle managers and workers alike now say, "so it's crazy for me to be loyal to it." Instead of the company, many people are now strongly loyal to their direct supervisors. Also, leadership training has helped managers encourage loyalty to themselves.

A cluster organization shifts the focus of loyalty. Since most people no longer have a direct boss, they shift their emotional attachment to the work group. A fierce loyalty develops to the cluster and to those who make it up.

Is this a positive or negative development? I have listed it here as a limitation because many top executives still believe there is still much loyalty to the firm itself among their employees. They do not realize that loyalty in a hierarchical organization today is almost always personal attachment to a boss, not to the firm. (A major exception is IBM: The company goes to great lengths to build loyalty among its employees to the firm itself.) Since those executives believe that considerable institutional loyalty exists, they fear to see it lost to a cluster.

But in reality, building loyalty to a cluster may ultimately attach the individual even more strongly to the firm of which the cluster is a part than does loyalty to a particular boss. So clusters may on net add a strong bond to the firm rather than reduce it.

Why Clusters Are Successful

To be successful a business organization must be well adapted to two environments: its economic environment and its human environment. The managerial challenge is to balance demands that the firm places on its workers as a result of changing business conditions with the expectations and aspirations of the people who make up the firm. Only when such a balance is achieved does performance in the company reach its potential.

Although adaptability is a great advantage in a rapidly changing world, it is possible that the cluster is no more suited to today's economic climate than the hierarchy or matrix. Instead, the genius of the cluster organization may be its better fit to the expectations and aspirations of today's work force.

In past decades there has been a tremendous advance in the educational attainment of a majority of people in industrialized societies. With increased schooling has come a steady evolution in aspirations. Expectations are no longer limited to living standards. Today, people have aspirations about the nature of their work and their role in business organizations.

By and large, the structure of organizations has not kept pace. We are confronting the work force of the late twentieth century with the organizational form of mid-century. The result is dissatisfaction and less than optimal performance.

In the past, blue-collar workers in manufacturing were the dominant employee group in our society. The administration of businesses was in a form that was expected by them and that had proven effective on the plant floor. The hierarchy, with its strict supervision and accountability, was central to this mode of management. There was, however, a subordinate system for professionals, especially in the research and development functions of big companies and in the professional service firms (e.g., lawyers and investment bankers) since these had difficulty fitting into the prevailing mode.

Now professionals are more numerous and significant in our society than blue-collar workers. The result is that the cluster system finds its roots in the old subculture of research and development and in the culture of professional service organizations. Those who look to the old industrial system as the norm for today's organizations are somewhat out of date in their thinking.

The informality of the cluster organization fits the more casual lifestyle of today. People look for warmth, enthusiasm, and fun—not only in their private lives but at work as well. Older-style managers are uncomfortable with these expectations, and the traditional hierarchy militates against them. Reporting requirements, direction and oversight by superiors, and differential status within the firm all work against the informality increasingly desired by employees.

It is possible that informality is merely a stage and that its current vogue will pass. I think this is unlikely, at least to any great degree. Instead, informality reflects a deeper longing concerning the relationships of human beings in advanced societies, where most people are reasonably well educated. This is not an egalitarian longing but rather one for openness and accessibility—whatever the wealth and income levels of those involved. It is the end of social class, not of economic differences among people.

I am aware that this distinction is not acceptable to those people who insist that economic differences are the basis of social class. Certainly this was true a century ago, when living standards were far lower, political structures less democratic, and education far less broadly acquired than today.

The result of higher living standards, political democracy, and widespread education has been to alter our world beyond recognition by the concepts of the nineteenth century. Those who continue to insist that these two very different concepts—social class and economic situation—are the same are simply extending without warrant observations about the mid-nineteenth century into the late twentieth century.

There is an antiestablishment flavor about many cluster organizations. Participants draw a special pleasure from the knowledge that they are challenging more traditionally structured firms. They delight in besting the others in the marketplace and are disappointed when flag bearers of the new form are defeated.

The motivational impact of the antiestablishment crusade can easily be overestimated, but it is not insignificant. People draw additional commitment from working against something.

Finally, there is in Western societies today among all levels of the work force an aspiration toward professionalism, to which only the cluster organization has responded. For example, in interviews with blue-collar and clerical workers, people continually referred to themselves in such terms as *professionals*: "I am a professional bus driver" or "I am a professional bartender" or "I am a professional secretary." These individuals were also quick to point out that their employers do not think of them as professionals, and they complained about the disrespectful, uncaring manner in which they are treated. In lengthy interviews with 150 Americans between the ages of 21 and 41, only two individuals indicated that their companies treated them with what they considered reasonable respect, and these two tied the respect they felt to opportunities to set standards for their own work and for learning new skills.

In the United States today, more than 70 percent of the work force has some college education. (This figure is higher than the official government statistics, which ask years of school completed, a quite different concept.)

Most working people think of themselves as well educated and entitled to respect for the contribution they make. They wish to have a role in designing their own work, to have its quality judged by others who know the field, to have access to learning opportunities about their field, and to perform their work in a dignified manner.

In effect they aspire to a professional form of work, along with the independence and respect that accompanies participation in the traditional professions. Denied the opportunity, they become embittered, discouraged, and hostile to their managers. Despite their aspirations to perform well, performance suffers.

The cluster organization, through its flexibility and informality, meets these aspirations toward professionalism at all levels of the work force. It permits people to do more. It provides elements of enjoyment, warmth, and enthusiasm in work. Because it meets the aspirations of people, it is not surprising that cluster-type settings often achieve far higher productivity levels than do hierarchical or matrix organizations.

Evolution Toward Clusters

It is common for people to believe that clusters are most readily established in start-up companies. Long-existent firms with traditional structures are hard to change, they argue. There is much truth to this, and Chapter Fourteen will describe the sometimes extreme measures that executives employ to break an old culture and move to one with clusters.

But clusters also emerge naturally, as it were, in the evolution of long-established companies. George Land has written about the evolution of the corporation through three stages. In the first stage a firm is dominated by the entrepreneur who founded it. This period is characterized by a search for whatever pattern will make the company a success.

The second stage involves improving the pattern by making it more effective and efficient. Policies are developed, procedures emerge, the organization is now run by professional management, and a bureaucracy takes root. The company begins to lose touch with its customers. More and more activity is internally focused. After a period of success, new competition emerges and the company's profit margins decline. In an effort to restore past profitability, executives sponsor a back-to-basics effort.

But a return to the fundamentals that worked before is no longer sufficient. The company has outgrown that stage of its evolution. A third stage is at hand in which executives encourage a transformation of the organization. They seek renewal and increased commitment. The organizational form best associated with this stage is the cluster. Hence, as part of the evolution of many firms, clusters seem a natural step.

Finally, clusters are valuable accompaniments to a vision-driven organization. Vision, a concept of the future that can be articulated to all employees as a basis for their activities, is frequently suggested today as an alternative to a firm whose executives rely on financial targets to move it forward.

Visions have become part of standard managerial behavior in America. Even traditional hierarchies are going through ''visioning'' processes. But often visions appear as mere supplements to a traditional managerial style. Whereas the vision is supposed to guide the company, the quarterly earnings per share are still in the driver's seat.

A truly vision-driven organization is an alternative way of managing. Financial success is expected to flow from the pursuit of other goals. Financial goal setting itself is no longer the driving force. Instead it is a forecasting exercise. Will a vision-driven firm experience a steady increase in earnings per share? Probably not since that is not a normal business phenomenon in a world of rapid change, economic fluctuations, and other unpredictable events. A vision-driven firm pursues its long-term goals and stabilizes earnings to the extent that financial actions make possible.

Some cluster organizations that exist within larger firms continue to use such management processes as goal setting, targets, and managing by objectives. These are not how the clusters are managed. They are instead translations of what goes on in the clusters into a language understandable in the traditional hierarchical organization.

Clusters are the proper organizational form for a vision-driven firm. They give employees the maximum opportunity to exercise their initiative and discretion in pursuit of the vision. Clusters free management from the morass of administrative detail that too often derails a vision. Hence, as firms move toward visions as a key element of strategy, the cluster organization moves to the forefront.

Can a vision-driven organization be managed in a traditional fashion? Linda Medin, an independent management consultant who has helped to establish several vision-driven units, insists that it cannot. Layers of the hierarchy are not needed to direct the work done by the clusters. Nor are middle managers needed for performance reviews, compensation adjustments, and similar activities since they also are performed by the clusters in conjunction with the residual hierarchy. If the full hierarchy is retained and middle managers perform their customary activities, they simply interfere with the effective operation of the organization.

A vision-driven organization uses significant human involvement to give people the greatest opportunity for contributing to the vision's fulfillment. The cluster organization is the form that participative management will take in the 1990s.

CHAPTER ELEVEN

Boxes and Circles: The Distinctive Organization Chart

A cluster organization does away with the currently ubiquitous boxes and lines of a typical organization chart. In its place are boxes with circles in them, each standing for a semiautonomous cluster, without solid or dotted lines to the managerial structure. Some clusters employ that strangest of all diagrams of an organization: a group of concentric circles. Foreign as such a chart looks, several companies have already begun to diagram their organizations in just this way to express the revolutionary differences between clusters and hierarchies.

A hierarchy is easily diagrammed. It may well be that this has contributed to its persistent popularity. It is common to observe executives moving boxes on an organization chart, much as a decorator arranges furniture in a room, apparently with the conviction that they are thereby rearranging actual roles in the organization.

A matrix is not so easily diagrammed because of the problem of representing its relationship to the top executives of the organization. The connections between the work unit and both project and functional managers are readily depicted in the crossing lines and cells of the diagram. But as diagrammed, the matrix appears to operate quite effectively without top management—a result that may have contributed to its lack of wider usage.

The cluster is the least amenable of all to a satisfactory diagram. Hence it is tempting to avoid diagrams entirely, except many people might conclude that any form of organization that cannot be reduced to a diagram is not an organization at all.

Some proponents of cluster organizations are so hostile to diagrams that they have refused on principle to make diagrams of their organizations. Apparently, they think a diagram would cause people to behave as if they were still in a hierarchy. Despite this point of view, cluster organizations can be diagrammed, and there is much to be learned about the new form from the exercise.

British Petroleum Engineering's diagram, for example, shows free-standing clusters represented by "boxes within circles"—that is, boxes unconnected by any lines to other elements of the organization. Let us turn for a minute to this BPE organization.

Figure 9 is a pictogram of the new organization structure in BPE. At the center of the pictogram are the clusters of engineers through which BPE now conducts its business with clients. In the upper left hand third of the surrounding circle is the general manager of engineering resources and the staff resource managers who report to him. This unit is hierarchical in form. In the other thirds of the staff support circle are the general manager of business services and his direct reports and the general manager of technology development and his staff. Dashed (not dotted) lines, which represent a reporting relationship, lead from each of the general managers to the managing director of BPE. The lines are dashed—not solid—to indicate that in the spirit of participative management the relationship between the managing director and the general managers is more collegial than boss-subordinate.

The managing director, general managers and their staff constitute the residual hierarchy of BPE.

In the clusters there is no formal hierarchy, and there are no direct reporting relationships to the general managers. In a sense, however, all clusters report to the managing director. Certainly there is extensive

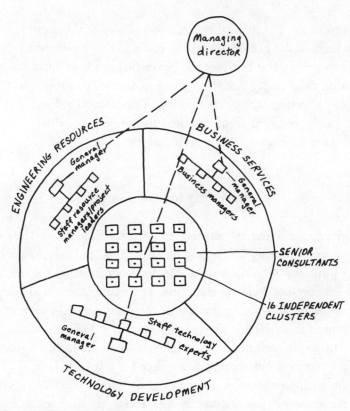

Figure 9   The BPE Organization

communication between the clusters and both staff elements and the managing directors.

In the terminology that was presented with Figure 1 in Chapter One the clusters are business units, the staff groups are staff units, and the managing director and the three general managers constitute a core team. BPE also has some project teams, not shown, but at this time lacks alliance and change teams.

The representation in Figure 9 is very powerful. It shows the engineers who compose the business units and who are in direct contact with BPE's customers as at the center of BPE's organization. The importance of customer contact is visually depicted.

Staff units, even though they are composed of managers, are shown not in positions of authority and direction but in a supportive posture to the business units. The managing director is shown in the upper right-hand corner as befits his or her key leadership role and the responsibility exercised for BPE as a whole. But the lines and boxes that in a traditional hierarchical organization chart imply that the managing director controls everything by pulling on puppetlike strings are missing. The managing director is seen as a leader, partly divorced from moment-to-moment activities. The pictogram tells how BPE works and gives hints of its ethos as well.

Engineering for the Future

It is crucial to note that the clusters are self-standing units. They do not have any direct reporting link to any functional leader. Each cluster has one senior consultant, who is responsible for coordinating the interaction between functions and cluster members. For example, he or she helps the resource manager assigned to the cluster evaluate trainees' progress toward journeyman status. He or she might help the business manager and resource manager assigned to the cluster find available engineers for specific jobs or pick out the right engineer for a specific task. The senior consultant is not responsible for work supervision. Engineers within a cluster are more or less self-managing, based on their experience and qualifications.

Each of the three functions has at least one individual assigned to service each cluster. For example, Engineering Resources has resource managers whose job is to review assignments and career progress for the 45 to 50 engineers contained within a cluster. Business Services designates someone to handle contacts and solicit business on behalf of a particular client. Technology Development designates someone to handle technology issues for a particular client.

Whereas BPE makes use of the box and circle approach, other organizations, such as Royal Trust and Åke Larson, represent their clusters with overlapping and touching circles. When using concentric circles to diagram a cluster organization, it is important to remember that a residual hierarchy remains. There needs to be a way of depicting not only the clusters themselves but also this limited structure of authority. For this reason, a cluster organization is usefully depicted from a different perspective than that ordinarily used in hierarchical organizations.

Hierarchies and matrices are best represented from the side, as in a cross section. A cluster organization is better viewed from above.

Royal Trust

To obtain an advantage over its rivals, the Royal Trust Company of Canada, one of Canada's largest financial institutions, has improved the speed and flexibility of its customer service. As explained by Paul Starita, executive vice president for marketing, a typical retail banking customer wants a transaction to be executed as quickly as possible.

For routine things like check cashing, this is readily done. The company's information systems allow a teller to identify a depositor, check the balance in an account, and provide currency for the check—all in a brief, one-stop process. But for most transactions this is not the case. In arranging a loan, the customer fills out an application and waits for the financial institution to process it. This step can take weeks.

To speed the processing flow, Royal Trust has reorganized its procedures, systems, and organization. In its annual report, the company noted, ''We believe that companies with traditional hierarchical organization structures will find it increasingly difficult to respond to the rapidly changing financial services environment.'' The Royal Trust report continued with a two-page pictographic representation of a circular form, somewhat like an amphitheater, that it described as an organization chart (see Figure 10).

''Royal Trust's circular organization chart,'' read the text ''represents what we strive to be—a non-bureaucratic group of people focused outward on our customers and shareholders. We have few reporting levels, which ensures quick response to customer needs. We work through informal networks and work groups defined by client needs rather than internal considerations. Our people share a sense of urgency and accountability in their work.'' Finally, just to be sure no one missed the point, the report added, ''We are organized to serve our customers, not to build internal hierarchies.''

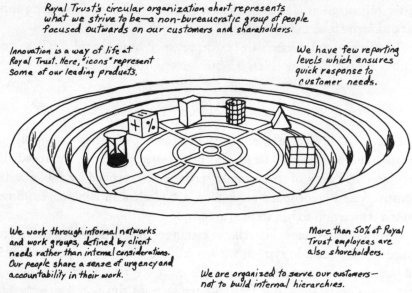

Royal Trust's circular organization chart represents
what we strive to be—a non-bureaucratic group of people
focused outwards on our customers and shareholders.

Innovation is a way of life at
Royal Trust. Here, "icons" represent
some of our leading products.

We have few reporting
levels which ensures
quick response to
customer needs.

We work through informal networks
and work groups, defined by client
needs rather than internal considerations.
Our people share a sense of urgency and
accountability in their work.

More than 50% of Royal
Trust employees are
also shareholders.

We are organized to serve our customers—
not to build internal hierarchies.

Figure 10   The Royal Trust's Pictograph

Åke Larson Group

Established a few decades ago, the Åke Larson Group, a Swedish international construction management firm, has expanded rapidly. From its inception, the group has had an informal, nonhierarchical organization. Each project manager is fully responsible to the clients for his or her projects. Staff functions are recognized as support functions, and every person in the group has the right and obligation to communicate with and seek support from anyone in the organization.

The company operates without job descriptions, and every employee is sent to Sweden for training in how the group operates. As shown in Figure 11, the firm's organization chart is a series of concentric circles. At the center is the coordination and support function. Control groups surround the center, and on the periphery are clusters specialized for different types of construction and different nations.

The system has certain limitations. There is some confusion about where responsibility lies because there is no clear administrative or managerial career path.

196

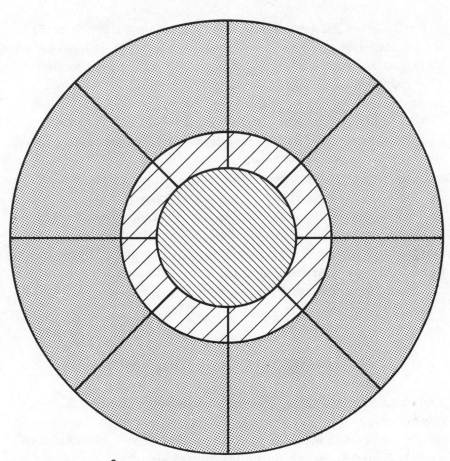

Figure 11   The Åke Larson Organization

But there are great strengths also. The group has low overhead because it has a minimal administrative structure. There is high flexibility in using its resources because individuals can easily move to different assignments in the absence of a more rigid organizational structure. Meeting customer needs is facilitated by the authority each employee has to initiate activities on a customer's behalf and to involve others in the company to satisfy a customer's desires.

Moreover, the internal environment of the firm is highly entrepreneurial—challenging and encouraging employees to develop business through their contacts with customers—which permits the individual to develop his or her own talents. Communications are not restricted by the boundaries of functions and by levels of a hierarchy. Instead they are quite open and are made easy by extensive use of the newest technology. Thus people spread out over many countries can remain in close touch with one another.

In the highly competitive and uncertain world of international construction the strengths just listed far outweigh the limitations. As a result, the group has prospered and grown.

The circular representation that Royal Trust uses is valuable in depicting the company's objectives for how it operates. But the company's pictograph is not really an organization chart. The pictograph describes on a wheel various functions that the business intends to perform. But the elements depicted on the wheel are not organization units. The pictograph is instead a visual representation of the firm's objectives, not a diagram of the organization units that are to accomplish the objectives. The BPE pictograph is far more informative.

Developing a Cluster Diagram

The use of concentric circles is a most unusual and challenging attempt to diagram a cluster organization. Figure 12 presents such a diagram, not of a specific organization but a generic representation. Specific applications will differ, of course, just as they do for hierarchies and matrices.

The figure suggests that a cluster organization can be conceived as a group of tangent or interlocking circles. At the center is the chief executive officer, whose overall responsibility for the organization justifies a central and separate position. In the circle adjacent are the top officers, followed by a group of subordinate managers; finally, represented as a series of circles at the periphery, are the working groups, which contain most of the organization's personnel.

The concentric circles indicate that unlike a conventional hierarchy, there are no unique lines of reporting and supervision. People in the second circle—marked "officers"—interact with others in the adjacent circle as necessary and appropriate but without the degree of structure inherent in a hierarchy.

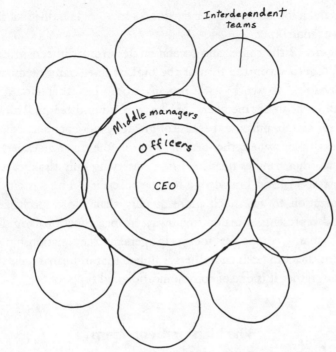

Figure 12   The Use of Concentric Circles to Depict a Cluster Organization

For example, a cluster can have a sudden need for additional personnel. If the officer whose expertise is human resources is available, representatives of the cluster will go to him or her. But if that person is unavailable, the cluster representatives will go to whoever is available, trusting that officer to set in motion the steps necessary to resolve the problem.

Alternatively, an officer concerned with cost escalation in certain activities will go to the cluster involved to discuss the matter. If a disagreement results, other officers may become involved. The one-on-one process of a subordinate reporting to a superior is absent. In its place is a more flexible process of continual interaction around problems and opportunities in which officers may deal with anyone in the organization.

Reports are made through the company's information system and need not be an element of the formal organization. There will be officers specializing in particular functions, of course, and there will be small staffs with specific expertise. But there is more movement of people among functions and a looser tie of specialized tasks to a single individual than in a hierarchy or matrix.

In Figure 12 the center and second circles ordinarily constitute a core team and together run the firm at the highest level. Any member of the team is available to work with persons from the other circles on any matter, though some members of the top committee will always be preferred for certain purposes because of greater experience and expertise.

For example, when the person who is the finance expert is not available, another handles financial issues, reserving only those that require the utmost specialized knowledge for the specialist. This system permits the organization to act much more quickly than more specialized hierarchies and represents a major step away from a functional rigidity that dominates many companies today. In general the relationship among members of the core team and others is unlike that of formal reporting and supervision; rather it is one of communication and support.

The Management Team

The cluster organization rests responsibility both in individuals and in teams. Although this seems to some managers a sure recipe for indecision, it often is not. Many companies with elaborately defined hierarchical organizations are in fact operated by top management teams.

Because of a widespread prejudice in the United States that committees are ineffective, most major U.S. firms choose not to show top management teams on their organization charts published in annual reports or otherwise made public. Nonetheless, the charts that are used internally generally show them. When I asked about this peculiar practice, a top corporate executive responded, ''We don't want people to think that we're a committee-run company. We want them to think we have only one boss.''

In a cluster organization the top management committee can preserve an element of top officer control, just as a lower-level cluster can. When a deadlock occurs in a top committee (e.g., Du Pont's core committee), it can be broken by the chief officer. In a lower-level cluster such a deadlock can be broken by the team leader. In this respect the new format preserves an element of the hierarchy. Most of the time, however, the activities of the group are determined by a collegial agreement rather than by the decision of one person.

The numerous working groups at the periphery of the concentric circle are interdisciplinary. They interact as need suggests with members of the management ring. You may think of the interactions between working groups and managers as similar to the interaction between computer memory chips and a central processing unit (CPU).

Random Access Characteristic

There is no need to run through long, slow preset channels to get data from the memory chip for the CPU. Necessary channels are created and released at random. Any bit of information on the chip is just as easy for the CPU to reach as any other. Hence the reference to memory chips as *random access memory*, or RAM.

One of the greatest differences between a cluster and a hierarchy is now apparent. Unlike a hierarchy, the cluster has few functional units. Turf battles prevalent in hierarchical organizations, struggles over budget for this and that function, and the reluctance of officials in one function to deal with those of higher or lesser rank in another function are all minimized.

In a cluster people do not consider themselves so specialized that they are reluctant to work outside of their classification. Pay systems are not so closely tied to job content that a person working out of his or her specialty is thereby involved in an issue of what is the proper pay for the additional duties. In fact it is a prime purpose of the cluster organization to break down the artificial barriers to communication and efficient work practices that the functional organization creates.

The random access characteristic of the cluster organization provides a substantial additional strength. Because people are free to communicate without regard to hierarchical structure, full utilization of the firm's communication network is permitted.

Dynamic Fluidity

The cluster organization can continually create and extinguish new elements without the complex issues raised in a hierarchy by reorganization. Clusters are of shorter or longer duration, depending on the needs of the persons involved and those of the organization. Thus there is a dynamic fluidity to the organization, which is akin to that of task forces in a hierarchy and serves the same purposes of rapid response to changing needs. But the cluster organization possesses this flexibility to a far greater degree than does a traditional hierarchy.

It is common to think of a firm that is continually reorganizing as floundering. Too much reorganization is viewed as evidence of indecision and ineffectiveness. Yet fluidity in an organization can go much further than we ordinarily think without being counterproductive.

For example, one large computer company reported to its managers recently that more than half its employees had been with their present managers less than one year. This short period was primarily a result of rapid movement of the managers among assignments.

The company is not organized on a cluster basis but instead has a pronounced hierarchy of many levels. Employees build clusters, however, or "networks," as they more often term them, to accomplish their work. These informal groupings survive the come and go of managers.

I discussed the role of middle management in a cluster organization earlier. But before we leave the computer company just mentioned, it is useful to comment on this role. When a company has such rapid movement of managers, each cannot be expected to be an expert in the area under his or her authority. The ability of the manager to analyze business problems, make decisions about them, and direct subordinates in how to resolve them is limited when he or she has spent little time in the unit.

In the computer company one manager on a new assignment told of going to see his new group of subordinates. He said, "Hello, I'm your new manager. Do you mind telling me what it is that you do here so I can try to be of help to you?"

This situation is common in a cluster organization. There are very few managers and their time is divided among many work groups. It is impossible to be expert in all that is being done. What then is a manager to do? That is our topic in Chapter Twelve.

Communication Channels

Figure 12 embodies a residual hierarchy of four levels: the CEO, officers, middle management, and rank and file. This is, in fact, a picture drawn from the actual structure of a retailing organization with some 2,500 locations in the western United States and some 7,000 full-time employees.

If the organization were viewed from its side, it would appear to be a flattened hill with a broad base and gently sloping sides. At its top would be the CEO, with a vantage point from which to observe the organization as a whole and its environment. To carry the illustration just a bit further, the interior of the hill, unseen by outside observers, would be honeycombed with working clusters connected by a network of communication channels.

There is in a cluster organization a greater reach of communication among individuals than in a traditional hierarchy. A company that has a computer-based communication infrastructure will see it used much more extensively when, in the absence of functional barriers, people contact those whose assistance or cooperation they need to do their work. There can be far less of the ''I do my job and my job only'' attitude, which in practice is a way of refusing to accept responsibility for the broader purposes of the worker's activities.

Communication among the groups is also informal and occurs primarily through the personal networks each member of a group develops and maintains to perform effectively. Within a group, communication is facilitated by frequent meetings of the entire group.

There is the danger that a system so dependent on meetings may degenerate. Meetings might be held for their own sake with little productive accomplishment. This need not occur if the group members, and especially the person running a meeting, exercises sufficient self-discipline to run the meeting long enough to do necessary business but short enough to leave sufficient time for members to get things done elsewhere. The need to allocate carefully what is otherwise insufficient time is common in our society.

For example, when parents work, there is too little time for the children, a situation many people find themselves in today. One answer is to improve what is accomplished in the time available for parent and child—hence the concept of quality time. The committees that make up the new structural form seek a similar concept: quality time in the meetings.

At the extreme, a cluster organization may have no hierarchy at all. Some partnerships and other small business organizations operate in this fashion. In the future larger groups may also do so as communications improve and as the external world becomes more accepting of organizations without a hierarchy. The loose alliances of professionals that now exist in some fields, as well as those emerging among corporations in certain industries, are early examples of organizations without formal hierarchies.

Diagramming

At the core of the cluster concept is the recognition that the work of many organizations is performed by professional or semiprofessional people who cooperate to achieve their purposes, rather than by persons working at narrowly circumscribed tasks under close supervision. In consequence, many organizations that have formal hierarchies can usefully be diagrammed as if they were clusters because, in fact, the organization actually operates in this way.

General Motors is a strong hierarchical organization. Yet when asked to draw a diagram of the firm, one executive drew not an organization chart but a series of disconnected boxes (one labeled Pontiac, another Buick, and so on). He commented that the firm's most basic problem, to his mind, was that the connections and relationships among the elements were incorrect. GM as he knew it, he was saying, was a collection of large clusters that did not know how a cluster organization should work.

An executive from another Fortune 500 company depicted the organization of his division not with a traditional chart but as a group of clusters connected by stronger or weaker communication channels. The resulting drawing (Figure 13) was rather like a wiring diagram.

Large Publishing House

A diagram of a large, New York-based publishing company, which its CEO drew, is reproduced here as Figure 14. The company is more than 100 years old and has a fully developed hierarchy. It also possesses a complete, traditional organization chart. But a few years ago, when the company was struggling to adapt to a changing business environment, the CEO began

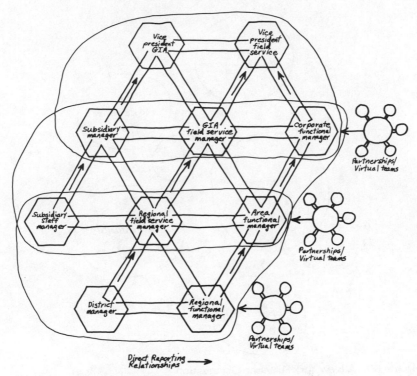

Figure 13   A Fortune 500 Firm's Interlocking Teams

to think of the company as a group of separate but interacting clusters of people. There was the top management; aggressive and younger middle managers, whom he labeled the younger managers; a group of professionals, of whom the editors were the most significant; and numerous persons in marketing, production, and the like.

At that time, the core of the company's situation was a distinct split between the senior management team (with the exception of the CEO himself) and the young turks. The senior management team believed that the company's existing business difficulties were merely a short-term reverse that would soon straighten out if the company adhered firmly to its previous business strategy. The young managers were convinced that the industry had changed profoundly and that the company required a radical reorientation of its strategy.

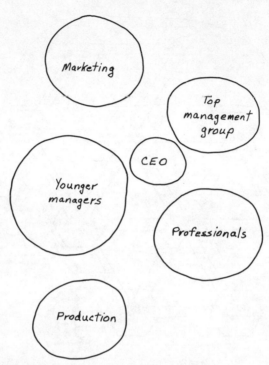

Figure 14 A New York Publishing Organization

The CEO agreed with his middle managers and visualized moving them into a position to direct the company's future. He recognized from his mental diagram that the transition had to be done all at once. Otherwise each young turk, promoted in the usual way up the chain of command, was likely to be coopted by the executive committee members. Even worse, if not coopted, they would be frozen out of any significant influence on the company as a whole by the old guard zealously protecting its own turf from the new ideas.

By visualizing his company as a group of clusters, the CEO was able to initiate processes by which the young turks could be moved into positions for determining the company's future course. He accomplished his plan by changing a number of corporate practices. For example, the CEO delegated down more authority and control over budgets to the young turk level. He also created a new internal "board" to formalize the process of resource allocation among the different market areas the firm covered and then he assigned a number of young turks to it.

Simultaneously, the CEO created new positions in the hierarchy to which he "promoted" the old guard. Thus he protected their status and kept their experience available to the company until retirement.

At the core of the CEO's success in this instance was his recognition that the firm had actually become a cluster organization, even though it was structured as a hierarchy. Many executives do not recognize this fact. Rather, they think of their companies as hierarchies when they actually operate as clusters. The consequences can be unfortunate when people believe their firm to be one thing when it is really something else.

CHAPTER TWELVE

The Changing Role
of Middle Managers

Driven by new technology, social trends, and economic pressures, many traditional middle-management functions are disappearing. Some are migrating upward into the hands of senior executives, aided by computers. For example, data once compiled by middle managers and submitted in their reports to top executives now go directly via information systems to the top. Other middle-management functions, including analysis of business situations, decisions about what to do, and direction of the work force are migrating downward into the work groups.

What remains is a smaller group of managers with a very different role in the corporation. In hierarchies this evolution results in the concentration of more and more decision making at the top of the firm. The cluster represents the only true alternative: a radical delegation that makes even better use of emerging technology. The new role of middle managers is to consult, persuade, and coach employees whose own responsibilities have been radically upgraded. (This topic was touched on in Chapter Eight. In this chapter, it is treated in greater depth.)

Between 1980 and 1985, major U.S. firms shed 500,000 middle managers, even as growth among smaller firms was creating a rise in total management employment. Why are large companies shedding managers? The common explanation is that executives were foolish. In the 1970s they allowed firms to become fat by hiring excess middle managers and by empire building. Then, in the 1980s, facing eroding bottom lines, they turned middle managers into cost-reduction targets. For example, John Sheridan noted that in an *Industry Week* survey, 91.7 percent of respondents were trying to cut overhead costs and that the biggest overhead—"people costs"—comprised mainly employee health benefits, nonproductive use of time, and layers of line management.

There is an element of truth in this explanation, but there are more fundamental factors at work as well.

First, the traditional hierarchy left many employees underutilized: working with their hands and not their heads. In the past this led to entrepreneurial spin-offs among aggressive and self-motivated people looking for improvement in conditions, and management tolerated this situation as a necessary byproduct of doing business. Today, competitive realities dictate that firms fully tap their resources. They can no longer afford poorly motivated employees. If this means yielding some managerial authority to employees and firing some middle managers in the process, it will be done.

Second, senior executives have been given a far broader reach inside their own firms. They no longer require the same degree of analysis of information and reporting by middle management as in the past. They can get much of the information they need for strategic and long-term decision making for themselves directly from computer data bases.

Third, operating decisions and analysis are now directly augmented and displaced by computer programs. Informal rules of thumb can be codified into programs that mimic human experts. Such systems can frequently generate solutions in situations in which routine decisions are required more quickly.

The net result of these three forces is a decrease in the demand for middle-management services and an altered role for those who remain.

What Does a Middle Manager Do?

The traditional answer to this question is fourfold. Middle managers report events to top management, direct employees in required tasks, analyze business problems and opportunities, and make local decisions within corporate policies or guidelines.

These functions have typically been exercised on nonroutine problems. Routine problems have been the responsibility of employees, using established procedures, and nonroutine ones have required managerial attention. When more nonroutine problems confront a firm, middle managers have more analysis, decision, direction, and reporting to do, and businesses find they need more of them.

This is what happened on a large scale during the 1970s. Rapid inflation, increased foreign competition, government deregulation, and other influences created an unusually hectic environment and nonroutine problems for middle managers in many businesses.

Each problem had to be taken through a process of structuring for companies to cope with it. I will describe this process with the assistance of a diagram, Figure 15, which places problems along a spectrum according to their degree of structure.

A structured problem is one that has been encountered so often its resolution is routine. An unstructured problem is something new for which a creative response must be found. Semistructured problems lie in between. The distinction is that unstructured problems need active managerial intervention, whereas structured problems allow employees or automated systems to respond with standard procedures.

As unstructured problems appear in the business environment, managers employ investigation, analysis, and trial and error to reach initial solutions. Then, as these problems reappear, managers learn which solutions are the most effective, and in this process, move the problem from right to left along the spectrum. Eventually, the most effective response becomes so routine that it passes into procedure for employees, or programming code for a computer, to follow. The organization can be said to have fully "structured" the problem.

In the past most of a firm's human organization handled routine procedures within fully structured processes. Middle managers largely engaged in supervising and reporting on these activities, thus putting the human balance firmly on the left side of the problem characteristic spectrum. This is what the blue-collar and clerical work forces of large U.S. firms are still doing. But the future will be different.

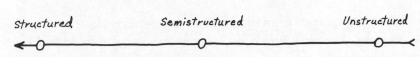

Figure 15 Problem Characteristic Spectrum

Automation Creates a Professionalized Work Force

Today, computers are handling many structured situations. Robots and other automated equipment perform routine tasks, from speaking phone numbers on telephone information lines to monitoring heart patients to painting automobiles. Many such mentally dulling activities can be performed more efficiently by machines operating on simple programs.

As automation increases, human activity in business is shifting from structured to unstructured problems—or from left to right on the spectrum in Figure 15. This automation process is well established in such capital-intensive manufacturing companies as Electrolux, General Dynamics, Whirlpool, Badger Meter, General Electric, Northrop, LTV, IBM, AT&T, Deere, and others. Just now starting in the service sector, it can be seen in some new companies that have taken advantage of the new technology.

Dent-a-Med, which offers the first credit card specifically designed for the health-care industry, is an example. Its card is available to persons who have been, for the most part, refused major credit cards (Visa, American Express, and MasterCard).

Dent-a-Med's profitability depends on minimizing losses, which requires careful evaluation of applicants' credit risk. Until recently, this required human analysis and intervention. Today, computers can use credit scoring systems to determine whether to advance credit in all but the most unusual situations. Dent-a-Med, which has assigned only a few employees to watch the system perform the routinized task of making credit decisions, devotes most personnel to marketing the product.

A field sales force does not require the same organization and skills as a central data-processing and screening operation. It needs people who can handle unstructured situations, take initiative, and work well without supervision. It does not need middle managers. It does require, however, good communications systems.

211

This development is of the utmost importance. Instead of doing routine tasks, like most employees, many encounter unstructured situations, whose resolution calls for initiative and imagination.

In the manufacturing sector, today's steel, oil refinery, and utility workers, for example, watch billions of dollars worth of machinery, which is fully capable of managing routine operations for itself through built-in monitoring devices. Employees have to intervene only in unusual circumstances. In such situations the traditional managerial functions of analysis, decision, direction, and reporting are performed by regular employees, aided by computers, not by managers.

An organization that moves its human center of gravity to solving unstructured problems faces different conditions than its predecessors. It does not need large numbers of supervisors and middle managers to maintain tight spans of control over its employees. It needs creative, thinking employees.

When clusters are not adopted and the organization remains a traditional hierarchy, problems develop. Excess supervisors and middle managers become an overhead burden. Or worse, they cause friction over work jurisdiction. There are three reasons for this.

First, the number of employees requiring supervision is sharply reduced by automation. Consider the example of the East Peoria, Illinois, transmission factory of Caterpillar, Inc. Caterpillar installed a computerized inventory control system that compressed the average time taken to run clutch housing parts through the plant from 20 days to 4 hours. By employing cellular manufacturing technology, Caterpillar reduced the staff required to machine, burr, balance, and wash these parts from 11 to 2, who now work as a team in a manufacturing cell of six machines. To maintain a full hierarchy where the work force had shrunk by 400 percent or more would lead to tight spans of control—perhaps one or two workers per supervisor.

Second, the skills required of production workers sharply increase with an automated process. Also, the additional productivity of capital equipment usually justifies cross-training, which often makes production employees just as literate and articulate as managers would be in a more traditional work environment.

Highly skilled employees are just as capable as supervisors at monitoring machines, reviewing manuals, making necessary nonstandard adjustments on a trial-and-error basis, and documenting activities for reporting to senior managers via on-line systems. Caterpillar explicitly recognized this capability by sending shop floor machinists to supplier plants to aid quality teams evaluating and certifying these operations. After all, it is the shop floor—not its manager—that has to work with what the quality teams bring back.

Third, solving unstructured problems in an automated environment requires flexibility and speed that a traditional hierarchy cannot deliver. Skilled operators receive most of the data they need to solve production problems directly from the equipment. It would cost hours of production time for the operators to write down problems, call their supervisors, describe the problem, wait for the answers, and then try the solutions. It is easier to delegate responsibility to those closest to the problem with the information to solve it, treat them like professionals, and pay them well for keeping up quality. These are the hallmarks of a "high-discretion" cluster organization.

The pressures placed on middle managers by this trend are illustrated by Carrier Corporation, a United Technologies subsidiary that builds heating and air-conditioning equipment in Syracuse, New York.

Under a compensation and employee involvement plan Carrier adopted, everyone from top to bottom in its plant gets the same percentage bonus, which generates a strong incentive to pull together to improve cost performance. To enhance communication, plant productivity information is posted daily on a bulletin board, and workers are encouraged to give plant managers ideas they have for improvement.

For example, when workers complained to a manager that five supervisors were too many for their shift and thus were reducing bonuses by pushing up costs, one supervisor was dismissed. "We seem to have created a shop floor full of managers now," said the manager. "Many first-line supervisors are afraid of losing control of the shop floor. The old-timers are saying, 'Give me back my baseball bat.'"

Expanding Senior Management's Reach

This book stresses the role of the cluster organization as an alternative to a traditional hierarchy. But the hierarchy as we know it is not unchanging.

Under the impact of improved information and communication technology, hierarchies are evolving toward greater and greater control from the top. To resist this trend, many firms try to decentralize, but the inherent tendencies toward central decision making in a hierarchy are frustrating these efforts. The fundamental fact of modern management is that the new communication technology, when applied in a hierarchy, draws senior managers ever more deeply into detailed running of the company. The only way to resist this evolution effectively is with radical delegation and decentralization—that is, with clusters.

Traditionally, top executives complained about rigid organizations and were frustrated by the time it took to get information from them. Reporting became a time-consuming function for middle managers.

Today, some corporate executives are much more able to be deeply involved in even a large business—an ability brought about by new information technology. One observer cites estimates that roughly 10 percent of top executives in the United States are hands-on computer users. The companies in which they work include Gillette, Polaroid, Xerox, Lockheed-Georgia, Pan Am, Kraft, Southwestern Bell, and ConAgra.

Powerful personal work stations, programs that convert tables of numbers into more usable graphs and charts, and the keyboard-bypassing "mouse" (which allows computer use without learning to type first) are combining to allow executives unparalleled access to operating data. As comfort with technology increases, many executives are cutting back the use of middle-management and corporate staff to analyze data for them.

Examples of how senior management can rely on computers rather than people to perform middle management tasks can be seen at Duracell, Mrs. Fields, Toys-R-Us, United Airlines, Acme Cleveland, and Benetton.

At Duracell

C. Robert Kidder, CEO at Duracell, used an information system to review productivity of Duracell's U.S. and overseas sales forces. Using the mouse attached to his work station, he told the machine to access records stored in the company computer and to assemble comparative performance data on his salaried work forces. These data indicated that the U.S. staff produced more sales per employee than did the European staff.

Kidder investigated further by calling up more numerical breakdowns to track down reasons for the difference. When he finished, he had determined that Duracell's German sales force was too large and that it was calling on too many small stores. As a result, Duracell reduced its German staff and signed on distributors to cover small stores instead.

The same information could have been produced from paper records, but the computer produced it faster, without sending memos or staff around asking questions that would create delays or trigger rumors about layoffs. "The system has been useful," says Kidder, "and we are a long way from getting the most out of it."

At Mrs. Fields

Run by Randy Fields and his wife, Debbi, this cookie company has nearly 500 stores in 37 states. Although it recently consolidated operations and broadened its product line to address bottom-line concerns, Mrs. Fields's management systems still represent a major innovation that are being marketed to other firms.

Mrs. Fields uses a computer network to perform analysis, decision, direction, and reporting functions usually assigned to middle managers. This system enables the Fieldses to retain control of their organization, while maintaining a structure that appears to be almost flat.

Each store is equipped with a personal computer connected to a central minicomputer at headquarters. Every day, store managers use their machines to call up the Day Planner program, which generates hourly production schedules for each product and which is designed to match cookie production to daily sales goals.

Day Planner uses various information sources in developing this schedule. First, daily sales projections are established, based on the previous year's sales plus an adjustment for growth. These projections are then adjusted to account for special factors (e.g., weekday or weekend, school day or holiday). In addition cash registers feed sales data to the computer so that it can monitor performance and make suggestions to the manager.

For example, the system checks customer count and average sales and tells the manager if either are down. If customer count is down, the system may suggest that the manager promote the product by giving out free samples. If the average sale is down but the customer count is within standards, the computer may question whether the employees are doing enough suggestive selling. Further, if for some reason sales continue to vary significantly from the daily estimate, the computer can alter the manager's schedule accordingly.

Headquarters stays in voice contact with the field through phone mail. Store managers call in several times a week to check their phone mail messages and often receive a message from Debbi Fields. Announcements made in her voice are much more personal than a memo, and they transfer information more quickly. Usually she shares news that she is excited about, but she also talks about her concerns. Further, managers can call her directly if they desire. She promises that either she or one of her staff will respond to their messages within 48 hours.

This kind of communication system speeds up the process and helps managers feel that they are important. The computer and communication systems work together to enable the Fieldses to control their company without franchising—an amazing feat for a company with nearly 500 stores.

With analysis, decision, direction, and reporting done by the computer, the store managers can focus on managing employees and serving the customer. Mrs. Fields pays people for what they do best and not for what a machine can do for them.

The subsequent result is a lean administrative staff, with just one staff member for every five stores. This is a great reduction over industry standards. By comparison, PepsiCo's chain of French bakery/sandwich shops, La Petite Boulangerie, had 53 headquarters staff people to administer the chain's 119 stores. After Randy Fields acquired this chain and finished restructuring it, he had reduced the headquarters staff from 53 to 3 people.

At Toys-R-Us

Applications of information technology are also being made in toy retailing. Rather than having a management team project demand, analyze results, and then make decisions about store inventory and product place-ments, Charles Lazarus, Toys-R-Us chairperson and founder, lets his computer system decide how much of each product to reorder.

Since 1978, Toys-R-Us has been an outstanding performer. Sales have grown at nearly 28 percent per year to an estimated $3.17 billion for fiscal year 1988, resulting in a record $200 million in earnings.

At Toys-R-Us, cash registers in each of 313 stores send sales data to a central computer, which totals, records, and reports daily figures for each item. It compares these figures to data for the previous day and year and the year to date. Then it automatically projects sales and orders the appropriate number of items according to its analysis.

The computer is able to spot "hot" items quickly and place orders immediately to keep stock on hand. Duties that were previously managerial responsibilities are now performed by the computer with greater speed and accuracy.

Although Lazarus has been skeptical at times, he has learned to trust the computer. He did not think that Cabbage Patch Kids would sell, but the computer quickly perceived the high demand and ordered accordingly. His computers also saved him from overstocking by anticipating the end of the Trivial Pursuit fad. A number of major retailers, such as Lord & Taylor and Wal-Mart, for example, use much the same techniques to keep close to the customer and maintain a lean administrative staff.

At United Airlines

A computer network that makes decisions about price, frequency of service, and capacity is the system United Airlines developed in response to competition from Midway Airlines. United wanted to compete with Midway, which was providing cheaper service out of Chicago, but did not want to lose its reputation as a full-service airline. It wished to continue to offer reserved seating and other full-service features on some flights, while selling discounted seats on others.

United responded to Midway's challenge with Friendship Service—cheaper, no-frills flights, on densely packed planes. United's computer network balances its need to compete with its desire to maintain its reputation as an upscale, full-service airline. With dozens of variables and flights to juggle simultaneously, a cadre of professional planners and their managers would be required to make such a system work without a computer. Indeed, it might even be impossible to operate. The machine, however, handles the challenge with ease.

At Acme-Cleveland

The National Acme unit of Acme-Cleveland Corporation, a maker of multiple spindle automatic screw machines, is experimenting with pushing profit-and-loss responsibility down to the lowest possible level. At its main plant National Acme initiated a pilot project in a 17-person department headed by a supervisor and a sales/service representative, each with a desk on the factory floor.

Under the new concept, customers communicate directly with the factory floor to order products and obtain status reports. In many firms customers deal with someone in a sales management role, who contacts the production-control department, which sends expediters to the floor to find out what is going on. At National Acme, the customer makes a direct call and may even talk to the supervisor, who is really the product manager. The end result is that fewer people, including managers, are needed.

At Benetton

This European garment maker discovered that a superior production facility is useless if distribution remains chaotic. Moving 50 million pieces of clothing worldwide in a year is a tremendous logistical burden. Benetton's difficulties are not unique; the garment industry is notoriously slow, and retailers seldom bother to reorder as they know deliveries will be backed up.

Benetton discovered that by creating an electronic loop linking sales agents, factory, and warehouse, it could shorten order processing. Today, if a salesperson at a Benetton shop notices that the store is short an item, he or she can call a Benetton sales agent, who enters the order on a personal computer, which sends it on to the mainframe in Italy. Since the item was originally created on a computer-aided design system, the mainframe has its measurements stored in digital code, which can be transmitted to a knitting machine in the factory.

The machine then knits the item and factory workers put it into a box, with the particular shop address noted in a bar code. The box moves on to Benetton's automated warehouse. (The firm maintains one warehouse for its 5,000 worldwide outlets. It cost $30 million and is run by eight people, moving 230,000 pieces of clothing a day by using computers and bar-code reading robots.) Including manufacturing time, Benetton can get an order to a shop in North America in four weeks—one week if the item is already in warehouse stock.

Factory workers who would otherwise move the garments, label the packages, clear the freight, and handle the flow of paper associated with distribution in a more traditional system are simply not needed. And the managers who would supervise, direct, and report on activities are not needed either—key employees and machines do the work themselves.

Faster Problem Resolution Through Expert Systems

As middle managers are being squeezed by both the expanding reach of senior executives and the growing professionalization of blue-collar workers, they are also seeing their jobs disappear into the computer. The process of converting unstructured situations to routine ones, which can be automated, is accelerating as more sophisticated computer programs are developed.

Today, computers can be programmed to make ever more complex decisions on steadily less solid information. Human judgment previously supplied by middle managers is being replaced by the judgment of expert systems—computer programs designed to replicate the thought processes of human experts more rapidly and completely.

Expert systems usually contain a series of "if/then" rules that when applied to a problem, move through a logical process to arrive at a reasonable solution. Although still largely in the development stage, they are currently operating effectively in a number of areas, including credit analysis, financial planning, and design of parts for military aircraft and computer circuits.

American Express finds that in the highly competitive credit industry, where companies attract customers by offering special services, expert systems are a valuable asset. One such service that American Express's customers are particularly fond of is credit cards without preset spending limits.

Although useful in attracting customers, this service presents a difficult administrative challenge because of the complex procedure that must be followed to determine whether a purchase should be approved. This procedure requires access to a network of 300 authorizers and up to 13 different data bases. The American Express system relies on a statistical model that determines whether the pending purchase is congruent with an individual's spending habits. Purchases that do not represent significant aberrations from the norm are approved automatically by the expert system, whereas decisions about purchases outside normal spending patterns are passed to administrative staff for further evaluation and subsequent approval or denial.

American Express estimates that the system increases the productivity of authorizers by 20 percent to 30 percent. More important are the savings produced by reducing fraud and unpaid charges. In the credit industry, where such losses are measured in hundreds of millions of dollars, reduction by even a fraction of a percent is significant.

Another application of expert systems is in financial planning. Developing a financial plan is a complex process in which the planner balances the unique characteristics of each client with a wide-ranging set of constraints, including tax and real estate laws, expected inflation and interest rates, insurance coverage, and previous investments. Programmers at Plan-Power have an expert system that replicates this process.

Currently, PlanPower recommends that financial planners use its system as a support rather than letting it perform the procedures alone. They explain that with the expert system as an aid, a moderately complex plan that would take 50 hours can now be completed in 10 to 15 hours, an improvement in efficiency of between 70 percent and 80 percent.

Northrop Corporation uses expert systems to increase productivity by reducing errors in process planning. Producing military aircraft such as the F-18A requires fabrication of more than 10,000 individual parts. Each part requires a process plan describing the steps and method of manufacturing.

Each plan requires eight to ten hours to complete, and if errors are not discovered until the plan is in the shop, required revisions may result in tool reworking, production delays, and even scrapped parts. Northrop's expert system reduces the time required to produce a process plan by several hours and helps uncover errors before the plans reach the shop floor.

Hewlett-Packard uses an expert system at its Lake Stevens facility in Washington State. The program looks over the designs submitted by engineers and recommends changes to improve assembly (e.g., replacing parts that require screws with parts that snap together). Over the past three years the process has cut failure rates for the facility by 84 percent and manufacturing time by 80 percent.

Expert systems are only one step beyond the traditional rigid computer program. Another step will be artificial intelligence (i.e., learning systems)—programs that reconfigure themselves as they are fed new information. The generations of programming are shown in Figure 16.

Figure 15 and Figure 16 are combined in Figure 17 to show how middle management is yielding to the computer. In Figure 17, problems from the environment enter the firm (and diagram) from the left and move to the right as they are solved. When novel situations arise, middle managers initially react to them. As situations are structured, however, automated systems take over.

Figure 18 and Figure 19 capture situational dynamics. The dotted lines, which run parallel to the diagonal line from Figure 17, reflect the impact of changing pressures in the environment. In Figure 18, the shift is to the left, indicating situations such as those in the 1970s, when environ-

Rigid Algorithms (circa 1960s)
- Apply only to fully structured problems
- Rigid and inflexible in application

Knowledge-based Systems (circa 1990s)
- Apply to semistructured and fully structured problems
- Relatively flexible in application

Artificial Intelligence Systems (circa 2010?)
- Apply to most management problems
- Fully flexible (can "learn" independently)

Figure 16   Generations of Computer Program Characteristics

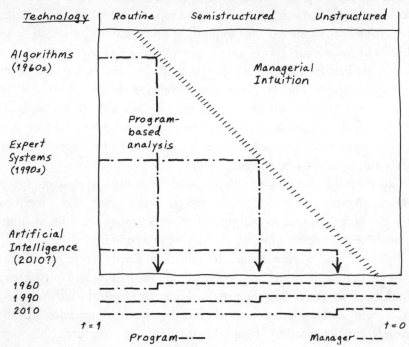

Figure 17   The Shrinking Role of Middle Managers

mental turbulence led to increased pressure for managers. In Figure 19 the shift is to the right, indicating situations much like those expected for the early 1990s: a reduced flow of problems.

These figures illustrate three points. First, as the bottom of Figure 17 suggests, as succeeding generations of programs emerge, they are permitting computers to be involved in resolving problems at earlier and earlier points in the process. This shortens the amount of time the problem is in managerial (i.e., human) hands and is progressively limiting the scope of middle-management activity to ever more unstructured situations. Second, even if the environment were to become turbulent (i.e., Figure 19), it is hard to see how managers could recapture much territory. The programs are improving so rapidly that they can handle increased turbulence without much additional human intervention. Third, if the environment were to

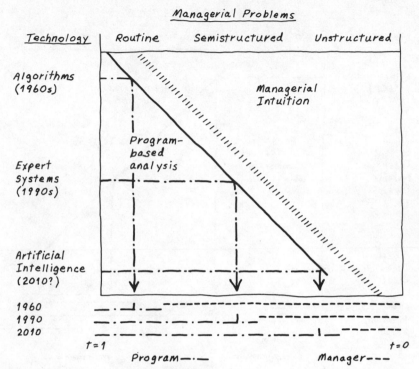

Figure 18   Increasing Environmental Pressures

become less turbulent (i.e., Figure 18), the process of substituting programs for managers would occur even more quickly. Fewer problems would require intervention to start with and more of them would move quickly into routines.

Responses to the Trends

The evolution of expert systems to aid decision making, the expanding reach of senior executives into data analysis, and a more professional work force are all nibbling away at middle-management territory by taking away the four basic functions of reporting, directing, analyzing, and decision making in larger companies. In effect middle managers are being pushed into new functions and duties, or out of larger companies altogether and

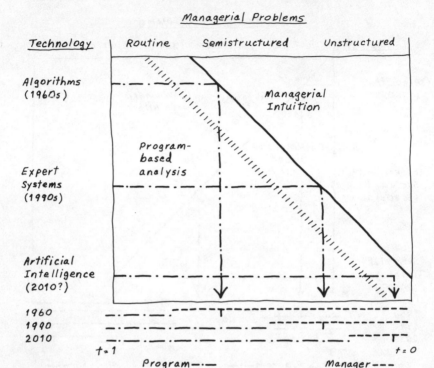

Figure 19 Decreasing Environmental Pressures

into smaller companies that are less technically advanced, where they can behave more like senior managers.

When the process by which a firm encounters and masters its environment is conceived in this manner, corporate executives can be seen to have something more important to do than simply cut middle-management fat. Instead, top management must monitor the relationship between firm and environment, whether or not there is an excess resource. When redundancy occurs, executives must make strategic decisions. Should they reduce the excess to save money, or should it be utilized in new corporate activities?

Firms have differed in their response to redundancy of middle management. Some have thinned the ranks. Xerox Corporation, by aiming at administrative and support functions, hopes to save as much as $600 million over the next several years through attrition and redeployment of workers whose jobs are being eliminated. As people costs are 60 percent to 80 percent of a typical overhead function, people are the first to go.

Other firms have used leverage created by computers to grow more rapidly or take on new businesses. Allen-Bradley installed computer-integrated-manufacturing (CIM) technology in its industrial computer business. As a result, the company reduced its direct labor costs by a factor of ten and cut its overhead costs in those factories in half. Implementation of CIM and proliferation of computers in the company—a process Allen-Bradley CEO Tracy O'Rourke calls "capitalizing the employees"—has allowed the firm to triple revenues while cutting employment from 15,000 people to 12,500.

Let me simplify a complex picture by dividing the spectrum of responses to the fundamental trends into two extremes. First, there are firms that under the pressure of increased competition have cut to take advantage of the new technology. Second, there are firms that have embraced the new technology completely, using it as a competitive weapon to grow quickly, with (what have been by previous standards) thin middle-management ranks.

In both instances middle management has declined, in the first case because of overt reductions, and in the second as a proportion of total company employment (measured by past standards). In neither instance does describing the process as one of shedding "fat" help our understanding of the more fundamental trends now underway.

Change Without Technology

It would be easy to conclude from preceding sections that technology is the only force squeezing middle management, helping the work force to professionalize, and aiding executives in managing data. This is not true. Some firms are making changes without altering technology. Such examples indicate that there is more than just technological development underpinning these trends; social forces are at work as well.

A company making mechanical, pneumatic, and electronic industrial equipment is Amot Controls. When Amot was taken over in 1983 by Steven Fox, it faced a poor labor-relations environment. The firm's major customers in the oil and gas sector had problems in the 1985–1986 price slump, and Fox had to persuade his staff to be more interested in their jobs and Amot's business if it was to survive.

Fox brought in a new manufacturing manager, Robert Miner, who shared his views on reducing the gap between labor and management. Miner was convinced that the division of labor embodied in many plants was antihuman, that to create a sense of involvement, people's jobs had to let them think, too.

Miner knew that modern manufacturing concepts such as just-in-time process flow had been proved in big facilities, with limited product lines and large production runs, but not in smaller plants like Amot's. Amot was a discrete manufacturer with short runs and many different products. When Miner tried to have outsiders advise him on how to involve workers in designing jobs and letting them make one piece of equipment at a time, they suggested it would be difficult to do so.

To prove them wrong took nine months of planning and work force training. The production teams Miner created ended up grouping existing lathes, drill presses, and other machines on the floor into cells, or clusters, as opposed to traditional long lines. In this way the whole production process could be seen at one time, bottlenecks would stand out clearly, and each worker could see his or her teammates so that a feeling of group responsibility for the product was created.

Another critical step was the visioning process. Team members worked out for themselves the best way to arrange the equipment. They talked about what things should look like, bouncing ideas around, until there was consensus.

Today, Amot's workers are organized around clusters of machines. Tools and stock move to the clusters and the workers both perform and manage work. The approach has generated improvements: Cells were shifted so that parts moving from production to assembly could be checked and rerouted back to the machinist if problems occurred, work tables were built that fit around equipment to prevent slippage, and new methods of changing setups were developed to reduce time requirements.

The payoffs have been dramatic. Production costs on one standard line have been cut 25 percent; it now takes only half the labor to produce one best-selling product as before. On-time deliveries of Amot's air-logic devices have increased from 60 percent to 98 percent. Throughput times on all product lines have been reduced: The time required to cast a fully machined part is now 1.5 days versus 22 days. One cast iron valve that needed 22 days for assembly can now be done in 7 minutes. Scrap has been cut 50 percent and inventory 10 percent.

Said an executive, "America has became notorious for the 'quick fix.' We Americans have become automation junkies. What we've done is taken nonsense and spent fortunes making it more efficient. In effect we make waste efficiently. We keep treating the symptom instead of finding the cause and fixing it at its source. . . ."

Amot is proving that technology in isolation is not responsible for the changing role of middle management, that gains can come from rearranging the power structure and hierarchy within a firm, even without new equipment. Others have noted similar gains.

One particularly interesting example involves a computer company that chose to achieve gains without new technology. The company is Entre Computers, where the operating manager of product logistics refused to spend additional money on equipment. Instead, he preferred to spread responsibility to lower levels in his organization and to provide extensive training, job rotation, and profit sharing. The result: Turnaround on orders declined from three or four days on the average to three to four hours.

The cluster form, and its delegation of authority to professionalized workers, is thus dependent not just on technology but also on new ways of thinking about what people ought to be allowed to do. These forces are currently expressing themselves in traditional organizations as a need for "employee involvement." As these ideas spread, middle-management roles are being altered and reduced. Technology will be a driving force, but not the only one.

A New Way of Managing

Under the impact of these forces, the role of middle managers is changing into something very different. In delayered organizations a few managers are responsible for legions of employees. No longer can those managers closely direct each person's work. Employees are either going to be directed tightly by computers or they must be largely left to direct themselves.

Today, middle managers are too few to stay on top of work in detailed fashion. Nor does the well-educated work force that many companies have require such close supervision. Where computer direction of employees is eschewed because of fears of excessive rigidity, the cluster offers an alternative role for those middle managers who remain. The new role of middle management involves consulting, persuading, and helping develop the competencies of employees whose own responsibilities have been radically upgraded.

Workers must be consulted because they know most about what is going on. This is easily recognized when one visualizes a group of employees in a traditional profession, but it also is increasingly true of what were once blue-collar and clerical staffs. In the age of automated work, employees generally are acquiring an element of professionalism.

When decisions have to be made about alternatives, middle managers still must choose, including the choice about whether to try to seek consensus on a course of action.

Managers must persuade. Only when today's professional and quasi-professional workers have the opportunity for input, and have the reasons for decisions explained to them, do they feel obliged to carry out a manager's choice diligently. Persuasion through consultation is key to motivation.

Managers must also coach and be concerned with the development of the cluster's individuals and with their smooth functioning as a team.

Because the cluster form embodies these changes in the role of middle managers, it is ideally suited to permit them to assume their new role successfully. The hierarchy, in contrast, continues to require middle managers to behave in the old fashion by expecting from them decisions that are in fact made by top management and programmed into computers, and by insisting that they direct the work force when they are themselves too few, and computers are increasingly doing the direction.

CHAPTER THIRTEEN

Breaking New Ground at Du Pont

The managers were gathered in a small group. Tension born of frustration roiled the atmosphere. For months, they had tried to change the way their unit operated. In the mind of each was a different vision of how they should do business. They were struggling to put aside the focus each tended to have on her and his own function and instead look to the success of the unit as a whole. But it was very difficult.

Despite their best intentions each seemed to slip into preoccupation with his or her own job. In some instances it was even unclear that the specific positions individuals filled were crucial to the organization. Those people began to fear for their jobs and to withdraw even further from cooperation with the others.

Finally, one manager, who had been many years in his position, voiced what was bedeviling each of them:

> I'm ready to give up my own job, if that's the only way we can make this work. I've got to have cooperation from the rest of you; I can't do my job without your help! But I don't think I'm getting it. I don't think any of us is getting support from the others. We're all in our own little pea patches. But I'm so fed up I'm willing to say let's get on with trying to build a team out of this place, even if it means my job is the first to go.

Andrew Harriss, manager of the Du Pont Fibers Department Information Systems (I/S) group, listened intently. Behind that outburst lay his own long desire to bring a different set of attitudes and a different way of working to his unit.

Harriss, a 27-year Du Pont veteran, became manager of the information services unit in 1984. His prior career had consisted of plant, planning, supervision, and management assignments—all in the Fibers Department and its plants. He had been involved with Fibers I/S since its conception in a 1978 study.

Harriss's unit was part of Du Pont's Fibers Department. This department contributed about 17 percent of Du Pont's annual sales of $30 billion and 30 percent of after-tax operating profits in 1987. (Du Pont as a whole has about 200 manufacturing plants and 140,000 employees.) Fibers I/S provided computer services to the department, supporting local computer installations and working with internal customers to analyze and fulfill management information system needs.

Du Pont's Traditional Culture

Although Fibers I/S was a relatively new unit, its initial culture sprang from long-standing company traditions and practices. Du Pont had had years of success after its entry into the textile fibers business. Patents gave it a monopoly on nylon and Orlon from about 1940 through the 1960s, and though competitors sought alternatives, they found few. With control in the founding family's hands and with patent insulation from market pressure, success became ingrained in the culture.

The firm, with a strong element of paternalism in its culture, maintained virtual lifetime employment for both regular and salaried employees. Although Du Pont released individuals for gross misconduct (e.g., deliberately causing industrial accidents), it was very difficult to terminate for lesser reasons. The preferred approach to performance-related issues was to transfer people from jobs where they performed poorly in the hope of finding a better fit for them elsewhere.

Paternalism was reinforced by compensation, promotion, and recruiting policy. Once an individual joined the Du Pont ''family,'' he or she was fully supported. Du Pont prided itself on giving generous fringe benefits.

The firm always tried to promote from within, confining its recruiting to young people from high schools, colleges, and military services. There were always steady jobs in a Du Pont plant town, and several members of a single family could frequently be found on the same site.

Plant cultures were firm on discipline. In some locations, production employees were not allowed to sit down during a shift for fear their attention would wander from their responsibilities and production would be halted or otherwise affected. There were also clear lines of authority and sharp delineation of status among plant managers, supervisors, professionals, clerical workers, and plant floor employees.

One effect of these practices was the building of strong networks among managers and staff. Du Ponters tended to move through the ranks together, utilizing a common network of contacts and associations first encountered at plant sites and then in corporate offices. People could date eras in their careers by referring to those who had been a boss or a boss's boss in the past. Often, key supervisors, tagged as fast trackers, would attract a following of subordinates who paced them as they rose in seniority.

Observers noted that promotion seemed to be a three-part process: one, doing the right work; two, being seen to do the right work; and three, getting these observations passed to the right people. Successes seemed to have many fathers but failures were orphans. On some occasions, doing the right work did not mean doing the work right. With transfers sometimes seen as a signal of concern over performance, people worked networks hard so that moves were always upward and perceived as promotions.

Pressures to Change

With patents on key products expiring and the marketing of new ones just getting underway, Du Pont experienced turmoil in the 1970s. The old formula for "spinning money" by running plants and making fibers stopped working.

Margins in chemicals and fibers businesses eroded rapidly as oil prices rose after the 1973 oil shock. Du Pont was caught between rising production costs and a slowing economy without patent protection.

These shocks led to a new cost discipline. The firm made layoffs in the name of improving efficiency—despite the "lifetime" employment practice. It hired contractors without Du Pont benefit packages for jobs deemed temporary. There was also a shift in attitude toward the use of internal services. Du Pont sent directives to plant managers giving them freedom to price services from outside contractors and to take the best terms offered.

Fibers I/S, 1984–1985

Harriss faced the same pressures as other Du Pont service groups. Customers seemed unhappy with quality, cost, and delivery times. Both focus groups and contacts, in effect, were saying, "Do it fast, do it cheap, and please make it work the first time."

Fibers I/S seemed to be lagging because its approach to customers was still rooted in tradition. The unit had been able to dictate to plants what they needed, when they could have it, and what they would pay for various projects. Pleasing users had traditionally been a secondary concern as department executives had paid the bills, not plant managers. Current reality, however, indicated that without willing customers budgets would be cut. Fibers I/S now had to convince its users that its services were worth having.

Rising concerns about cost, quality, and delivery times prompted Harriss to start a cost-cutting and service improvement effort during 1985. He felt that costs could be reduced by trimming overhead and improving productivity and that service could be improved by instilling new attitudes toward customers.

Defining quality was a key issue. Technical concerns like error-free programs, documentation, and user support were only part of the answer. Prompt service and cost management were also important. These were not so easy to measure as programming errors or satisfaction with user training programs.

Speeding service and holding down costs required Fibers I/S managers and staff to develop new customer relations skills. Technical programmers had to be able to work with users to define their needs without dictating answers.

This task was not easy as the user community was a diverse group. Some managers saw computers as instant answers to many problems—even ones in which more effective managerial judgment was the real solution. Others wanted nothing to do with computers at all.

Even those managers who understood both the usefulness and limits of computers frequently did not grasp the complex logistics of major software projects, and they often had artificially high expectations of what was available. Sometimes they demanded delivery in a short time period or requested functional flexibility that was difficult to provide at reasonable cost.

Recasting Fibers I/S

Harriss's new approach to customers was to recast Fibers I/S as a consulting service rather than as a group of staff experts. His concept went beyond Fibers Department customers. He also wanted to create an external customer base, which would help Fibers I/S in two ways: First, the group would gain credibility with senior Fibers Department executives by earning revenue—thus elevating Fibers I/S to operating plant status in the culture, albeit on a small scale; second, it would build credibility with internal customers, who could see other firms buying from Fibers I/S. To make this approach work, Harriss had to change his unit's operating culture.

Programmers and others would have to work with their customers before throwing technology at them. If these discussions were conducted in an atmosphere of mutual understanding, both delivery times and cost performance would improve. Thus programmers and engineers had to improve their understanding of customers' businesses and learn new communications skills.

Managers and supervisors also had to learn new habits. They had to recognize that programmer/consultants—not themselves—would have responsibility for customer contact on a daily basis. This meant giving autonomy to programmer teams, which did not need regular communications with supervisors to slow down customer service.

Another critical change lay in the composition of Fibers I/S staff and skills. To build up a consulting base, people who were trained in plant operations or business analysis were needed to work with technically oriented programmers. This meant a different recruiting focus and a greater emphasis on teamwork to merge technical and business analysis skills.

Harriss also believed that Fibers I/S would be better served if the number of supervisors were cut. First, resources would be freed to hire programmers and analysts or to cut price quotes. Second, supervisors would be pushed away from a close management style by a widening span of control. This would free the programmers to manage more of their own work and increase their involvement in it.

By increasing reliance on programmer teamwork, Harriss also sought to enhance productivity. In this he was echoing a broad change occurring in management information departments elsewhere in industry. With technology becoming more complex, it was more difficult for a single person to stay abreast of all developments in a multiple range of technologies. Thus the assignment of projects to single programmers was giving way to team assignments, so that insights could be developed and shared through interaction among professionals.

There was also a changing social context. Thus Harriss decided that a supervisor-driven style would be inappropriate for the Fibers I/S work force, but a style recognizing programmers' professional stature might well yield greater productivity.

However, Harriss was unwilling to loosen all bounds. To retain some direction, he altered key management roles. Supervisors became responsible for administrative functions of staffing, budgets, performance reviews, and team assignments. Team leaders picked from the staff managed technical issues inside the work teams.

Changing Direction at Fibers I/S, 1985–1986

During the 1985–1986 period, Harriss tried to make his vision work. He left supervisory slots empty to widen the managerial span of control. He held many meetings to get management to buy into the vision of Fibers I/S as a consultant. However, these internal efforts somehow never clicked; the old culture appeared to be too strong.

Harriss eventually reached a critical juncture. He could request staff transfers for managers to shake things up, and he was about to do so when Kris Yadav brought the Pecos River program to his attention.

A Du Pont industrial engineer, Yadav had worked with Harriss at Kingston, New York, and Charlotte, North Carolina, before joining Fibers I/S in Wilmington, Delaware, as manager of Human Resources in 1986. He had both a professional and personal interest in new approaches to learning and had come across Pecos through his external contacts.

The Pecos River Conference Center was located on a ranch outside Sante Fe, New Mexico. Its program was a combination of physical and mental exercises designed to open people up to new ideas, to put them in touch with their emotions, and to make them more trusting and supportive of each other. Its goal was encouraging people to put these new and more cooperative behaviors to work in team settings to solve problems and speed work flow.

Yadav came back very impressed by what he had seen. He had watched some cynical managers from another major U.S. corporation make significant strides toward openness and cooperation in their activities. He reasoned that this process might help Fibers I/S establish a more team-oriented and open environment along the lines that Harriss wanted.

After some persuasion, Harriss agreed to send some employees, including himself, to Pecos. His initial reluctance was reinforced by a negative signal he received when he floated the idea to senior Fibers Department managers. They were concerned about supporting what looked like a vacation for employees on company time.

Pecos's Major Impact

The initial Pecos session had a major impact on Fibers I/S managers. It revitalized their commitment to changing their business and led to a novel idea for structuring it in support of its new consulting mission.

During the session, the managers were challenged to develop a novel vision of their organization. They decided to propose a visual image of the unit. After long discussion, they agreed that the best image of the traditional hierarchical structure was of a large Plexiglas box with opaque dividers, many levels, and multicolored Ping Pong balls, which represented the organization's 500 workers. Each cell in the box was filled with balls of the same color.

The managers also agreed that there was a different and, in many ways, more important informal or quasi-formal structure. This they imagined as separate, small boxes of project teams. Each of these boxes was filled with balls of varied colors, representing the skill mixes necessary to meet customers' needs.

The teams were not necessarily ad hoc and of short duration. One, a computer support group, had been in existence for nine years. It was these teams that performed the significant work of the firm but were nowhere represented in its formal organization.

If the multidisciplinary teams performed the work of the business, the managers asked themselves, what purpose did the formal organization, with its distinct and single-colored cells, serve? Drawing on a simile taken from their years in secondary schools, the managers answered that each cell was like a home base to which a person reported each morning to have attendance taken before going to class—that is, to the teams where the work was done. Also, they said, having the formal structure, the home rooms if you will, made sure that no one was left out.

Who would be likely to be left out? Those who really did not have much to contribute was the answer. Why? Because they would not be missed in the project teams. Hence the formal organization made sure that they had somewhere to go and a place to sit while others did the work.

Was this necessary? Was it productive? Could the managers find a more productive and less frustrating way of working? The answer was a simple one, but like all simple ideas, difficult to see at first.

The management group attending the Pecos program had to create some form of team structure to house the professional staff and reorganize the other Fibers I/S managers around it. Programmers would do the work and the managers would be the supports.

Management Teams at Fibers I/S

Heartened by this new understanding, the management team returned to Wilmington. Several multidisciplinary groups were drawn from the senior managers to address the critical issues raised by the team-oriented structure. These issues would have previously been in Harriss's jurisdiction, but to reinforce the newly opened atmosphere, he turned to these larger collective groups, creating an "overlay" of teams on the existing managerial hierarchy.

Among the management teams were a customer team, a people team, and a technology team. These were ongoing efforts—not task forces—although it was unclear if they would continue with their original memberships after completing their initial missions. It was anticipated that additional relevant issues would surface from time to time and require the attention of one or more of these teams. A special management forum known as the core team was also created around Harriss and his immediate managerial reports as time passed.

Customer Team

The mission of the customer team was "to define and implement an optimal interface between the I/S organization and its customers that provides for the identification of needs and delivery of products and services . . . so that we can better respond to our customers' needs thereby contributing to the overall success of our customers' businesses."

The customer team proposed a business approach for Fibers I/S in which a new role—the customer account specialist (CAS)—played a central part. A CAS would be assigned to each customer to identify customer needs and propose initial solutions, coordinate Fibers I/S service efforts, monitor customer satisfaction, and gather intelligence from different customers so that Fibers I/S could anticipate and coordinate activities across customers.

Once a CAS solidified a request, a proposal development team (PDT) would be assembled "to collect and evaluate the requirements of a customer's tasks and develop an estimate for a delivery team." A PDT would be responsible for working with a CAS to ensure continuity between current and previous requests for the customer, preparing cost estimates (but not detailed studies), evaluating requests to see if better approaches were available, auditing proposals for accuracy as delivery teams completed development phases, maintaining competence with technology to identify "best" solutions, and making sure that customer proposals met overall business directions.

When a proposal was finalized, it would be passed to a delivery team (DT) for execution. These DTs were of three types, based on the requests Fibers I/S typically received: application development, service, and application support. Application development teams would do programming. Service teams would provide training and other assistance to customers. Application support teams would handle inquiries from customers needing to use the system. Development and service teams were to be project-oriented with a finite life span; members would be reassigned after the project ended. Support teams were "evergreen" and stayed in business as long as the system they supported.

The DTs were to be ultimately responsible to the management core team for meeting objectives. Support teams were to be reviewed at least semiannually for effectiveness. All DTs were to define their own ongoing membership as part of their self-managing responsibility.

People

The mission of the people team was to review the ways in which Fibers I/S would manage people. Its charter stated, "the People Team shall be responsible for creating a framework for managing the human resources in I/S. It shall provide the leadership for creating new processes and systems which will maximize individual contribution, growth, job satisfaction, and fun as stated in the I/S vision."

The team was working on four key issues: performance appraisal in a team setting, career planning based on individual desires, a transfer policy, and a new recognition and reward system that gave Fibers I/S staff more incentive to meet team goals.

The most important issue was incentives and recognition. Fibers I/S had to operate within a corporate pay system that recognized individual contributions—not those of the team—since the broader corporate culture was not as team-oriented as Fibers I/S.

The broader corporate system also had limited financial flexibility and reward assignment. Promotions were largely fixed by "time in grade" considerations, and financial rewards were tied to overall corporate levels. This system presented special challenges to the people team. Several of their attempts at change had died after failing an informal employee review.

Thus the team would have to redouble its efforts in view of these earlier setbacks.

Technology Team

The mission of the technology team was "to provide strategic leadership in the selection, assimilation, removal, and appropriate use of computing technology, in a way that: simplifies and accelerates application delivery; facilitates construction and enrichment of infrastructural assets; [and] enables the migration of application development to the customers."

Its responsibilities were divided into three interrelated segments: end-user application development, Fibers I/S application development, and underlying hardware infrastructure. The team was trying to develop a set of principles that would guide Fibers I/S and unify its approach to technology issues.

Core Team

Led by Harriss, the core team was an extension of line management, with responsibility for career management, technology decisions, and review of significant proposals. In a core team meeting, any manager could raise issues and Harriss was always prepared to listen. It welded Fibers I/S management into a collective by helping those who could not resolve issues among themselves to do so in a group context.

This team grew out of a special managerial forum established when Harriss initially cut back on the levels of management. The forum's purpose was to coordinate information and ensure that the remaining managers and supervisors saw Harriss regularly to maintain contact. Although Harriss had originally hoped to flatten the organization completely, some formal structure turned out to be necessary, and so the core team evolved.

In the beginning all supervisors and managers were invited to core meetings, but as Fibers I/S grew, that became unwieldy. The issue of who reported to whom also arose because managers and direct subordinates attended the same meeting. This resulted in a decision to restrict the meetings to Harriss and those who directly reported to him.

The supervisors responded by establishing their own forum. One of the core team managers always attended their meetings as well as the core team meeting to act as an conduit between the two groups. It was unclear if the core team would retain its shape or if it would assume more or less power as circumstances changed.

Spreading the Pecos Word

After the initial Pecos session, Harriss changed his mind about its effectiveness. He reasoned that if Pecos could have a positive effect on his management team, despite some stumbles along the way, it was bound to help the rest of the staff, too. He decided to gamble by sending all Fibers I/S staff to Pecos in three quick waves, before the managers above him in the chain of command raised too many objections.

Every employee who went seemed to remember a different aspect of the program. For some, it was physical experiences like the "trust" fall, in which a person fell off a low wall backward into the arms of teammates. For others, it was the indoor experiences like the listening exercises, in which attendees had to pick up enough information in a short period of time to tell someone's life story to the group or be embarrassed by having little to say.

Incidents of new attitudes at work began to surface for weeks and months after the staff groups returned from Pecos. A wooden sign appeared beside the coffee and candy machines with "Trust" written on it. Payments for coffee suddenly exceeded the cost of the coffee being used. Previously there had been a deficiency in the change pot and someone had to go around to collect money.

In retrospect, the need for a broad program became evident. Fibers I/S had a diverse work force. Young graduates in business administration and management information systems mixed with older employees who had considerable work experience and a strong focus on technical computer programming. White, male supervisors with military backgrounds and a technical focus on computer programming or systems engineering mixed with younger white males having nontechnical business backgrounds. Black, Hispanic, and Asian men and women with both technical and nontechnical backgrounds were a significant and growing segment of the employee population. Recent groups of recruits to Fibers I/S had been 60 percent to 70 percent female and 10 percent to 15 percent minority.

Deliberately limiting supervision of such a demographically diverse work force, without instilling a unifying common culture that stressed cooperation and trust at its base, seemed to be a receipt for anarchy to many, and they refused to give up their old managerial and supervisory styles as a result. The realization that culture concerns underlay the resistance to change led Harriss to undertake additional efforts.

Making the New Organization Work, 1986–1988

In the initial change process, Harriss had created a role known as the team leader—to work with the existing programmers, supervisors, and managers. As conceived, team leaders were not administrators but had responsibility for work leadership. This was a fine distinction that tended to blur in practice.

Harriss also installed a recruitment and career management program to speed the influx of new skills at Fibers I/S. This program drew heavily on Pecos and was used in part to establish the common work culture necessary to make the new organizational structure work more effectively.

Finally, Harriss looked for opportunities to try his ultimate organizational objective—converting work teams into self-supporting clusters by removing as much supervisory authority as possible and substituting a process he called ''team guidance'' in its place.

Complications Around the New Role

Fibers I/S was like other technical organizations in that it had two career ladders. One was administrative, leading through supervisory positions to senior Du Pont management. The other was technical, leading through specialist positions to senior consultant status.

Both roles were of tremendous value to a science-based organization like Du Pont. Some specialists needed to remain as such to ensure the maintenance of key skills. Others had to become administrators so that the "promote from within" personnel policy could be maintained.

Corporate compensation policy generated difficulties for Fibers I/S as it tried to maintain a balance between those on each ladder. Although both were well paid and promotion meant substantial jumps on either side, the administrative side had more attractive benefits and a higher ultimate end point in senior management.

Technical promotions were linked to time in grade and were contingent on good performance, but they could occur even if a person did not switch projects. Administrative promotions, however, depended on the availability of openings as well as performance and implied a need to change jobs. It was difficult to switch ladders once an individual had risen past a certain point on either side.

These factors implied a substantial risk in abandoning the technical side for administrative positions, particularly in Fibers I/S, where intermediate positions were limited by the flat organizational design. One could become a supervisor and remain there forever. On the other hand, remaining on the technical ladder meant completely giving up ambition for the ultimate pay, perks, and power attached to higher rungs in administration.

The situation was further complicated by the influx of staff with nontechnical backgrounds and a focus on business problem solving over technical programming. These people were naturally biased toward an administrative career—in Fibers I/S, at a Fibers plant, or elsewhere in Du Pont.

The team leader role, with its supervisory overtones but lack of formal authority, thus confused many when it was introduced. Some saw team leaders as supervisors although they were not responsible for performance appraisal or promotion and pay reviews, did not create or change assignments, and had limited disciplinary authority. These impressions became reinforced when team leaders were pushed by the wide span of control to provide input to key processes such as performance appraisal to support supervisors who could not get to know all of their people well enough to evaluate their work.

Others saw team leaders as being the coequals of their teammates. These employees felt that the team leaders should be doing detailed programming work, if only to keep their feet on the ground, even as they struggled to help others, answered client calls, and conducted team meetings. These impressions became reinforced when some employees, whose pay grade was lower than that of the more experienced programmers around them, were chosen as team leaders after limited exposure in the company.

One team leader articulated the actual job duties as follows:

1. System oversight (keep "big picture" in mind)
   - Keep systems up to date
   - Manage documentation
   - Control quality/cost
   - Ensure deadlines are met
   - Estimate and set priorities for work to be done
2. Team management
   - Motivate people
   - Help others with problems
   - Keep tabs on day-to-day team events
   - Plan team activities
   - Discover strengths and development needs of members
   - Do limited programming
3. Customer management
   - Communicate with system users as well as I/S management
   - Ensure that people are informed when things go wrong
4. Technology management
   - Ensure that systems are using best available equipment

Harriss was convinced that many of these concerns would work themselves out as people became more accustomed to the new approach and the actual job description for a team leader evolved. He had hoped to avoid defining it so that it would remain as flexible as possible. Not everyone agreed with this approach.

Recruiting and Managing Employees

All new professional employees after 1986 were made part of the *Active Career Exploration* (ACE) effort. The ACEs received career mentorship from James Fossler in Fibers I/S and development experience from their assignment supervisors. Each ACE was expected to complete three rotational assignments in the Fibers Department, including Fibers I/S and plant sites, and then to choose a permanent assignment with the help of those with whom he or she had worked.

The ACEs received a number of benefits, including automatic entry into a strong and growing network of present and former ACEs. Most ACE administration and social activities were coordinated by existing members of the program with the active support of Fossler and his human resources staff. The ACEs filled key slots in the Fibers I/S interviewing process and participated in special interviewer group meetings in which candidate qualifications were discussed.

The 1988 ACE group, which was roughly 15 percent minority and about 67 percent female, was working on a special job-posting scheme to aid in internal placement of members. This would act as an internal labor market, allowing managers in plants and other parts of Fibers to see the Du Pont experience and ratings of ACEs, and allowing ACEs to see available opportunities.

Some supervisors and team leaders in Fibers I/S were concerned about the effects of rotation, feeling they were being asked to invest heavily in socializing new employees only to have them leave after a year or so. On the other hand, they were very happy to get experienced ACEs from others. It appeared that compromises in the internal market were being worked out.

Transfers across departments and plants for more experienced Du Ponters were also handled differently. Harriss and other Fibers I/S managers began using their contacts to offer good people to different parts of the Fibers Department and the company. This was in sharp contrast to past practices. Fibers I/S people began turning up in Fibers Marketing, in other departmental I/S groups, in the Information Systems Department (a corporate Du Pont staff group equivalent in rank to the Fibers Department itself), and elsewhere in the company.

Another critical aspect of people management involved breaking barriers with respect to education in key positions. In several instances high school and two-year college graduates, with considerable on-the-job experience but a lack of formal credentials, were promoted around barriers in the compensation system by becoming consultants to Du Pont and then rejoining the regular payroll at higher levels.

Fibers I/S also strove to promote female programmers and analysts into team leader positions. Fibers I/S was roughly 50 percent female, versus a Du Pont average of about 31 percent, and had many more female leaders than most other Du Pont groups.

The Information Systems Department (ISD) also had a high proportion of female employees, but its female supervisors tended to leave after stints of three to five years as their life priorities shifted toward family concerns. Fibers I/S did not as yet have this issue to contend with, but it had set up a special part-time program, also modeled after an ISD effort, with improvements, which was just getting underway. This program was designed to address the issue of professionals who were becoming mothers by offering part-time and home working situations.

Each of these new policies was generating some concerns. Some opinions about the relative ranking of technical proficiency, experience, and sex in designating team leaders had surfaced. Although team leaders were not formally designated as supervisors and remained on the technical pay ladder, some felt Fibers I/S was moving too quickly in designating recent female recruits as team leaders.

It was unclear how much of this concern was actually related to technical shortcomings or lack of experience. It was clear, however, that some projects were falling behind and that some female team leaders were extremely effective in their positions.

Among the byproducts of ACE was an emerging network in which the members were fully integrated on the job and off. A concern among some more experienced people was that these ACEs, having never experienced the older Du Pont culture, would encounter adjustment difficulties as they moved into plant or other settings where the cultural values were different and where they were not seen as the "chosen few."

Team Guidance

As practiced at Fibers I/S, team guidance was a system of management that encouraged programmers who made up work teams to take responsibility and initiative for their work rather than to accept assignments and direction from supervisors. Where team guidance was operational, supervision was limited to managing team members as opposed to managing teams' work—recruiting them, assessing their progress against career objectives, and finding new assignments for them when projects ended.

This system was in contrast to the operating culture of Du Pont in general, which relied heavily on supervisors to generate initiatives and take responsibility for carrying them out, while employees carried out assignments under strict direction. It also went beyond the self-managing team concept as practiced in many companies, as supervisors had a limited say in how teams organized themselves to perform work and in how team members carried out much of the administrative detail themselves with help from formal planning materials.

Harriss believed this system would ultimately help the programmers be more productive by recognizing their professional stature and their desire to be involved in work planning and direction. He felt that as programmers were the closest of all staff to Fibers I/S customers, they had to be more involved for Fibers I/S to succeed in cost reduction and service improvement.

The team guidance system was slowly going into effect among programmer teams through 1988. Harriss and his supervisors were concerned that the initial adoption go smoothly, both to encourage the programmers with early success and to avoid difficulties that might jeopardize the process with senior executives and customers.

Changing the Physical Space

Late in 1986, Harriss saw an opportunity to reinforce the changes being made in his organization in an entirely unexpected way. Rapid growth in the Fibers Department spawned by the success of a new carpet fiber necessitated construction of new office space at Du Pont's Chestnut Run Plaza site. Fibers I/S was given the opportunity to design its own floor. (See Chapter Fifteen for a description of "caves and coves" and how the process of office design fed back into the culture change.)

Retrospective

Early in 1989, Harriss paused to reflect. The experience since the initial Pecos meetings had both encouraging and discouraging sides. The previous year had seen both substantial progress and some frustrating slowdowns.

On the negative side, the new Fibers I/S culture, with its emphasis on teams and cooperation, was interacting with the older, more traditional Du Pont culture around it with some unwelcome results. Confusion about the status of team leaders had been a particularly difficult issue. Those in client groups around the department were only slowly coming to understand who these individuals were and that they should place their trust in a team leader and team judgment instead of seeking out a formally designated supervisor.

Rapid growth in the Fibers I/S group had caused it to be split not only between the Charlotte and Wilmington sites but also within the Wilmington site. Some teams found themselves split between sites, while other teams found themselves isolated from the main group at customer sites. Closeness to Harriss, even in an environment of openness, still seemed to count for a great deal in the minds of the programmers. Harriss tried to set an example for his managers by getting out to meet all of the new employees as they went through the Pecos experience and by visiting as many of the isolated sites as possible. Unfortunately, not all the managers could follow suit.

Rapid growth also was accompanied by expansion of the supervisory ranks. Several of the more experienced team leaders had been elevated to full supervisor status, and this gave the management structure an appearance of turning back into a hierarchy, although the spans of control were still extremely wide.

Yet another sign of concern was the issue of an organization chart. Harriss had refused to issue or use a formal organization chart, reasoning that it would be a throwback to the old hierarchy and would send out the wrong signal. Some staffers had surreptitiously created their own chart so that they could locate each other and their bosses in the organization.

On the positive side, there was recognition that something different was happening in Fibers I/S. Some of the subjective measures of productivity and quality had started to improve. Client complaints about losing touch with the programmers were diminishing, although some projects did lag behind their projected completion dates.

The reactions of staff members to the culture change were generally positive. Said one team member of the changes, "I like the new system. We are all treated equally and operate as a group, even though there are differences of experience and training between us. We are all specialists, but still exchange data to get our system to work."

Said another,

Where else is someone out of school less than five years going to get a chance to have such an impact on a major corporate system? I am the only one in my team working on my piece of the project—if my piece won't fit, the whole thing won't work . . . and that is a lot of responsibility in a hurry.

But we need to do it this way. It's too expensive to have two or three people on each piece. We have to have idea-sharing meetings all the time and document what we are doing. Since documentation around here isn't always the best, those meetings are very important.

One team leader with considerable service was heard to remark,

It seems ironic, but the most junior people here may be the best at answering certain questions. After all they studied it last year . . . and I've been out for awhile—for 20 years in fact.

The ACEs know how things are done today. We have to respect that, even if some impractical ideas come out too. If I, as team leader, don't get them [new recruits] to share fully in our work—for whatever reason—the project suffers. One of them might save a customer thousands of dollars, but only if they are encouraged to open up.

The thing about Pecos I remember most was learning about the others who were there. It wasn't falling off the pole or riding the zip-line; it was meeting them and finding out what made them go.

Senior Fibers Department executives were asking Harriss why his group was suddenly so successful in recruiting and retaining minority and female employees. Those in Fibers I/S pointed out the Chestnut Run space, the team guidance system, and their new culture (backed up by Pecos and the ACE mechanism) as key reasons.

PART III

The Opportunity for People

CHAPTER FOURTEEN

Empower Me:
Catalysts for Clusters

Gaining full benefit from a cluster organization requires different attitudes and behavior than those that usually exist in a hierarchical organization. To break old patterns and instill new ones, many companies are turning to surprising and sometimes bizarre activities. These catalysts are intended to help people understand their roles and opportunities in the new organization.

Support Each Other

Andrew Harriss of Du Pont stood at the edge of a cliff staring into the emptiness below. A slender cable stretched from his perch 100 feet above the river to a goalpost on the flat earth ¼ mile away. He was strapped securely into a harness that was to carry him along the cable and across the river. In his mind he knew there was no danger. But still he had to jump off the cliff and fall for a while before the cable snapped up his harness and sped him down the line to the landing beyond.

The young man who had strapped Harriss into the harness said, "You've done this several times, so you know it's all right."

"I've done it eight times," Harriss answered, "once with every group of employees we've brought out here. But I never get over being scared to death when I look down at those rocks in the river below. I know it's not rational for me to keep being frightened, but people just weren't meant to jump off cliffs."

"Go on, Andy, you can do it," several employees from Du Pont called out. Each of them was going to make the same jump after him. Across the river at the goalpost, he could see a group of his associates who had preceded him on the cable. They were standing and yelling for him to come on.

Harriss hesitated only a moment more, then gritting his teeth, hurled himself over the cliff and into the open air. He fell breathlessly until he was jerked upright as the cable tightened and yanked on his harness. Now he was speeding down the cable, the wind blowing past his face, the river and the ground beyond rushing toward him. Suddenly, he was sliding into the goal. The cable ended and he hung suspended above the ground, swinging in his harness.

Hands reached up to pull him down and free him from the harness. A surge of exhilaration rushed through him. He had forced himself to do something once again despite his fears. He knew that he had to have support to do it. "I could never have jumped, not once, without those other people standing with me on the cliff and encouraging me," he admitted to himself. And he felt a surge of gratitude and warmth for his coworkers. "With people like this," he thought, "we can accomplish great things, both here and back at the business."

Mistakes Are Okay

Two rugs had been placed on the conference room floor. Underneath each was a simple electronic grid. In front of each rug a team of people was milling around. Each team was to find its way across the rug through a sort of maze created by the concealed grid. The exercise was nonverbal: Words could not be used as a means of communication among team members. One person at a time entered the maze from each team, and as he or she took steps on the rug, a buzzer would go off when feet strayed from the proper path. The purpose of the game was to get across the rug (i.e., through the maze) before the other team without setting off a buzzer.

Initially, a member of each team picked his or her way gingerly across the rug. When a buzzer sounded, the next person took over, trying carefully to remember the false step the previous person had made. Each person was trying carefully to plot his or her own path through the entire maze. Fearful of making an error and setting off the buzzer, each person proceeded with great care. It was a slow process.

Suddenly, a person on one team had an idea. Rather than only one person on the rug at a time, several went on, each following directly in the footsteps of the person ahead. Now there was no need for caution. When the leading person set off the buzzer, the one just behind simply stepped the other way. Nor was there now any need for delay. As soon as one person was buzzed out, another was there to go ahead. Quickly the team made its way across the mat and claimed its victory.

What was the secret of the winners' success? They had learned that it was okay to make mistakes. Initially, each person had tried to avoid an error. So they proceeded slowly, laboriously. But when they worked as a team, it no longer mattered whether one member succeeded, for if not, the next one would. Mistakes, rather than something to be avoided, were now seen as the very method by which the team made progress. Each person's misstep helped the team determine the correct path. And equally significantly, it no longer mattered which teammate crossed the mat correctly since that team was going to win whoever finally made the entire trip without error.

Is there a lesson here for the business world? Could it be that mistakes are okay, as long as others learn from and act on them? Could it be that rather than living in fear of the consequences of an error, time could be better spent in teamwork, where errors become an education?

Surely the answers to these questions are yes. Risk taking is necessary to innovation and successful change. But risk taking involves the chance of error. A strong organization learns to profit from errors; a weak one tries at all cost to avoid them.

Mistakes are not always okay, of course. Some are due to heedlessness or neglect and cannot be justified. In general, mistakes are okay when three conditions are met: first, that the mistake occurred on purpose in pursuit of the mission of the organization, that is, in trying to make the vision of the group a reality; second, that the person who made the mistake learned from it; and third, that the learning is shared so that the group as a whole learns from it.

Many errors meet the first standard—that is, people make them trying to bring about a vision. Somewhat fewer result in learning for the person who made the mistake. Fewer still result in learning for the organization. Not many firms provide an environment in which people are prepared to admit their errors to others and what they learned from them. But in a trusting atmosphere, this kind of sharing can occur, and it contributes to the growth and increasing competence of the firm.

Pull Together

Five teams stood at the ends of five ropes radiating from a center like spokes from a wheel. Each team was engaged in a tug of war with the others over a "pot of gold" situated in the center of the circle formed by the five ropes. The winning team would be the one that pulled the pot of gold from the circle in its direction. On a signal, each team pulled mightily, heaving against one another. Once the pot shifted slightly toward one team, but the others redoubled their efforts and the pot returned to the center. They struggled on and on, wearing themselves out but not budging the pot more than a little bit. Finally, all gave up in frustration. The lesson is clear: When people pull against one another, nothing happens. If they want to win they have to pull together.

Trust Others

What was John Temple doing on a wall about 6 feet above the ground? He was more likely to have been found in the large New York headquarters of the corporation of which he was president. Instead, he was in the desert looking uncertain and concerned.

Behind his back and below him were ten employees of his company. Some were smiling; some were serious; all, like Temple, seemed uncertain about what was about to happen.

The company had been having difficulties, and many of the people in the group blamed Temple. Although they liked him personally, they also resented him because of the company's situation. In fact several of the people who now stood in the group behind him had been suggesting quietly that he should resign from his position. Temple knew there was dissatisfaction but he was unsure who felt it most strongly.

Temple had been told that he was to let himself fall backward off the wall. If all went well, he would be caught by the people standing behind him. But would they catch him?

In his mind Temple could picture all too readily some people stepping aside here or letting their hands slip there, and himself crashing, apparently accidentally, to the ground. It was not an ordinary occurrence for a person to fall off a wall, and he was not embarrassed to be apprehensive. Still, he had to try to show courage. After all, he was a leader.

Some of the employees in the group behind him were unsure what would happen. They thought the president would not dare to fall, that he would find some excuse to step down from the wall. He was a person who seemed to have such difficulty making decisions that the whole company was now in trouble. They would be amazed if he could bring himself to decide to take the risk of falling off the wall.

Others in the group were more sympathetic. They believed that Temple was less to blame for the company's difficulties than circumstances. Still others thought Temple would summon sufficient courage to fall but wondered whether they and their colleagues would bother to catch him.

Finally, steeling himself against his fear, Temple leaned backward and fell suddenly off the wall. Below him, ten pairs of hands went up instinctively, clutched him as he fell, and gently lowered him to his feet.

Temple stood facing the people who had caught him. He smiled with gratitude. Then, with a sheepish grin, he said, "If I could trust you to catch me when I fell and could have been injured, then I ought to be able to trust you to run the business, shouldn't I?"

"Yes," one answered vehemently, and then all cheered.

Reach—Stretch Yourself

Susan Driscoll looked at the slender pole rising 20 feet above the ground. At its top was a small circular platform just big enough for her two feet. From a nearby tree, a trapeze bar was hanging.

"Just climb the pole," said a voice in her ear, and she looked with a doubtful expression at the person who had spoken. "It's no problem," the voice insisted; "there are rungs all the way up the pole."

And indeed there were. Susan could see them clearly. But she was unsure that she wanted to climb them. Again she looked suspiciously at the speaker. "What am I supposed to do up there?" she asked.

"I'll go up the tree," the speaker answered, "and swing the trapeze out to you. You reach out, grab it, and swing down."

"Oh," Driscoll said, not at all reassured.

Her companion read the doubt in her voice. "It's all right," he insisted. "I'll climb up the pole after you and put you in a harness. Even if you should fall off the pole, you won't go very far. And there's a net here, too," he said, pointing to a light netting that was spread beneath the pole about 5 feet above the ground. "If you fall, the net will catch you. So there's really no danger at all." Driscoll saw that considerable effort had been taken to ensure her safety, and she recognized that there was no physical danger. But her emotions disagreed.

Driscoll had run out of questions. She had also run out of time. In the distance she could see others of her team going through the exercise that followed this one. She was the last in her group, and she knew the others had been up the pole. Still she had trouble suppressing the fear that rose in her.

"I'm afraid of heights," she told herself. "Surely that's different from the others. It gives me a reason not to go up." But she knew it was no different and that she had to go. Otherwise she'd look like a coward, and that she wasn't prepared to accept no matter what she had to do.

As Driscoll began to climb the pole she noticed to her horror that it moved. No, not just moved: It swayed, it swung, it spun. "This darn thing isn't strong enough to support my weight," she said to herself and started to back down. But then she felt the pressure of a hand on her back. Turning to look, she saw her companion grinning at her discomfiture.

"The pole always does this," the man reassured her. "It's strong enough."

And so, with trembling, sweating hands, Driscoll pulled herself slowly up the pole until she stepped, cautious and frightened, onto the platform at the top. From below the perch on which she crouched her companion fitted her with a harness. Finished, the man said, "Now stand up while I go over to the tree."

Slowly Driscoll straightened up, trying to place even pressure from her feet on the platform so that it would not move at all. Finally, she was standing, balancing precariously like an acrobat on a wire high above the crowd in a circus tent. She refused to let herself look down.

She discovered that if she chose a leaf on the nearby tree to stare at and squeezed her knees together, the pole would stop shaking. Some friends at the bottom of the pole were calling encouragement to her.

From across the clearing she heard her companion's voice. "Here's the bar. I'm going to swing it over to you from the tree; you reach out and grab it." The man paused, took the bar in his hands, then pushed it away from the tree. "Here it comes," he called.

Driscoll saw the bar coming and began to reach for it. Suddenly, the whole pole moved. Frightened, she froze. The pole vibrated a bit, then returned to stability. The trapeze, however, had peaked in its flight and returned to the tree.

The man in the tree seemed not at all nonplussed as the bar swung back to him. He pushed it toward the pole again, calling, "Here it comes."

Bracing her feet, Driscoll reached a little further toward the approaching bar, but the pole swayed alarmingly and she pulled back.

"Here it comes," called the man in the tree as he pushed the bar again toward the pole.

Again Driscoll missed the bar as the pole swung. With each reach for the bar she went further and the pole twisted more violently. But slowly she was recognizing what she had to do. She had to stretch out for the bar without regard to her perch on the pole. Let the pole bend as it might, she had to reach.

On the next swing of the bar, Driscoll pushed off the pole with both feet and stretching her arms grabbed for the trapeze. The pole bent wildly

257

and sprung back to full height, swaying violently. No one atop the platform could have retained balance. But she was no longer on the platform. Instead, she was falling through open air reaching madly for the trapeze.

By the tips of her fingers she caught it. Hanging on for dear life, desperately trying to move her grip forward over the bar, she swung with the bar toward a safe landing at a shelf built onto the tree.

Caution had discouraged her from reaching for the bar. "Don't leave your perch," she had heard the voice of caution insist; "don't take the risk. Stay where there is something solid beneath you."

But she had overcome the pleas of caution. She had reached further than she had thought she dared—so far that she had abandoned her place of safety, and in grasping so far she had won the prize. She had been carried successfully to a new place.

"I had to reach," she told herself. "To do it, I really had to reach."

It's Harder to Lead Than to Follow

The seeing were to lead the blind. Half the group had been blindfolded. Then the whole group assembled in pairs, one person blindfolded and one seeing. They were in the desert amid rocks, gravel, cacti, and steep gullies. There was danger all about for anyone who made a misstep.

It was a simple exercise. Those who could see were to lead those who could not on a half-hour walk through the rough country. Each pair of participants was to work out a set of signals, without talking to one another, by which they would progress. Some worked out a sort of dance. Others had the blindfolded person simply place a hand on the seeing person's shoulder and follow in his or her steps. A variety of arrangements was established, reflecting the diversity of human personalities.

Then, each pair took off on the course in the desert. At the finish line, those who had been blindfolded were relaxed. It had been a slow and pleasant walk. But those who had been able to see were hot, sweating, and uncomfortable. What made them this way?

"I was worried," said one, "that the person behind me would fall and get hurt."

"I had to make sure I didn't go too fast for her," said another, indicating the blindfolded woman who had been his responsibility. "I had to be sure she could follow easily."

"You know," said a man removing his blindfold, "I never before realized how much easier it is to follow than to lead. The follower just relaxes and lets the leader take the responsibility for where the two are going. The leader has to worry all the time about whether the follower is going to be all right. I had always thought the opposite was the case: that it is easy to be a leader and that the followers do all the work."

"There's more than that," said another person. "If the leader wants to delegate to the follower so that the follower can make his or her own way, the leader has to make sure that the follower has eyes to see ahead, like enough information in a business to decide what ought to be done next."

Rely on the Team

"I was amazed the first time I saw the wall," Georgia Irons said.

> The darn thing was 12 feet high and 25 feet long. They told me I was going to go straight over it, but I didn't believe them. The wall was made of smooth boards, freshly painted, and there was only a wide, dusty, open area in front of it. I had no ladder, no stones, nothing to stand on. I reached up the wall and tried to find a handhold, but there was nothing on which I could get a grip. I decided I couldn't get over it, and I told them so.
>
> So they told me I could have a team of people to help me. I wanted a rope or steps or a pickax; instead they gave me several people. And then they told me that we had to get everyone over the wall, not just me.
>
> There we stood in front of the wall. Everyone looked at it, then at each other. How to get over? We were given three minutes to talk, plan, and create a strategy, and afterward were allowed only to cheer one another on.
>
> We decided we had no choice but to do it by hand. We were going to have to push someone up to the top, then he'd have to reach down and pull another up, until by a human chain we had everyone over the wall.
>
> One of the men in our group was big and heavy—probably 250 pounds. When we looked at him, we knew no one was going to be able to pull him up over the wall. Because we would have to push him, he had to be the first one up.

259

After lots of hesitation, we all took up positions in a little huddle at the base of the wall. We probably looked like a rugby team all ready for a game. Then the big man started to climb up our backs. How we bent under the strain. But we found that if he put his hands on two people and his feet on two others, each person could handle the load. So we built a human pyramid and he climbed it until he could reach the top of the boards.

We thought we had it made. We wanted him to pull himself up to the top of the wall, sit there, and pull us up one at a time after. But he wasn't strong enough to pull himself up. So we had to make our pyramid steeper and slowly push him up to where, by standing on our backs, he was higher than the top of the wall and could throw a leg over to get into a sitting position.

We discovered that despite the prohibition on talking about our strategy, we could communicate in many other ways. It was easy to push several other people up and over the wall, with most of us pushing from below and him pulling from the top. Then, we began to run out of people. For the last two people, we had to build a human chain from the top of the wall down because the big man on top wasn't strong enough to pull two up at one time. So we had all those bodies hanging down from the top to get enough arms to pull the last two people up.

But we got everyone over, and what excitement there was then. We felt like we'd done a magnificent thing. We learned that by relying on the team we could do what none of us could even begin to do alone.

Trust the Process

The physical activities of the two preceding days had given each person a different perspective, but it seemed impossible to translate the new awareness into a business context. Group after group reported being stuck and frustrated at their inability to reach an understanding of what ought to be done back at the office.

The small group of people responsible for the conference as a whole, along with two facilitators, met after everyone else had gone to dinner. A litany of complaints spilled out. Nothing was going right. Nothing was being accomplished. The company had wasted its money coming here. Those who were responsible for putting this together were going to be in real trouble.

The group talked for a long time about what to do next. But despite many plans, several people seemed to have become despondent about anything being accomplished.

Finally, one of the facilitators spoke:

I've worked with groups like this for many years. I've seen many just where this one is. Nothing seems to be going right. We can see what ought to be done, but just can't find the way to do it. Because of the catalyst exercises, each of us now knows how it feels to trust others, to reach, to support each other. But we can't translate those attitudes into the business. Some people despair that anything good will come out of all this effort.

He paused, letting his words sink in. Then he continued. "But it's always like this. There has to be strain, frustration, pain, for us to break out of old ways of doing things."

"Trust the process," he urged. "Somehow, at some point, something will occur that breaks it open and the new ways come pouring in. I don't know when and I don't know how. But it always happens."

People looked at him suspiciously. They wanted to believe what he said, but didn't. "Always?" one asked. "Always happens?"

The facilitator shrugged. "Almost always," he conceded.

From the expressions on many faces he knew that they thought this was one of the exceptional times when things just weren't going to work out well.

He saw their disbelief and said again, simply, "Trust the process."

Metaphoric Learning

Think about this:

- Support each other.
- Mistakes are okay.
- Pull together.
- Trust others.
- Reach—stretch yourself.
- It is harder to lead than to follow.
- Rely on the team.

261

These are powerful lessons for a group of people who are trying to run a business. Instead of supporting one another, many people try to climb to their own success over the fallen bodies of their comrades. Instead of taking risks, many people try to avoid mistakes at all costs, fearing that any error will cost them dearly in promotions, pay increases, or even employment itself. Instead of working with others, many people wage a continual battle among departments, functions, and individuals. Instead of reaching for success, many attempt to do as little as possible, always protecting themselves from any risk of failure. Many people spend their energy thinking how much better things would be if they ran the business rather than its executives—forgetting that it is much easier to follow than to lead. Finally, many people shy away from challenges, not realizing the potential for success that is created when individuals work as a group.

Often a business finds it is in trouble because of these kinds of attitudes and behaviors. When the business is having difficulties and those in it want to do things differently, take more risks, and be more aggressive, the lessons just discussed are exactly what people need.

But lessons learned in catalyst exercises, no matter how pertinent, may not transfer directly to business. People may recognize the importance of trust but be unable to trust others in the work environment. They may see how important teamwork can be but be unwilling to give that much of themselves at the office. Or they may recognize the importance of all these lessons, and want to apply them at work, but be unable to do so.

Why might people who want to behave differently at work not be able to do so? First, the desire may be only shallow. After all, the workplace is far different from a conference center or an exercise field. Different incentives apply. The desire to overcome a challenge in the exercise environment may not carry over into the office.

Second, other people at the office may not have been through the same exercises or may not have absorbed the same lessons, and so they find the new attitudes and behavior of those who have, strange. Those who are not part of the new attitudes may actively obstruct the efforts of those who are. They may be suspicious of the transformation some have gone through or threatened by it.

Finally, the circumstances of the office may inhibit the extension of the new lessons. People who want to work as a team may not encounter one another. People who feel they should take risks may find themselves in a performance appraisal system that penalizes failures, without making allowances for the risks involved and the potential that had existed.

In general, transferring the lessons of exercises to business can be very difficult. As a result, it is often useful to think of a form of half-life for an attitude change. Every four weeks, half the new spirit gained in the exercises is lost, until after a few months virtually all is gone.

Moreover, things may be worse than before the effort to change. Matters may have deteriorated as a result of the process. People who have experienced the lessons and then been unable to apply them successfully at work may be frustrated and resentful. ''What has happened to the spirit of the conference center?'' they ask each other with anger.

The exercises are not business itself, of course. They are metaphors for business. Experiential learning is metaphoric learning, and it will not transfer without careful attention to the process of transfer. This is a crucial point.

Experiential learning is a marvelous catalyst for changing the attitudes and behavior of people in the workplace, but it is only a catalyst. It can only be used successfully when the ingredients are there to permit the desired reactions to occur in the office itself. Because Andrew Harriss recognized this fact and used experiential learning to help make the transition to the cluster organization, he derived benefit from the investment his company made in extrabusiness activities. Without the structural changes that the clusters embodied, the people in Harriss's unit would have been unable to apply much of their learning, and the experiential learning would have been wasted.

Harriss was looking for a way to create excitement around new ideas. He used the outdoor activities to break through old patterns of behavior. He and his managers at one point presented to others in his unit a skit in which he dramatized both the old managerial system and the new. His purpose was to develop a small core group of committed people, who could then serve as leaven in the organization in order to achieve change.

Radical Transformation

Establishing clusters requires significant alteration in an organization, and therefore requires a change process. Change is made difficult by inertia, by fear of the unknown, by attempts to protect established positions of privilege, and by lack of knowledge of how to behave in the new situation. Hence it is not enough simply to have a plan for a transition to clusters. The process of getting there also requires considerable attention.

In general people advance two sorts of objections to a radical transformation. First, they may say, "We're already doing that. We've been more open in our decision making; we're delegating more to people, and we're delayering. There's nothing more to do."

But this response is like that of a person who has lost a lot of weight and insists on wearing his or her old, ill-fitting clothing. There is much more to do before the full advantages of the organization of the future are realized.

Another objection is that in a cluster no one is in charge. A group without an internal hierarchy speaks to some of anarchy. It is like a scout troop without a leader.

"We're from too many different backgrounds," it is often argued, "and too many varying cultures. We have to have someone in charge."

These are powerful objections, less significant in logic than in the emotional commitment to the status quo that so often accompanies them. Logic alone cannot carry a radical transformation. Persuasion on the right side of the brain is also required.

Catalysts help break resistance to change, and they help create an environment in which change can occur.

What do catalysts accomplish?

- They provide a forum in which opposing views can be put on the table so that the change process is in the open rather than concealed and undermined.
- They provide a mechanism for letting go. This is most important because many people hold tenaciously to the illusion of command and control.
- They begin to build a basis of trust among people in which there can be honest communication. Most people can't work together as teams because of suppressed resentments that have their foundation in past misunderstandings or unresolved conflicts. Unless these barriers can be overcome, there can't really be cooperation. Honest

communications among people are less important when people work on their own, but in the cluster format communications are crucial.

How Do Catalysts Work?

In reality, of course, managers in a hierarchy can influence the behavior of employees only to a limited degree. Often, little can be achieved beyond minimal performance by hierarchical and directive approaches. Nonetheless, many managers believe that without control the business would slip through their fingers into chaos. And some employees find comfort in the thought that someone else is in charge.

Hence, letting go of the notion of control is a prerequisite to experimenting with clusters. This key to empowerment liberates employees to go beyond what they are told to do, and it frees managers to do more important things than closely supervise others.

Catalysts help people to let go of the old order and to understand that the new cannot be built without relinquishing the old.

Catalysts work by

- Creating an environment in which change can take place by making it okay to question how things are customarily being done
- Building a climate of encouragement and support so that teamwork—which is key to clusters—can develop
- Providing an opportunity to experiment with trust and self-disclosure in a group
- Being a forum for personal growth and change in which individuals can try out new attitudes and practice new behaviors
- Allowing opportunities to learn from others
- Taking the change process out of the solely analytic, rational, and linear and permitting instead a left-brain approach.

Simply thinking about moving to clusters is not enough to help attitudes and behavior change, so an effective catalyst involves emotions and lets people feel what the changes mean. This is a crucial element in the radical transformation of a company.

Alternative Catalysts

Physical activities are not the only type of catalyst, but they are important. Their method is to put people in situations that minimize positional power such as that encountered in hierarchies. In such exercises people can actually watch leadership rotate from those with titles to others who are more competent at the assigned tasks. For example, it is rarely the boss who comes up with the solution for how to get a group of people over the wall.

Further, physical activities put people in touch with fear and, when it is overcome, help to make it easier to overcome the fear associated with a new organization at work. Learning from the activities facilitates understanding in how to let go of control and to work in a freer organization.

In addition to physical activities, there are simulations and classroom-type exercises. To many people, simulations are less threatening than physical activities and often have a broader scope of acceptance. Also, simulations are less language-dependent and are therefore especially valuable with groups of many nationalities.

Case studies, such as those included in this book, help by showing what others have done and how they have solved problems.

Bonding exercises use self-disclosure to bring more of the whole person to the work group, thereby building trust.

Visioning exercises, which I will describe shortly, go beyond the purely rational, but without the sometimes perceived limitations of physical activities.

These various alternative catalysts stress different forms of communication. If the medium is the message, employing only words to help people understand clusters is to suggest that the process can occur only in one's head. To go beyond words, facilitators can turn to videos (including those of physical exercises to let people see themselves), music, skits, and so forth.

But Is It Brainwashing?

Many types of learning are offered to companies with the ostensible purpose of serving as catalysts to improve the attitudes and behavior of employees. Some are much more extreme than others. Many described in this chapter are relatively conservative, derived from military survival exercises, and stress the emotional uplift that comes from overcoming fears in oneself. Other processes involve substantial philosophical and even religious elements.

Most physical activities utilize several powerful psychological tools to assist in breaking through to a new set of attitudes for participants. Among these tools are

- Disorientation—taking people away from familiar surroundings and supports (including family and, for executives, their secretaries and other staff)
- Egalitarianism—removing the comfortable lifestyle many people now have and replacing it with more spartan circumstances in which people are grouped together and suffer minor deprivations
- Heavy workload (i.e., lots of planned activities)
- High emotional intensity
- Pressure, especially from peers, on the individual to perform
- Unfamiliar challenges

Emotional tension and pressure are necessary to get people to give the exercises a chance. If people were simply asked, "Do you want to go out in the woods and jump off cliffs?" or "Wouldn't you like to stand on a 20-foot pole and grab a trapeze?" many would say no.

Time and again I have watched people come to the end of these programs with a conviction that they have really gained something significant. However, there is also resistance to such learning. There are stories that in some business programs people have been injured and others killed (though I know of no specific cases). There are also tales of brainwashing and of exercises that violate some persons' moral convictions. According to the *Wall Street Journal*, some of the more bizarre of these programs have led to lawsuits against the companies that sponsored them. Clearly objections are primarily to physical activities and less so or not at all to simulations and case studies.

Most companies that sponsor metaphoric learning say they do not require their employees to attend. But participants say there is tremendous pressure to participate. If employees refuse, they may be left out of something that is important to the business and their careers may be

267

adversely affected. If people attend the program, they may often find themselves under great pressure from others to participate in whatever occurs. Thus they may be carried along by hierarchical or peer pressure, only to regret it later.

One of the reasons for resistance to these programs is that they have been confused with encounter groups, which have developed a bad reputation. Encounter groups generally operate from the presumption that a better bond can be created among individuals only by first having them be honest with each other about their feelings, including those that are negative. In effect, relationships are first broken down so that they may later be built up.

I have heard managers vigorously condemn these sorts of programs. "We just went through a program like that [i.e., encounter groups]," one told me, "and now half of us hate the other half." Another added, "I don't think I'll ever get some people in my unit to work together again."

Although encounter groups are sometimes used as catalysts in business transformations, many physical learning exercises are quite different. Experiential learning is positive from the start. People are confronted with physical challenges but are encouraged to believe that they can overcome them, and when they do, are praised for it. There is none of the negativism that initially accompanies an encounter group approach.

Strategic Visioning as a Catalyst

Experiential activities are not the only catalysts available to organizations that are attempting to develop new attitudes better suited to cluster organizations. An effective alternative has been developed that utilizes a visioning process supplemented by visual representations. Visioning may be used in conjunction with experiential learning, of course, but there are those who prefer visioning as an alternative.

"Visioning is a more powerful process," one consultant told me, "and you don't have to jump off cliffs."

As practiced at the Pecos Learning Center, the essence of the visioning process is to help people think about their business in a new way. From the new modes of thought come ideas about how to serve customers better, how to cut costs, and how to organize and work together more effectively.

"What's a car?" This is the kind of question with which a facilitator might start a process for a group from an automobile company.

"It's a method of transportation," someone in the company might answer.

"What else?" the facilitator asks. "How does the customer see it?"

"It's a lifestyle," offers another. "And there are many types of lifestyles, each of which needs a different kind of vehicle."

"It's a form of self-expression," adds another. "The car a person drives is a personal statement about the kind of person she or he is."

The group explores the concepts of lifestyle and self-expression as they apply to automobiles. What would it mean to how cars are designed, marketed, serviced? Insights develop.

Then the facilitator asks for yet another shift in how the group is thinking. This time ideas that appeal to the group are slower in coming, but finally a member observes,

> You know, if you think about how cars are used in our cities at rush hours, you get a different picture. They're in the middle of traffic jams. In the summer it's hot outside, noisy, smelly from exhaust fumes. Drivers are frustrated and angry at traffic jams. They're yelling and making obscene gestures toward each other. In that setting the car isn't so much a form of self-expression as it is a refuge. It's an island of contentment in a world of confusion. It's my own space where I can be myself and get away from all the bums outside. In summer it's air-conditioned and cool. In winter it's heated and warm. Its seats are comfortable and just fit me. The steering wheel is right where it suits me. The radio or tape deck plays the music I like. It's my place of escape from the hassles of the world. It's my sanctuary.

"That's really good," the facilitator says. Encouraging others to pick up on the idea, she asks them to think through its implications. How should the company design a sanctuary? How market it?.

Ideas pour out and are captured on flip charts or writing boards. The implications of novel ways of thinking about the product emerge. Slowly a plan takes form—often one that is radically different from the company's present mode of operation.

"Now what will keep us from getting to our new vision of the company?" the facilitator asks. "What are the dragons we'll have to slay?"

Answers pour from the group: This procedure and that structure—but also more than procedures and structures, for behind them lie the thought processes that put them there. Can we change the way we think?

"What do we have to do to let go of ourselves?" the facilitator asks.

As insights come from the group, everything seems clear. People are swept up in exhilaration at the freedom that lies before them. Everything seems possible at this moment.

"But what about tomorrow morning?" queries the facilitator. "Will the high last? Will it seem as clear and attainable then as it does now? Will we retain the vision?"

The group has to capture its vision. First, they put it into words. "We need a statement of what we want to be," the facilitator says. "It's got to be short and clear, and no jargon. It's not to be a page from the company's strategic plan. It should stress fundamentals. If we do these things right, then we'll be a business success."

Around and around go the thoughts. Short sentences are amended and become longer sentences. When they become too long, they are junked and the group starts anew.

"We want our vision to coincide with what the customer wants," suggests one group member. "The customer wants something that's not a hassle to obtain and that's fun to have."

"Easy to purchase and a joy to have," proposes another group member.

"You know," adds another, "if we really did that—made it easy for the customer to buy our product and made sure it was a joy for him or her to own—then we'd be a success."

"Only if we kept our costs in line," said another.

"That's right. There are lots of things that have to be done to make a business a success," commented the facilitator, "but keeping the customer first is probably number one. So we've made a good start. What else belongs?"

So it goes. An iterative, imaginative group process in which people grasp new ways of thinking about their business and their own role in it.

A vision statement is now on paper. Can it be rendered into graphic form? That is the specialty of a few talented artists who listen carefully to such discussions and portray them visually in full color. When converted to posters and circulated in the office, these pictures remind people of their vision and help keep it foremost in their minds even during the distractions of the day-to-day business environment.

Changing a Culture

The vision is complete. New attitudes and behaviors are promised by each member of the group to their coworkers. But not everyone in the company has been in the process. Can the culture of the whole company be changed? What are the catalysts to bring that about? Will it not be much harder actually to implement a new vision than it was to develop it?

Probably it will. An executive of a major pharmaceutical company told me,

> We had demoralization and absenteeism in one of our departments. We got the key people together and worked out a new vision of what the department ought to be. Then, we began to try to implement it.
>
> We beefed up the personnel function and proceeded to hire people very carefully. We screened them for work attitudes and previous behavior as well as work skills. We selected only those with outstanding dependability. On average in their previous jobs, they had attendance records far superior to those in the department they were joining.
>
> After six months we checked the attendance records of the department and the new people. We expected to find a marked improvement in the department's average absenteeism. But we were shocked to find no improvement at all. Worse, the new people we had so carefully screened before hiring, showed attendance records no better than that of the department as a whole.
>
> Rather than the new people improving the department, the department had worsened the new people. The new people hadn't changed the department. The new ones had been changed by the people already there. The new people conformed to their environments.
>
> I've never seen so strong a demonstration of the power of an established culture in an organization.

In an exactly similar way a few people coming back to an established organization with a vision and new attitudes are caught up in the old ways. And new people brought in from the outside are captured by the natives.

The traditional pattern of attitudes and behaviors in a human organization such as a business is a powerful force. Trying to get people to adapt to a new pattern, such as that which clusters require, is not at all easy. This is why many companies use catalysts such as those I have described in this chapter.

A firm can move to clusters through a communications effort only (i.e., telling people what is coming). But it can get there more quickly and securely with a program that serves as a catalyst to get supporting attitudes and behaviors in place quickly.

Using a catalyst to smooth the transition to a cluster organization can be helpful in overcoming the old system. But it is best if the catalyst is not so extreme in its philosophy that it alienates people. Also, while participation should be voluntary, it can nevertheless be encouraged. The important thing is to try to get a proper balance.

CHAPTER FIFTEEN

Caves and Coves:
Physical Space for Clusters

Clusters make different use of office space than do hierarchies. Needed are places for meetings; space for encounters and imagination; work areas organized for interchange, instead of separate cubicles in which people work in isolation. Furniture should encourage interaction. Even the architecture of a building should be different. Consider the following example.

A group of top executives from a large firm had met for several days away from the company's home office to discuss how to revitalize the business. The meeting was necessary because the firm was encountering substantial competition. For several years its rivals had introduced new concepts in the marketplace and had added new capacity at a far faster rate. Now the cumulative impact of its competitors' growth and its own stagnation was beginning to be felt in falling earnings. The board of directors was concerned.

So the executive team had developed a series of steps to put new life into the business. At the core of their plans were greater innovation, risk taking, and responsiveness to the marketplace. To accomplish this, red tape that had grown up in the company over decades was to be eliminated. Cooperation was to replace rivalry and nonresponsiveness among the many functions in the organization. Proposals for closer cooperation among the company's units were made and accepted. But could the good intentions be implemented?

"You know," remarked one executive as the meeting drew to a close, "I think we all want to work more closely together, but I think that corporate headquarters itself is one of the worst problems we have."

Seeing confusion on the faces of his colleagues he quickly explained:

I mean, our physical setup. We're all on different floors separated by elevator banks. I don't see most of you for days, except when we have a meeting. And I know my people often don't see their counterparts in many of your organizations at all. People don't even run into people from elsewhere in the company during breaks, because we each have canteens on our floors. I don't want to be a spoilsport, but I think we're going to have real trouble making all this cross-functional cooperation work the way our space is currently laid out.

As he spoke, the executive saw that confusion had been quickly replaced by agreement on the faces of most of his associates. Everyone seemed to recognize that being separated into little islands was a problem.

Commented another manager,

That's not all; I recognize that my people don't interact enough with people from other functions. But frankly, they don't interact enough among themselves. I mean, look at the way our own floor is laid out. You walk onto my floor and all you see are little cubicles. We use a space-facility system that lets us fill big, open spaces with hundreds of small work stations. The system has dividers or partitions that go up to a person's height, and inside the little cubicles our people do their work. The supervisors have permanent offices around the central core of the building—the shaft where the elevators, utility connections, and rest rooms are. It's been a good efficient layout as long as everybody worked essentially alone. But now we're trying to get people to work more as teams. Our business is so much more complicated that a person has to consult with specialists to get things done right. But our space doesn't give us any way to do that.

The only people in my area who have spaces large enough in which to meet with others are the managers, and those spaces are their own offices. I think we have one conference room on the whole floor. And the space itself, with all its high barriers and little broken up cubicles seems to shout, "Stand apart, work alone, keep to yourself."

The system we have is flexible, I guess. I can move the partitions about, and even lower their height a bit, but it's still all right angles and little cubicles. There's still no way for people to work together easily. We are telling people to work together but we don't give them the facilities and the space to make it possible.

The pause that followed this executive's comments was broken by the interjection of yet another executive's opinion.

"There's more," she said. "Our current work stations don't give us the space to install the wiring necessary for the new terminals, modems, and other equipment we need. The desk surfaces aren't always big enough to hold the new equipment, and even when there is enough room on top, there simply isn't any good way to do the wiring underneath."

A Strategic Role for Facilities Managers

Those responsible for the physical facilities of business firms are struggling today to understand how to accommodate the changing organization. For several decades, the design of office space and buildings has not altered a great deal. But now there is a new direction.

"We don't want just space," employees tell the facilities managers, "but an environment that embodies a new work system." Suddenly the design teams have psychologists on their staffs, and the design teams meet with those who will inhabit the space to try to understand how it will function. To meet the new demands, facilities managers have to get into the heart of the changing organization so that they can create a new physical environment.

But facilities managers today, rather than simply trying to cope with the changes that clusters bring, are in a key position to provide leadership. They can force change in an organization by creating a setting for innovation.

Facilities managers are an extension of top management. They have to think strategically about how the changing organization plays out in physical space. By asking questions of top management and of nascent clusters in the firm, they prod thinking and cause change to occur. Facilities management thus becomes a key catalyst for action.

Space Design for Interaction

In the past companies have focused on the work station in designing offices. This was a micro focus: an assumption that work was going to be accomplished by an individual working alone. But the cluster organization requires a different focus: on the environment, teamwork, collaboration, cooperation, and communication. Companies that want people to work together must make it possible.

Actually, of course, more is needed than mere permissiveness. Especially when what is desired is for people from different functions and disciplines to work closely together, the space the company provides should actively encourage collaboration.

There are precursors of the new architecture and space layout. Corning Glass's W. C. Decker Engineering Building, which was completed in 1981, is one of the earliest examples of what would now be called cluster design. As described by Peter Lawrence of the Corporate Design Foundation,

> Dr. Thomas Allen of MIT . . . noted that eighty percent of an engineer's ideas come from face-to-face contact with colleagues. The architectural firm translated these findings into a three-story structure that has optimum visibility on every floor, strategically placed ramps, stairs, and escalators to encourage vertical movement, and an open plan layout and informal gathering places to maximize communication.

Du Pont's Different Office

Andrew Harriss's unit at Du Pont went through a redesign of its space when it was making the transition to a cluster organization. It was late in 1986 when Harriss saw an opportunity to reinforce the changes being made in his organization by how physical space was handled.

Rapid growth in the Fibers Department spawned by the success of a new carpet fiber necessitated construction of new office facilities at Du Pont's Chestnut Run Plaza site. Fibers I/S was given the opportunity to design its own work space.

Harriss appointed a physical space team to embody the new philosophy in the office. Comprised of programmers, team leaders, and clerical staff (but without managers), the team found itself charged with meeting the architects and drawing the office plan.

Harriss tried to stay as far removed from this process as possible, only involving himself when requested by the team as they approached a key presentation. As the team worked through the issues, four key principles emerged.

Having Privacy

Everyone working in Fibers I/S at Chestnut Run would have some private office space. This space would be quite small, and it would be the same size and furnished in the same way for all staff and managers alike. This was unusual for Du Pont in three respects.

First, clerical staff would not normally have private space. Instead, they usually were in a position of visibility in the office. The team felt that visibility would send the wrong signals about the value of these individuals and their contributions, and so reinforce an artificial difference in status.

Second, contractor staff normally would have cubicles or other temporary facilities so that floor plans could be altered easily as the employees came and went. The team felt this would be divisive in an office where contractors were considered to be as close to "family" as possible.

Third, managers normally had more space than staff. Both Harriss and the team felt this also would send the wrong signals about status to those who needed to work together and about the approachability of managers in a cooperative environment.

All staff workers were given the opportunity to choose the material that would form their office walls. Harriss initially insisted on having no walls, with the idea that, as manager, he ought to be the most accessible person. After debate about the need for privacy when holding meetings with outsiders, he was convinced to choose glass walls and a location next to a conference room, also furnished with glass walls.

Most of the other managers and staff opted for partial glass walls so that people could see if their lights were on, if they were "at home," but they could not be seen from the hallway. After installation, an open-door norm quickly developed, so that if employees were in their offices they left their doors open, making them visible from the hall anyway.

Sharing Openness

The team also decided that no one—including managers—ought to have a private window and that hallways would be relatively large. Windows and hallways were to be considered public property and available to all, for two reasons. First, the principle of equality suggested that windows should be shared. Second, public windows and broader hallways would especially encourage those among the technically oriented, who might be tempted to remain invisible, to get out of their offices to interact with other people.

A significant number of filing cabinets and benches were placed under the windows. The filing cabinets forced people to come out of their offices to get information, and the benches encouraged them to do so.

Developing Team Spirit

The space team arranged the floor plan so that offices occurred in pods around a central open space, which was designed for, and equipped with, chairs. These pods were assigned as closely as possible to teams on the same project, so that a pod would house a team. People switched offices and joined a new pod when they switched team assignments.

Reinforcing the Message

The design team put a physical link into the empowerment experience through the office plan. For example, one interior hallway had no office doors. Several levels of benches ran down either side, and pieces of artwork from Pecos River ranch were hung on the walls.

The "Pecos Pit," as it was referred to on the office directory, was designed to simulate an Indian meeting place. It was used to invoke memories of the group building experience on occasions when business pressures tended to erode positive feelings.

Reactions of Others

The architects the employees worked with were accustomed to requests for larger offices with more window space, better carpets, and similar perquisites intended to reflect the status of executives. They were astounded at the different requests that were made by the representatives of the Du Pont employees. A traditional office layout was considered and is shown in Figure 20.

The team wanted lots of open space, smaller offices to conserve space for meeting areas, numerous places for informal meetings, window space reserved for the meeting spots, and similar furnishings everywhere. Every employee would have a small space of his or her own—a "cave," they called it, and they referred to the meeting spaces as "coves." The new layout is presented schematically in Figure 21.

Implicit in the requests was the idea that physical space should facilitate the accomplishment of work rather than serve as a statement about the status of individuals in the unit. The objective was to acquire space that would facilitate communications and offer opportunities for exchange and creativity. The design plan led to considerable discussion among the managers on the floor above and in adjoining buildings, which had been developed in the traditional fashion. Many people found their way to Chestnut Run just to see "what it was like."

On more than one occasion, Harriss was asked to show managers from other places his "real office." Other people, not seeing a secretary at the

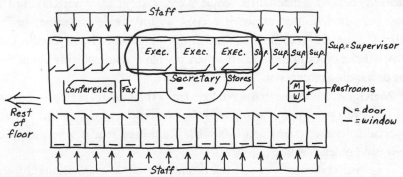

Figure 20 Du Pont's Traditional Culture

279

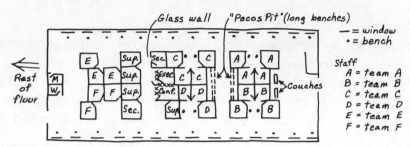

Figure 21   Fibers I/S, 1984–1985

main entrance, would wander around, getting lost while searching for a particular office.

The effects of the space were striking. Successful recruitment of professionals and others from within Du Pont in career transfers rose markedly. Also, the ratio of acceptances to offers extended to college students went up after Fibers I/S occupied its new space. Impromptu team meetings did occur more spontaneously, and doors remained open.

Office Layouts of Clusters

What does a cluster organization need in terms of space? Clusters need an environment in which people can see one another easily, and therefore are encouraged to communicate. In the past companies wanted to avoid this situation, believing that when people were talking, they were taking time away from work. But as work comes to involve less routine, because computers do the routine jobs, and more judgment about specific situations, efficiency can be increased when people consult quickly about how best to handle a circumstance.

Managers who are often separated from their own employees by rows and rows of eye-stopping work stations need to be closer and to have the opportunity for frequent consultation. They need places where they can easily hold quick meetings.

The spatial demands of teamwork are even more dramatically different from the work stations of the past. Teams need dedicated space that allows them to create group identification. They need a place to meet; tables on which to write, illustrate, and make copies; and the ability to bring team records into the meeting space easily.

So what will the office of the future be like?

It will have work stations, of course, but they will not be small cubicles fenced off by high partitions. Instead there will be lower dividers. People will be able to see their coworkers and, when they desire, to look over and speak to a colleague. Visual barriers will be minimized in favor of broad sweeps for the eye.

In place of the angularity of the current office, with its right angles and vertical surfaces, there will be an emphasis on curves and on the horizontal. Desk surfaces will curve gently, especially at the corners. Curved surfaces psychologically invite others to visit and exchange views. Curved surfaces also provide greater counter space, and the additional space underneath will allow for better installation of the extensive wiring required for modern technology.

Curved desk surfaces will sometimes end in podlike appendages that can readily be used for a quick and impromptu meeting. Where there are close-working teams, work stations will have two people at a curved desk surface, a bulge in the center giving visual separation to the spaces of the two individuals. Behind their chairs will be a similar configuration for two more people, and maybe for another at one side. In the middle space between the work stations will be a circular pedestal table, so that the entire group can quickly assemble simply by rolling their chairs to the table.

In the cluster organization the space between work stations becomes as important as that in the station itself. This is a substantial departure from the currently prevailing concept in which space between stations is merely lost and thus should be minimized. In contrast, this space in the future organizational setting is crucial to the incentive and ability to meet and confer. Hence it must be carefully designed and effectively utilized.

In the organization of the future the offices of managers will be close to those of their employees and will be configured in much the same way. The separated executive office, which emphasizes the hierarchical distance between manager and managed, becomes counterproductive and ineffi- cient. Today a manager's office cannot be mistaken for a rank-and-file work station. In the future the two will look much more alike. The manager's office will also use curved spaces and pods for meetings.

There is an element of the egalitarian in these physical arrangements. Employees are doing more "bosslike" work, and therefore their space will look more like that of the managers. Similar physical spaces will suggest a lesser degree of differentiation by status. This will be consistent with several elements of more competitive organizations, including high levels of commitment from all, regardless of their status in a hierarchy, and individual recognition based on expertise and contribution rather than on one's level in the organization.

Some companies have already determined that the new physical configurations are cost effective. A large insurance company reports that as it has experimented with clusters, it has discovered it can now move people, if necessary, without moving their personal space. The result is a savings of millions of dollars on space and design.

The Building of the Future

Thus far I have described the office layout of the cluster organization. To acquire such a layout will not be unduly difficult because much space that is devoted to old-style work stations can be converted to the new without structural changes to the building itself.

But buildings themselves will need some adaptation, and this may have to wait in many companies until leases expire or new structures are erected. What will the office building of the future be like?

In the past only managers gathered for meetings. Today, in the collaborative organization, employees will meet often among themselves and also with managers. Hence, a building layout must provide considerable communal space that can be used for meetings.

Equally important will be the need to permit persons of different functions and disciplines to work together. A building will have to provide contiguous office space for managers of different departments, without sacrificing unduly the accessibility of a manager to those with whom he or she works in the same department.

For a large organization, these needs imply broad, short buildings of few floors and considerable space on each floor. Numerous elevators and broad staircases will facilitate movement among floors.

The office skyscraper is a dinosaur. Its many stories and difficulty of access between floors Balkanize the organization and make difficult the cross-fertilization that is at the heart of a cluster organization.

Where are the office systems and buildings of the future to come from? Fortunately, they are already appearing in the marketplace.

Steelcase Corporation

As the largest producer of office furniture, Steelcase introduced in 1989 a new line that fits very well with the needs of the cluster organization. Featuring gentle curves, low visual barriers between work stations, soft colors that invite people to think and interact, and circular pods for meetings, it fits to perfection the needs of the modern organization.

Steelcase itself already utilizes its own product. At the corporation's Grand Rapids, Michigan, headquarters, a corporate development center was opened in 1989. The building is a low, flattened pyramid, large at the base, and offering lovely views of the midwestern plain. At night, the building is lit in such a way that it seems to be the launching pad for a great rocket ship. Inside, the company's new line of furniture creates comfortable, collaboration-inducing space. Meeting spaces line the inner walls around the building's central core. On one floor, all managers of the different functions housed in the building occupy offices around an atrium. By this propinquity, the designers of the building thought to encourage close cooperation among the managers of the various functions.

On each floor, there is a canteen equipped not only with food and beverages but also with flip charts and blackboards. The purpose is to encourage the interchange of information and ideas in the informal setting of coffee and lunch breaks.

The building and the configuration of its interior are consistent with the strategic purpose of the center. The building houses planning elements of all functions that have a role in the development of new products. The strategic purpose is to facilitate innovation much more quickly than has been possible previously.

Through the redesign of offices and office buildings, the impediments to increased collaboration among the functions and disciplines in large organizations can be removed. Cluster organizations, so ill fitted to the current configuration of most office space, will blossom in the new environments. The barriers to improved competitive performance that are posed by current spatial arrangements—so clearly perceived by the executives at the outset of this chapter—can be swept away.

CHAPTER SIXTEEN

Working in Clusters at GE Canada

The work force had been downsized by 40 percent and work had been centralized at headquarters. How was the leaner organization to do as much work as previously? A new organization was the answer.

What is it like to work in a cluster organization? Employees in the financial services unit of GE Canada tell us in this chapter.

Edward Johnson is head of Pooled Financial Services—GE Canada. Over the past several years, he has led a redesign of the unit, eliminating two organizational levels and approximately 40 percent of the employees while improving productivity and quality. The goal of the redesign was to combine the economies of scale and resources of a large company with the flexibility, creativity, and motivation of a small and entrepreneurial one.

A wholly owned subsidiary of the General Electric Corporation, GE Canada, for its first 70 years, operated like a smaller version of the parent company, serving as the pilot site for the decentralization of GE during the 1950s. During the late 1960s and 1970s, changes in tariffs and increased competition from Europe and Asia provided impetus for GE Canada to restructure.

The goals of the restructuring were to increase profitability, to refocus the company, and to expand from a primarily Canadian market focus to global markets. William Blundell, chairperson and CEO of GE Canada, described the restructuring of the company in the 1987 annual report to shareholders:

> For the past few years the management of GE Canada has been structuring the company for a future very different from the past. This was done in the belief that fundamental changes to the company were required to remain competitive in an increasingly complex and global marketplace. Included in this restructuring were the rigorous rationalization of a number of our manufacturing operations, clear identification of those areas where we believe we have a competitive edge operating from a Canadian base, and change of product mix to reflect the increasingly global nature of the market.
>
> For GE Canada, the key elements for success were: first, flexibility of our work force through multi-skilling; second, teamwork through information and responsibility sharing; and third, a commitment to both quality and to becoming the most productive work force in North America. We are making progress in developing the kind of work force that the future will require. We have had considerable success, most notably at our Bromont facility [a factory] in developing self-directed, multi-skilled work groups.
>
> To reduce costs and improve operating efficiencies the financial and some administrative activities of GE Canada's corporate and Toronto-based businesses have been pooled and the resulting organization has combined a mix of people, service, and technology that is professional, responsible and cost-effective. The organization was designed with self-managed work teams which provide employees the opportunity to share in the responsibility and the results.

Self-managed work teams share many characteristics with clusters, and so are important sources of insight about what it is like to work in the latter. The example of GE Canada's effort is especially valuable because it demonstrates that self-managed teams, or clusters for that matter, are not strictly linked to decentralization. The GE effort involves a delegation of what had been managerial functions to the teams but is also part of a recentralization of activities that had previously been conducted in the field. Self-managing teams and clusters are forms of organization that can be utilized in a centralized or decentralized environment.

Redesigning at GE Canada

In late 1984 Johnson was chosen to head the consolidation of the financial, employee services, facilities maintenance, and information technology services at GE Canada. Before his selection, he had been responsible for financial resources at the Bromont, Quebec, plant. In this position he had observed the innovative design of the manufacturing operations, a process that was viewed as a tremendous success and resulted in significant cost savings; increased productivity; and improved flexibility, speed, and quality of production. The mandate given to Johnson by Blundell in 1985 was to reduce the work force by 40 percent over the next two years while continuing to provide high-quality financial and administrative services to GE Canada's business units. Johnson described his assessment of the task confronting him as he assumed his new position:

> A steering committee of senior financial and administrative managers throughout GE Canada was formed by the CEO who served as an active member of the committee. In our initial discussions we clarified our vision of the new organization and developed a set of guiding principles that could be used to initiate the redesign process.
>
> We agreed that a combination of: 1) centralizing similar work, 2) analyzing and simplifying work structures and processes, 3) exploiting information technology (especially new opportunities in office automation), and 4) developing a flatter and more responsive organization offered the best chance of achieving the goals of the restructuring. We knew that to achieve the necessary productivity, quality and levels of service with 40% fewer people we would need to make optimal use of each and every employee.
>
> As time compresses our business processes we can't afford the luxury of relying on a rigid organization structure to define communication paths and the locus of decision-making. As we downsized and de-layered the organization we needed to restructure so that a manager would not end up with a crowd of direct reports that he or she would need to control and manage. We believed that the shift to self-managing work teams would be critical for helping us cope with the effects of the downsizing and de-layering.

Over a three-month period of concentrated effort, an employee task force performed a technical, social, and administrative analysis of the financial structure, the business and managerial processes, and the work of each of the 360 finance employees. During this phase of the analysis, the task force actively worked with the majority of the employees in the organization to define their work processes, to identify ways in which the work could be simplified or consolidated, and to identify and eliminate problems that hampered productivity.

Recommendations were made for job redesign to increase the quality of the work for the employees while simultaneously increasing the quality of output for the customers. A steering committee monitored progress, ensured that the task force understood and remained consistent with the vision and guiding principles, and assisted the task force in removing any obstacles that could impede progress.

The task force report, completed in June 1985, summarized the major findings of the analysis:

> The current structure and culture within GE Canada evolved from and reflects the economic and social environment of the past 55 years—the depression years followed by the war years and the high-growth years—in which the strengths and weaknesses of the twentieth century North American smokestack industry environment were clearly displayed. The organization was structured like a steep pyramid with many layers of management.
>
> As the organization grew and diversified, it was broken down into separate business areas, and there was a tendency to duplicate staff and tasks in each area. Response time within the organization was very long because decision making on even minor issues was reserved for management. Jobs were highly structured and rigid procedures discouraged creativity, innovation, risk taking, and accountability. Communication within hierarchical reporting channels and laterally among employees who must work together to accomplish a task was very poor, and employees lacked the information needed to do their jobs. The organization demanded employee loyalty and in return provided a high degree of security to employees. Finally, employees were evaluated and compensated based on the length of service and their level in the organization, not on the quality and quantity of work.
>
> These characteristics may have been appropriate for GE Canada in the 1950s and 1960s. But in the late 1970s and 1980s, the company had evolved to a more focused, smaller organization in a much more dynamic environment. In order for our company to prosper the organization must change to a leaner and more agile structure, and the culture within the organization

must change to an atmosphere of openness, information sharing, account-ability, and entrepreneurism. A new organization structure and human resource strategy are needed that maximize the contributions of all employees by focusing on high involvement and commitment.

The task force recommended an organizational design that centralized most financial, administrative, and information technology services for corporate administration and the Toronto-based businesses into one unit, comprising five centers of work-related activities (control, analysis, employee services, information systems, and facilities support). Coordination of the five centers would rest with a Coordinators' Council consisting of a coordinator for each center and manager Johnson.

Within each center, the ongoing work of the unit would be performed through the creation of self-managing employee teams, and ad hoc work teams would handle the project-oriented work within a center and across centers. The task force report was presented to the steering committee, and it was approved with minor modifications. The steering committee charged Johnson with the responsibility for selecting the five coordinators who would join him to form the Coordinators' Council and gave the council responsibility for implementing the redesign.

From Hierarchy to Self-Managing Teams

The implementation of the redesign began in the summer of 1985 with the creation of the Pooled Financial Services organization through the centralization of the financial, administrative, and information technology services and the assignment of personnel to the five centers recommended by the task force. Johnson selected five people to serve on the Coordinators' Council, to develop vision and mission statements as well as an implementation plan. In early 1988 the vision and mission statements were revised, with input from all employees.

Early in the redesign process, each center was broken down into two or three self-managing work teams. Within each team, members often worked in smaller groups based on logical units of work adapted to the needs of the organization and the team members. Control of the quality and quantity of work, and the process used to accomplish it, was given to the team. Much of the traditional managerial responsibilities (e.g., planning, budget setting, hiring, firing, monitoring, and managing) was to reside at the team level. The Coordinators' Council was to provide leadership and strategic direction and to assist in integrating and coordinating the work of the teams.

A gradual transition occurred from a hierarchical organization to self-managing teams, which involved mutual adaptation between team members and the Coordinators' Council. Teams progressed at different rates, but on average it took 24 to 30 months from the announcement of team formation to the development of a functioning self-managing unit.

Fiona Cooper, a ten-year employee of GE Canada and a member of the payroll team, described some problems encountered in the transition to self-management:

> In the beginning we were all very unsure of what was expected of us. We really needed help. You can't just say "Now you are a self-managing team" and expect that we would know what to do. We had the initial course on team development and group process but then there was no ongoing follow-up and so soon we weren't meeting regularly and continued to rely on our previous managers for direction.

Recognizing the need for support for ongoing organizational development and human resource management, the Coordinators' Council recruited two human resource specialists to their group: Bev Davids and Marie Percival. Under their leadership and guidance, significant progress was made on the redesign effort. Davids described her role:

> I really see myself as a catalyst for change. I work with both the coordinators and the work teams to help them build the team administration and group process skills that will be needed to accomplish the transition from a hierarchy to a self-management team structure. I provide formal training courses, such as the Meeting Skills course and the Building Effective Interaction Skills course, and also respond to requests and initiate opportunities for training with teams and individuals.
>
> For example, I often meet with a team to help its members build meeting skills during their team meetings or to analyze work processes and redesign their work. When I first started at GE Canada, I realized that

members of the Coordinators' Council held meetings but did not consider themselves a team.

I worked with them to analyze their work processes and we found that over 70% of the tasks were highly similar and less than 30% were specific to their team. They were surprised at the overlap, and this was the basis for developing more of a team approach to their work. This also acted as a role model for the other teams and provided the coordinators with their own experience as a team member.

Percival also discussed her role:

My primary role is to provide human resource support in the areas of staffing, human resource management, planning, communications, and salary administration. I also assist Bev [Davids] as a resource to the teams to facilitate their development in the areas of team building, team administration and group process skills. I believe that the need for ongoing organization development support will decrease and that one person who combines both organization development and employee relations skills will be available on call to Pooled Financial Services. I already see a shift from "expert" trainer to more of a facilitator and support person in my work with both the coordinators and the work teams.

Davids and Percival provided extensive group and individual training. The formal training included programs on team development (16 hours), meeting skills (8 hours), and conflict resolution (16 hours). All programs included training about effective group processes and were supplemented with on-the-job feedback and informal training. As each team gained administrative and process skills needed to self-manage, more and more responsibility was shifted from the coordinator and former managers to the team. By December 1988, Johnson estimated that the organization had achieved approximately 50 percent to 60 percent of its goals.

Al Holden, a 25-year employee, had been a manager within an area of GE Canada outside of Pooled Financial Services. Holden voluntarily moved to Pooled Financial Services to become a member of the information systems development team. He described the reasons for his move and his impressions of the transition:

It was not easy to give up my management title and become a member of a team but I chose to do this because I believed strongly in the concept. I have always felt that as more people participate in the decision-making process, greater benefits accrue to the total organization.

I speak for many of the employees when I say that we never expected that it would take so long and be such an agonizing process. In the early phase of the transition people continued to come to me when they had problems and expected me to provide a solution. I had to work with them to help them develop their own solutions and to look to other team members for expertise and assistance. It was hard to break old habits. At times, I found myself biting my tongue during meetings to keep from jumping in and taking charge. I saw my role in the redesign process as helping the members of my team develop the management and administrative skills they would need to become fully self-managing. You might say that I gradually worked myself out of my previous job.

Holden also commented on the initial difficulties his team had in breaking down old organizational barriers:

Initially, we had difficulty breaking down the divisional barriers and thinking of ourselves as one team. Our team was formed from three distinct groups that had previously worked in separate operating units.

At first there was considerable conflict and confusion over whether we should remain as three subteams or become one large team. Over time we are beginning to think of ourselves as a single team and, as a result, we are gaining the benefits of the added skills and flexibility.

To help break down division barriers we reorganized physically, changing people's locations to promote new communication channels. We also changed the work itself to enable people to work on projects that crossed previously defined group barriers. Team members met regularly to discuss problems we had encountered and develop solutions. We formulated our own policies for hiring, staffing, performance evaluation, and budget development and monitoring.

We have definitely made major strides toward becoming fully self-managing but still have areas where more progress needs to be made.

Sid Clark, a member of the Coordinators' Council with specific responsibility for the Employee Center, described his view of the transition:

Before the restructuring I was in charge of Division Accounting—these functions are now part of the Control Center and Facilities Support Center—and had four layers of management between myself and the employees who worked for me. With the reorganization, they asked me to become coordinator for the Employee Center, and the first order of business was to cut 60% of the staff and remove all layers of management below me.

I decided that the best way to accomplish this was to conduct the layoffs as quickly as possible and then to proceed with the redesign of the organization to self-managing teams. I decided to take a desk in the large, open work area and work along with the employees to understand the day-to-day activities, meet the people, and get to know them.

After a few months, I ranked employees on a variety of skill levels and asked former managers to perform the same rankings of the employees that used to report to them. I then laid off based on the rankings, not by seniority. I knew that if we were going to get the work done with fewer employees as expected, we would have to keep the winners.

Now, I am in the process of helping the teams to become self-managing. That involves gradually giving them responsibilities that used to be reserved for managers. For example, to prepare the team to begin taking over the budget, I took them through last year's budget process and am currently having them do the expense tracking so that they can see how expenses are incurred. Next year they will prepare the budget and I will be available to answer questions and will review their final result.

Other teams were at different points on the road to self-management. Paul Vermette, a six-year GE Canada employee and a member of the end user support team, described his team's progress:

Our team has made considerable progress toward becoming fully self-managing. We are actively involved in the hiring process. We evaluate our work load and assign people to projects. We develop the budget, track expenses and make all our own buying decisions. We were also the first team to perform our own performance reviews.

When asked to describe why he felt that his team had made so much progress, Vermette said,

First of all, we are a small team with only four members, and, for the most part, we were very open to the concept of self-management. But the most important factor was that we had a former senior manager as a member of our team who believed strongly in the concept and was very skilled in helping and encouraging us to take on additional responsibilities.

He was very adamant about not taking a directive role. He pushed us and he pushed the coordinator to make changes happen. He not only taught us the mechanics of the various management functions (e.g., how to develop a budget), but he also shared with us his vast understanding of the organization (e.g., who to go to for specific information and how to use the resources available), and gave us tips on how to manage in the political environment. Without him, we would have had a very hard time knowing where to begin.

Since all teams were responsible for developing their own approach to self-management, there were no standard procedures for performance measurement and other managerial activities within Pooled Financial Services. Initially, the Coordinators' Council believed that the teams would find the peer appraisal process to be one of the most difficult to develop and implement. This did not prove to be the case for the teams that were currently performing their own peer appraisal. Vermette described his team's approach to self-appraisal:

It took us over 12 hours to reach consensus on the process we would use for peer evaluation. We all realized that, while the team would not make specific recommendations for salary and grade level upgrades, the evaluations would be used by the coordinators as important input in our salary determination.

We also knew that we would need to develop a process that remained consistent with the performance appraisal process used throughout GE Canada so that the results could be communicated in a way that the rest of the company could understand. We developed a process that meets the company's needs for a standard evaluation process and meets our own needs for feedback on our work and review of our progress.

The entire process takes about four weeks for each employee but we all feel that we are getting much better feedback than before. Most of us felt that our previous evaluations were very superficial and did not provide the kind of guidance and support that is a critical component to real growth and development.

The self-appraisal team evaluation process has been in place for two years and we have had no major problems to date. We have never had anyone contest their evaluation and we wouldn't think of going back to the old evaluation process.

Barbara Cromie, who was a member of the Customer Information Center, discussed her reactions to the new organization and described how her team had faced the very difficult task of terminating a team member whose performance was unsatisfactory:

Before the reorganization I worked as a secretary for one of the vice presidents, so I had no direct management responsibilities. The reorganization really expanded my opportunities and responsibilities, which at times can be somewhat intimidating but has made work much more enjoyable.

Since we make decisions as a team, we all feel more comfortable with those decisions. We learned to seek expertise from each other and from people all over the organization. We develop our own work procedures and are able to change or modify them as new situations and needs arise, and we handle problems as they occur. You don't have to write memos and wait weeks to get a response.

I feel that I have grown considerably in my management and group process skills through the formal courses that have been offered, through the support and guidance provided by the coordinators, the human resource support and my team members, and most important through the experiences that I have had over the past few years.

I'll never forget my first experience running a meeting. While I had been in many meetings before, I did not know there were specific things you could do—like setting agendas, summarizing action plans, and encouraging participation—which help to make meetings more successful.

The Meeting Skills course provided me with lots of practical skills and gave me a chance to practice those skills in a supportive environment. But, the first time that I had to stand up and run a meeting, I was very nervous. Since then, I have had the opportunity to run many meetings and now feel very comfortable. In fact, when I attend meetings I often find myself analyzing the process and thinking of ways that the meeting facilitator could do a better job of moving things forward.

I think that the most challenging management task that I have faced to date, however, was when our team determined that an employee that we had hired was not working out and would need to be terminated. The team decided that only one person should talk to the employee, and I was elected. I first talked with the coordinator and then sought out Marie Percival for support and guidance. Marie really helped me work through the steps I would need to take and the potential problems that could arise.

295

Since I had never faced this situation before, I did not know that I would need documentation and did not have hard evidence of the employee's weaknesses. She explained how to handle that situation and I learned an important lesson on the importance of documentation of weaknesses as well as strengths during evaluations. She also role-played the conversation that I would have with the employee to be sure that I would handle the situation according to GE policy and that I felt comfortable with the potential responses of the employee. At one point she asked me to think of the worst possible thing that could occur and then to describe how I would handle it. The actual meeting with the employee went very smoothly and our team learned a great deal in the process.

Information Technology Infrastructure

The redesign team recognized that information technology would be a critical factor for both supporting and enabling the new organizational structure and the intensive information sharing and communication that would be required. Each employee needed a personal computer work station that would enable him or her to access, analyze, and communicate information. There were no secretaries, clerks, or administrative assistants in the Pooled Financial Services organization. Not even Johnson had clerical or administrative support, so he did his own typing, copying, and mailing of correspondence, as did all other employees in the unit. Hence, software applications to support productivity (e.g., word processing and electronic calendars) were also needed.

Robots were purchased to deliver mail and supplies. Also, electronic mail, voice mail, and a fax machine were installed for all employees. Special data-base access programs were written to allow payroll employees to gain on-line access to critical employee and financial data and to facilitate the transfer of those data to spreadsheet programs. A separate application program was written to allow employees access to hotel information so that they could make their own travel arrangements.

Jane Roche, a member of the analysis and reporting team, discussed how information technology supports her work:

Since we no longer have secretaries the technology is critical for communicating with other GE employees. Everyone uses E-mail or voice mail, and we no longer send memos. I personally like to use E-mail since most of my communication is with people inside GE.

When I have a corporate report that needs to be done, I send out all my requests for data on E-mail and the divisions can send back the data to me on-line. That really saves time and improves accuracy since we are not re-keying data. I also use the special database access programs that were written to download data from the mainframe. The data can be loaded directly into the PC which I use for analysis.

The company is very supportive of us and is very willing to supply any hardware or software we need. They recognize that we could never get the work done with fewer people if we didn't have these productivity tools.

Marilyne Kapuvari, a member of the information systems development team, also believes that technology is a critical factor in the functioning of the new organization:

Technology has been critical in allowing us to work much more productively and effectively as a team and as individuals. I use E-mail to communicate within the organization, and use the word processing and spreadsheet functions to write documentation, do budgets and manage my projects.

The biggest timesavers for me are all the communication and work productivity tools on the PC and the information access tools on the mainframe. Top management—both Blundell and Johnson—encourage us to identify ways that technology can help us do our work in a more efficient and effective manner and are very willing to try out new technologies that we think may be of help.

Cromie depended on voice mail and access to the product information data bases to support her work in the Customer Information Center:

We have access to information through the Product Directory and other mainframe data bases. It's our lifeline for handling customer complaints and supplying information. When it goes down, which luckily is not too often, we can rely on paper directories of product information—but they are not as up-to-date—which can be a major problem in dealing with customer complaints.

We update the information files on a daily basis. I also use voice mail to allow customers to leave messages for me—although we try to give personal service whenever possible. When we first installed voice mail, about 70% of our customers complained stating that they wanted to talk to a real person.

But now we have shown them that we are just as responsive as before, and that they actually get better service since they don't have to wait on the line for us to get done helping someone else, they have become much more accepting. The complaints have decreased substantially.

Evaluation of the New Organization

In early 1988 Johnson reflected on the progress that had been made over the past several years in fulfilling the objectives of the redesign. The basic structure of the new organization and the supporting infrastructure were now in place. All employees were working in teams, which were in the process of transition to self-management. Reductions in the number of employees, required by Blundell, had been achieved without decreasing the level or quality of service to the customer.

With few exceptions, employees were experiencing personal satisfaction from the organizational design—more control of their own work through participation in team decisions, freedom to act, and more scope for personal development. Good progress was being made toward a highly committed work force.

And what did people think about the new organization? Cromie summarized her impressions:

> My job is much more satisfying and rewarding because of the increased responsibility and challenge and the opportunities to develop a wider range of skills. As a team, we have really grown in our ability to communicate and interact with one another. We have learned to really listen to one another and to consider each other's point of view while making decisions.
>
> Despite our growth as a team, there are areas where we still have difficulty. It can take us longer to reach a decision since we all need to come to consensus. We also have problems knowing where the responsibility of the team ends and the responsibility of the coordinator begins.

Yvonne Zeitoun, a member of the ledger team, expressed her views on the team concept:

> For me the transition to the self-managing team concept has been a very positive one. Prior to my current project with RCA, I had responsibility for fleet administration.

In the old hierarchy system I would never have been considered for that level of responsibility, because I had not risen to the appropriate level of management. Now I have many more opportunities and the potential for taking on all types of projects and responsibilities exists, and is even encouraged. I am learning new skills and the new experiences are broadening my knowledge of the business, the GE organization, and management processes.

Not everyone has been so fortunate, however. Some people are satisfied to do the job and don't want to get involved in decision making. I also think the change has been very hard on the senior staff who used to be managers. They worked hard to reach that level, then the organization changed. For those who became coordinators, they needed to learn to delegate responsibility and train others to do the jobs they used to do. For those who became team members, they needed to adjust to being part of the work group with equal say in how things will be done rather than making and enforcing decisions. Somehow it just doesn't seem fair for everyone.

Holden spoke of the impact of the new organization on former managers:

The transition from a hierarchical organization to self-managing teams was especially difficult for former managers. Early on, in the process, we did not have any special training to help us cope with the transition in our roles from manager/decision maker to a member of the work force. The employees did not know how to treat us and we had difficulty breaking down the old management/employee barriers.

We ended up accomplishing the transition in a phased approach. Initially, we [the former managers] operated as senior team members—continuing to function in the role of managers. Gradually, we worked our way out of the management role by training the other members of the team to take on more of the administrative and decision-making responsibilities.

We really needed help in understanding how to break down the traditional stereotypical management roles and in forming new roles based on self-management and a team approach. Early on we did not realize that the process would take time. As a result, in the beginning we felt that we were not living up to the expectations that had been set, so all of us felt very frustrated.

Cooper, a member of payroll, commented,

Since the reorganization, my job has definitely expanded and taken on more variety. The new structure encourages us to take on new responsibilities.

For example, shortly after the reorganization, one of the former managers quit. I had helped this manager in the past and knew how to carry out some of her responsibilities so I jumped in and did the work.

Before the change, work was dedicated to a specific person. If that person left, someone else was hired. Now, work is the responsibility of the team, so if some one quits the team meets to discuss ways of getting the work done. In some cases we may decide not to hire someone new but to split up the responsibilities among different team members.

We're a lot more flexible than we used to be. Another positive advantage of the team concept is that now I can voice my opinion and people listen. Before, decisions on how you did your work were left to managers who didn't have to live with the consequences of those decisions on a day-to-day basis. Now, there is no one looking over my shoulder telling me what to do and how to do it, so I feel less pressure even though I am doing more work than before.

But in addition to these advantages, there have also been problems. For example, we are told that everyone on the team is equal, but we are all paid differently and are at different grade levels in the organization. We are encouraged to take on new responsibilities, but we are not necessarily compensated for jumping in and doing the extra work.

Our pay needs to be more closely tied to the quality and quantity of our work. In addition our bonus systems are all designed to recognize individual performance, but we are expected to work together as a team. Finally, we are told we are supposed to be self-managing, yet we don't always get the information we need to make decisions. These inconsistencies make it difficult to live up to the expectations of what we are supposed to achieve.

Kapuvari also discussed difficulties with the new system:

The most difficult part of the new structure is taking on all the administrative responsibilities in addition to our regular work. We are asked to assume responsibility for scheduling the work of the team but often I don't know what other team members are doing. Because our team has not reached full maturity, I don't feel comfortable just going up to people and asking them what they're doing and I'm not sure how to ask them to help me when I need additional resources.

In early 1988 the Coordinators' Council decided to conduct an attitude survey of the Pooled Financial Services employees to get a broad range of opinions on the new organization. An ad hoc team of employees from different teams developed and administered the survey. The results highlighted positive gains as well as areas that still required attention. Davids described the key findings:

> The survey helped to highlight the areas of strength and weakness in the organization redesign, and provided a good picture of where we needed to focus in the future. It was clear that there was support for the new organization design.
>
> The majority of people felt that the self-managing team concept had provided increased responsibility, control and initiative to the team members in determining their work. They were positive about their team communications and the commitment of their teams to working together as groups. They felt that their personal roles and responsibilities were clear in their own minds but not in the minds of the team, and they were much less clear on the role of the coordinators. They felt that the coordinators were committed to the new organization but that communications with coordinators on the goals and objectives of the organization could be improved. They felt there was genuine concern on the part of top management for job quality, but were confused by how the administrative and team building responsibilities were translated into activities for them to carry out as part of their jobs.
>
> They were also confused about how the quality and quantity of their work were reflected in raises and compensation. A number of employees mentioned that they had not received recognition or commensurate pay for the additional work they had been asked to assume. Finally, the teams felt that ongoing training and support were critical for helping them to become fully self-managing.

The survey findings were presented to the teams in June 1988. Each team assumed responsibility for implementing action plans based on those results. The Coordinators' Council assumed responsibility for developing recommendations and for addressing overall concerns.

Davids and Percival described their efforts to respond to the survey results:

The critical issues highlighted by the survey that required immediate attention were:

1. The coordinator role needs to be more clearly defined and communication between (and among) the teams and the coordinators must be improved;
2. Reward and compensation systems need to reflect expanded job designs and must recognize both team and individual performance based on quality and productivity measures;
3. In some teams, the work had changed significantly requiring jobs to be re-examined; and
4. Career planning must recognize that the flatter Pooled Financial Services organization provides less opportunity for advancement into managerial positions.

In late summer 1988, GE Canada began to address these issues and by December 1988 had conducted training programs and developed some draft documents that could be reviewed by the Coordinators' Council and the employees. From the beginning GE Canada wanted employees to be involved in defining their roles and designing their jobs and to be responsible for continuously modifying and adapting them to the needs of the team, the organization, and their personal growth. The company recognized that this approach would make standard job descriptions obsolete.

From an organizational perspective, work was assigned to a team, not to an individual, which complicated the use of standard job descriptions. As a result, GE Canada developed a more general approach to organizational roles in which jobs were designed around three major areas: technical—job-related work of the employee/team and the technical requirements of the work; team administration—planning, organizing, leading, integrating, and controlling; and team process—participation, facilitation, and conflict resolution.

Afterword

I once attended a meeting of a company at which managers were asked which of the following they would do first:

Answer a call from a key customer.
Deal with an urgent production problem.
Answer a call from your boss.

When the responses were made by secret ballot, an overwhelming majority selected the third alternative: Answer a call from your boss.

This was not what the top officer of the company wanted to hear. He was trying to instill in his management team customer responsiveness as a first priority. But stubbornly the managers clung to the chain of command as their highest priority.

Why? Because each person's career depended on his or her relationship with the boss. No customer had that direct an influence on their lives.

This is the essence of the hierarchy. Every person has a boss who is the single most important reality in his or her business life. Everything else comes second; how could it be any different?

And yet, like the chief executive of the company of which we're speaking, many companies want it to be different. In fact, when the CEO in our example asked for a show of hands on the same question, a majority said they'd first of all answer a call from a key customer. They knew what he wanted to hear, and they gave him the answer he wanted. The secret ballot alone revealed their true feelings.

But what if the top priority of the boss is to meet a customer's need? Then isn't calling the boss first the same as responding to a key customer? Yes, to a large degree it is. But it isn't always the case that boss and customer are effectively one and the same. And waiting for the boss to take an interest before responding to the customer is the sort of time-consuming bureaucratic behavior that so many firms today are trying to escape.

Breaking out of the hierarchical mode of behavior is what this book is about. Only then can the people in an enterprise pursue its mission with their full attention and commitment. The very best customer responsiveness, the lowest administrative costs, the greatest productivity, and the most effective utilization of new information and communications technology can occur only when the traditional hierarchical organization is changed dramatically.

What do we want people in today's business to do? We want them to think customer, teamwork, bottom-line, innovation, and boss—in that order. Yet how can the boss be on the list and yet not assume first priority? This can't be done. So, ironically, to get the desired priority we have to remove the boss entirely.

Thereby we discover the cluster organization—a form of business in which people work together in teams without close supervision, yet preserve their individuality. No one has a boss, but work gets done and the company prospers. Management is accomplished by the exercise of leadership, and employees are truly empowered. The cluster is the organization of the future.

NOTES

Chapter One   Shortchanged by Traditional Ways

G. Bruce Friesen contributed to this chapter.

p. 19 "In this sense . . ."
John Markoff, "Computer Mail Gaining a Market," *New York Times*, December 26, 1989, pp. D1 and D8.

p. 19 "A manager at a major Canadian . . ."
Brian Dumaine, "How Managers Can Succeed Through Speed," *Fortune*, February 13, 1989, pp. 54–59.

p. 21 "We had to speed up . . ."
Ibid.

p. 21 "The more responsibility . . ."
Ibid., p. 56.

p. 22 "Give us the people . . ."
Robert D. Hershey, Jr., "As Labor Pool Ebbs," *New York Times*, December 22, 1989, p. D1.

p. 23 "I know how these things . . ."
Ronald Henkoff, "This Cat Is Acting Like a Tiger," *Fortune*, December 19, 1988, pp. 71–76.

Chapter Two   Changing the Fundamentals: A One-Way Ticket to the Future

p. 28 "Thus, for these to be . . ."
See, for example, Tom Peters, "The Destruction of Hierarchy," *Industry Week*, August 15, 1988, pp. 13–35; Peter Drucker, "The Coming of the New Organization," *Harvard Business Review*, January–February 1988, p. 45; John S. Mc-Clenahan, "Flexible Structures to Absorb the Shocks," *Industry Week*, April 18, 1988, p. 41; Neal E. Boudette, "Networks to Dismantle Old Structures," *Industry Week*, January 16, 1989, p. 27; and Ken Macher, "Empowerment and the Bureaucracy," *Training and Development Journal*, September 1988, p. 41.

p. 29 "A cluster says a major work guide . . ."
Norman Lewis, *The Comprehensive Work Guide* (Garden City, NY: Doubleday, 1958), p. 162.

Notes

―――

Chapter Four "It's Like a Beehive: How Clusters Harness
Cooperation and Competition

p. 73 "At Bay City, Michigan . . . "

Brian S. Moskal, "The Sun Also Rises on GM," *Industry Week*, September 5, 1988, pp. 100–102.

p. 76 "The cluster concept has come to the battlefield."

I am indebted to Lt. Col. Joe Austin of the U.S. Army and member of the 103rd Harvard AMP for providing information used in this segment.

p. 78 "The adoption of clusters at Swissair . . . "

See *Swissair: Annual Report 1988*, p. 7, for a description of the new organization and its philosophy.

p. 83 "The 400-person plant . . . "

Brian S. Moskal, "Supervisors, Begone," *Industry Week*, June 20, 1988, p. 32.

p. 85 "There are several types of service firms . . . "

See, for example, Robert G. Eccles and Dwight B. Crane, "Managing Through Networks in Investment Banking," *California Management Review*, Vol. 30, No. 1, Fall 1987, p. 176.

p. 86 "The Milwaukee automotive plant . . . "

John Hoerr, "The Cultural Revolution at A.O. Smith," *Business Week*, May 29, 1989, p. 66.

p. 88 "For the Swedish automaker Volvo . . . "

See Robert Taylor, "Why Volvo Is Planning to Go Back to the Future," *Financial Times*, June 9, 1989, p. 14. See also Jonathan Kapstein and John Hoerr, "Volvo's Radical New Plant: 'The Death of the Assembly Line?' " *Business Week*, August 28, 1989, p. 92.

Chapter Six Linking Strategy, Structure, and Attitudes:
The Corporation of the Future

G. Bruce Friesen contributed to this chapter.

p. 112 "This is fundamentally a different way . . . "

Steven Butler, "Cutting Down and Reshaping the Core," *Financial Times*, March 20, 1990, p. 14.

p. 114 "We've ended up with . . . "

Lynda Applegate, "IBM Canada, Ltd.: Restructuring for the 1990's," Harvard Business School, April 1990 (mimeo). See also Tom Corcoran, "And Now for the E Word," *Dialogue*, IBM Corporation, 1989.

p. 118 "As described by the 'Seven S' . . ."

Thomas J. Peters and Robert H. Waterman, Jr., *In Search of Excellence* (New York: Harper & Row, 1981).

p. 120 "A Green-Field Plant"

A Green-Field Plant is adapted from *"Sedalia Engine Plant (A),"* a Harvard Business School Case (481–148).

Chapter Eight "What Would You Like to Do Here?": Surviving and Prospering in a Cluster Organization

p. 144 "Managers do not supervise . . ."

David R. Altany, "Decision-Making Trickles Down to the Troops," *Industry Week*, April 18, 1988, p. 34.

p. 146 "The secret to . . ."

Harry Gittler, "Foremen: The Ultimate in Overhead," *Industry Week*, July 18, 1988, p. 56.

p. 147 "These individuals . . ."

Steven J. Stowell, "Coaching: A Commitment to Leadership," *Training and Development Journal*, June 1988, pp. 34–38.

p. 149 "And the fourth was . . ."

G. Bruce Friesen and D. Quinn Mills, "Elements of Managerial Style," unpublished survey research.

p. 150 "The key to success . . ."

D. Quinn Mills, *The IBM Lesson: The Profitable Art of Full Employment* (New York: Times Books, 1988).

Chapter Nine New Visions versus Old Habits: Managerial Practices for Clusters

G. Bruce Friesen co-authored this chapter.

p. 154 "These range from . . ."

See Kenneth A. Merchant, *Control in Business Organizations* (Boston: Pitman, 1985) Chaps. 3, 4, and 5, for further discussion of results and personnel control mechanisms.

p. 156 "More than 30 years ago . . ."

Harold J. Leavitt and Thomas L. Whistler, "Management in the 1980's," *Harvard Business Review*, November–December 1958, p. 41.

---

p. 157 " 'Those reports,' Reichert says . . . "

Brian Dumaine, "How Managers Can Succeed Through Speed," *Fortune*, February 13, 1989, pp. 54–59.

p. 157 "When the bank . . . "

Ibid.

p. 158 "The extra cost . . . "

See John P. Wanous, *Organizational Entry: Recruitment, Selection, and Socialization of Newcomers* (Reading, MA: Addison-Wesley Series on Managing Human Resources, 1980).

p. 159 "The benefit of reducing . . . "

James Kochanski, "Hiring in Self-Regulating Work Teams," *National Productivity Review*, Spring 1987, pp. 153–159.

p. 160 "It is thus possible . . . "

Roger Plant and Mark Ryan, "Managing Your Corporate Culture," *Training & Development Journal*, September 1988, pp. 61–65.

p. 161 "And if it is a problem . . . "

Dumaine, op. cit.

p. 161 "Says Monaghan . . . "

Ibid.

p. 162 "Many firms invest . . . "

Jude T. Rich, " 'Reincenting' America," *Industry Week*, November 21, 1988, pp. 53–54.

p. 163 "Otherwise bonuses . . . "

Ibid.

p. 163 "A survey by . . . "

Nancy J. Perry, "Here Come Richer, Riskier Pay Plans," *Fortune*, December 19, 1989, pp. 50–59.

p. 163 "Being able to do so . . . "

Carla O'Dell and C. Jackson Grayson, Jr., "Flex Your Pay Muscle," *Across the Board*, July–August 1988, pp. 43–48.

p. 164 "Pay-for-knowledge . . . "

See Fred Luthans and Marilyn L. Fox, "Update on Skill-Based Pay," *Personnel*, March 1989, pp. 26–31.

p. 165 "To deal with this situation . . . "

W. Christopher Musselwhite, "Knowledge, Pay, and Performance," *Training & Development Journal*, January 1988, pp. 62–65.

p. 165 "The supervisor-employee ratio . . ."

Steve Donahue, "New Ways to Divide the Pay Pie," *Labor Relations Today*, U.S. Dept. of Labor, September 1988, pp. 1–2.

p. 165 "Said Dick Dauphinais . . ."

Perry, op. cit., p. 58.

p. 169 "About 40 percent . . ."

"Many Middle Managers Find Bosses Uninspiring," *Wall Street Journal*, November 5, 1989, p. 18.

Chapter Ten   The Fourth Form: From Mob to Hierarchy to Matrix to Cluster

p. 182 "John Cooke described . . ."

Larry Reibstein, "Follow the Leader: Workers Face Dilemma When the Boss Is Sinking," *Wall Street Journal*, March 10, 1988, p. 29.

p. 185 "The company goes . . ."

See *The IBM Lesson: The Profitable Art of Full Employment* (New York: Times Books, 1988).

Chapter Twelve   The Changing Role of Middle Managers

G. Bruce Friesen co-authored this chapter.

p. 209 "For example, John Sheridan noted . . ."

John H. Sheridan, "Attacking Overhead," *Industry Week*, July 18, 1988, p. 49.

p. 211 "This automation process is well established . . ."

See Thomas M. Rohan, "Special Report: Factories of the Future," *Industry Week*, March 21, 1988, p. 33.

p. 212 "Consider the example . . ."

Ronald Henkoff, "This Cat Is Acting Like a Tiger," *Fortune*, December 19, 1988, pp. 71–75.

p. 213 "These are the hallmarks . . ."

Daniel Yankelovitch and Sidney Harman, "Managing a High-Discretion Workplace," *Industry Week*, December 5, 1988, pp. 64–65.

p. 213 "Many first-line supervisors . . ."

Nancy J. Perry, "Here Come Richer, Riskier Pay Plans," *Fortune*, December 19, 1988, pp. 50–58.

p. 214 "The companies in which . . . "
Therese R. Welter, "Tools at the Top," *Industry Week*, November 21, 1988, pp. 41–45.

p. 215 "The system has been useful . . . "
Jeremy Main, "At Last, Software CEOs Can Use," *Fortune*, March 13, 1989, p. 77.

p. 215 "Although it recently . . . "
See Buck Brown, "How the Cookie Crumbled at Mrs. Fields," *Wall Street Journal*, January 26, 1988, p. B1.

p. 216 "After Randy Fields acquired this chain . . . "
Tom Richman, "Mrs. Fields' Secret Ingredient," *Inc.*, October 1987, p. 56.

p. 217 "A number of major retailers . . . "
Subrata N. Chakravarty, "Will Toys 'B' Great?" *Forbes*, February 22, 1988.

p. 218 "The end result . . . "
Sheridan, op. cit., p. 52.

p. 219 "And the managers who . . . "
Brian Dumaine, "How Managers Can Succeed Through Speed," *Fortune*, February 13, 1989, pp. 54–59.

p. 221 "Northrop's expert system . . . "
Dwight B. Davis, "Artificial Intelligence Goes to Work," *High Technology*, April 1987, p. 16.

p. 221 "Over the past three years . . . "
Dumaine, op. cit., p. 55.

p. 224 "Xerox Corporation . . . "
Sheridan, op. cit., p. 49.

p. 225 "Implementation of CIM . . . "
Ibid., p. 49.

p. 225 "A company making mechanical . . . "
William Pat Patterson, "Tackling Sacred Cows," *Industry Week*, October 17, 1988, p. 65.

p. 227 "We keep treating . . . "
Ibid., p. 69.

p. 227 "The result: Turnaround . . . "
Ira P. Krepchin, "The Human Side of Competitiveness," *Modern Materials Handling*, February 1988, pp. 64–67.

p. 227 ''These forces are currently . . .''
See Brian S. Moskal and Thomas M. Rohan, ''A Much Tougher Line Faces Line Managers,'' *Industry Week*, April 18, 1988, pp. 29–30.

Chapter Fourteen   Empower Me: Catalysts for Clusters

p. 267 ''According to the *Wall Street Journal* . . .''
Martha Brannigan, ''Employers' 'New Age' Training Programs Lead to Lawsuits Over Workers' Rights,'' *Wall Street Journal*, January 9, 1989.

Chapter Fifteen   Caves and Coves: Physical Space for Clusters

p. 276 ''The architectural firm translated . . .''
Peter Lawrence, ''Building Design: More Than Meets the Eye,'' *The Journal of Business Strategy*, July–August 1989, p. 17.

INDEX